A Gift For

_____

Presented By

_____

_____

AN ILLUSTRATED COLLECTION

THE Bible's MOST
FASCINATING PEOPLE

AN ILLUSTRATED COLLECTION

THE Bible's MOST FASCINATING PEOPLE

Stories from the Old and New Testaments

R. P. NETTELHORST

Reader's Digest

The Reader's Digest Association, Inc.
Pleasantville, New York/Montreal/Sydney

A READER'S DIGEST BOOK

This edition published by The Reader's Digest Association, Inc.,
by arrangement with Quarto Inc.

Conceived, designed, and produced by
Quarto Publishing plc
The Old Brewery
6 Blundell Street
London N7 9BH

For Quarto
Project Editor: **Michelle Pickering**
Art Editor: **Natasha Montgomery**
Designer: **Elizabeth Healey**
Picture Researcher: **Claudia Tate**
Art Director: **Caroline Guest**
Creative Director: **Moira Clinch**
Publisher: **Paul Carslake**
QUA:HCH

For Reader's Digest
U.S. Project Editor: **Mary Connell**
Canadian Project Editor: **Pamela Johnson**
Australian Project Editor: **Annette Carter**
Project Designer: **Mabel Zorzano**
Associate Art Director: **George McKeon**
Executive Editor, Trade Publishing: **Dolores York**
Associate Publisher: **Rosanne McManus**
President and Publisher, Trade Publishing: **Harold Clarke**

Library of Congress Cataloging-in-Publication Data
Nettelhorst, R. P.
  The Bible's most fascinating people : an illustrated collection :
  stories from the Old and New Testaments / R. P. Nettelhorst.
    p. cm
  Includes index.
  ISBN: 0–7621–0888–6 (978–0–7621–0888–6)
  1. Bible--Biography. 2. Bible stories, English. I. Title.
  BS571.N48 2007
  220.9'2--dc22   2007022101

We are committed to both the quality of our products and the
service we provide to our customers. We value your comments,
so please feel free to contact us. Address any comments about
The Bible's Most Fascinating People to:
The Reader's Digest Association, Inc.
Adult Trade Publishing
Reader's Digest Road
Pleasantville, NY 10570-7000

For more Reader's Digest products and information,
visit our website:
www.rd.com (in the United States)
www.readersdigest.ca (in Canada)
www.readersdigest.com.au (in Australia)

Color separation by Modern Age Repro House Ltd, Hong Kong
Printed by 1010 Printing International Ltd, China

1 3 5 7 9 10 8 6 4 2

Contents

Introduction

For millions of people the Bible is the Word of God, but in fact the "good book" is also the work of many authors writing over the centuries. The tales they tell are not of plaster saints but of vibrant and often flawed men and women who accomplished great things even though they frequently made wrong choices.

Their stories are told in three separate and distinct parts of the Bible that are not revered by all religions in the same way: the Old Testament, the New Testament, and the Apocrypha. Jews and Christians accept the Old Testament as scripture, while only Christians consider the New Testament as sacred. Jews and Protestants reject the Apocrypha, while Roman Catholics and the Eastern Orthodox churches consider it a part of the Old Testament and therefore holy writ. Each major section of the Bible is divided into "books"—there are 39 in the Old Testament and 27 in the New Testament. The number of books in the Apocrypha varies, with Roman Catholic, Eastern Orthodox, Oriental Orthodox, and Eastern Catholic churches each accepting different apocryphal books as canonical scripture.

God appears as the leading character in Genesis, the first book of the Bible, and is a presence throughout all of the others, sometimes as an actor on stage but more often as the director behind it. In the Old Testament God is called Yahweh, translated as "Lord" or "Jehovah" in English.

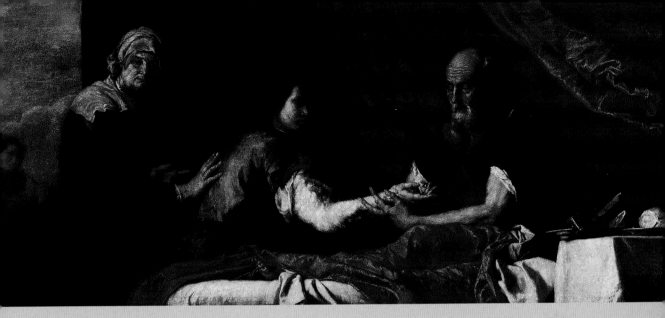

The authors of the Bible tell stories, myths, and legends of the ancient world, and their reactions to them, rooted in their own experience. *Enuma Elish,* the Babylonian creation epic, describes the violent emergence of their many gods, who treat humankind as their servants. The Bible, in contrast, portrays only one God who creates humans to rule the Earth. Babylonians had a polytheistic view of the world that held gods to be local and national, while the Jews saw only one God who cared for all of humanity.

Is the Bible true? Are Shakespeare's plays? Drama is written for entertainment, not to teach history, and the Bible, likewise, is neither an encyclopedia nor a history text, but a work with a theological purpose. It can be compared to a grand painting that reveals a God who loves people despite their flaws. He takes them as they are and does not wait for their perfection, but in the process of engaging them changes them. Jesus' own summary of the Bible was simple: "Love the Lord your God with all your heart" and "Love your neighbor as yourself" (Matthew 22:36–40); St. Paul later made the same point (Romans 13:8–10).

In this book you will find the stories of the most fascinating people in the Bible. Ancient genealogies show the connections between them. Their lives illustrate the overarching theme of love in the Bible.

All dates are approximate. Names in boldface within each profile indicate that there is a separate article about that person.

THE OLD TESTAMENT

The Old Testament, as it is most commonly called by Christians—or the *Tanakh*, as referenced by Jews—was composed over a period of several hundred years by many individuals. Written mainly in Hebrew, with some small parts in a related Semitic language called Aramaic, it is mostly an anonymous work. Although the contents of the Old Testament are identical for Protestants and Jews, the order and categorization of the books differ. Roman Catholics and Eastern Orthodox believers add some extra books called the Apocrypha.

A certain culture shock will face any modern reader of these materials. Urbanites may be puzzled by the details of ancient farming methods. Citizens of industrialized nations who expect precision in measurements will be shocked when it is not there. Moderns will read the word "Earth" in the Bible and picture a blue ball spinning in space, whereas the original authors knew it only as the dry land they could see stretching to the horizon or bounded by oceans.

Westerners may struggle with the storytelling techniques of the Bible. While modern novels are often slavishly tied to the chronology of the events being related, ancient authors of scripture often allowed thematic elements to overwhelm the time frame.

In Genesis, for instance, the creation narrative that begins the Bible—details of how God proceeded over six days—does not follow an exactly chronological pattern. Related ideas are arranged thematically. Notice that on the first three days God prepared empty spaces, while on the last three days, those empty places are filled with objects: On the first day, light and darkness—day and night—appear, while on the fourth day, the sun fills the day with light and the moon and stars fill the night. Likewise, on the second day, God makes the waters in oceans and clouds, while on the fifth day he fills them with fish and birds. On the third day, dry land separates out from the waters, while on the sixth day animals and human beings inhabit the surface of the Earth. God then rests on the seventh day.

Likewise, when poetry appears in the Old Testament, it fails to perform according to modern expectations. Rather than rhyming ending sounds of words, biblical Hebrew poetry uses parallel ideas, reworking identical thoughts with different words. This format often intrudes into the way stories are told, with the same incidents being revisited but from different points of view.

The author of Genesis, for example, first details Sarah's role in God's promise of a son, and follows it immediately with Abraham's, retelling the same story all over again (Genesis 17 and 18). Unwary readers might imagine they are reading about an entirely different incident, rather than the same one told twice, with only a shift in perspective.

Another peculiar aspect of the Bible for modern readers is the genealogies. One purpose of the family trees was to connect the original readers of the Bible to the people portrayed in the stories within. A second purpose was to demonstrate the value of the individual. Not just the nation was important; individual human beings who made it all happen mattered, too.

CONTENT AND CATEGORIZATION OF THE OLD TESTAMENT BOOKS

The Law of Moses (Pentateuch): Genesis; Exodus; Leviticus; Numbers; Deuteronomy

History books: Joshua; Judges; Ruth; 1 Samuel; 2 Samuel; 1 Kings; 2 Kings; 1 Chronicles; 2 Chronicles; Ezra; Nehemiah; Esther

Wisdom books: Job; Psalms; Proverbs; Ecclesiastes; Song of Solomon

Major prophets: Isaiah; Jeremiah; Lamentations; Ezekiel; Daniel

Minor prophets: Hosea; Joel; Amos; Obadiah; Jonah; Micah; Nahum; Habakkuk; Zephaniah; Haggai; Zechariah; Malachi

Apochrypha (New Revised Standard Version): I Esdras; 2 Esdras; Tobit; Judith; Additions to Esther; Wisdom of Solomon; Ecclesiasticus, or the Wisdom of Jesus the Son of Sirach; Baruch; Letter of Jeremiah; Additions to Daniel, including the Prayer of Azariah and the Song of the Three Jews, Susanna, and Bel and the Dragon; Prayer of Manasseh; 1 Maccabees; 2 Maccabees; 3 Maccabees; 4 Maccabees; Psalm 151

Old Testament Genealogies

The 39 books of the Old Testament, called the *Tanakh* by Jews, are sacred scripture to Jews and Christians alike. All Israelites are descended from one of the twelve sons of Jacob. Jacob also goes by the name Israel. The Bible is filled with the genealogical listings of the people within its pages. This family tree gives a simplified overview of family relationships in the Old Testament. Several unnamed generations often intervene between names on the branches. Additional genealogical information is provided within each person's article where appropriate.

The Mountains of Ararat

This genealogical engraving depicts how the Earth was peopled by Noah and his descendants after the Great Flood. The mountains of Ararat are named in Genesis 8:4 as the place where Noah's Ark came to rest after the flood. (English, 1749)

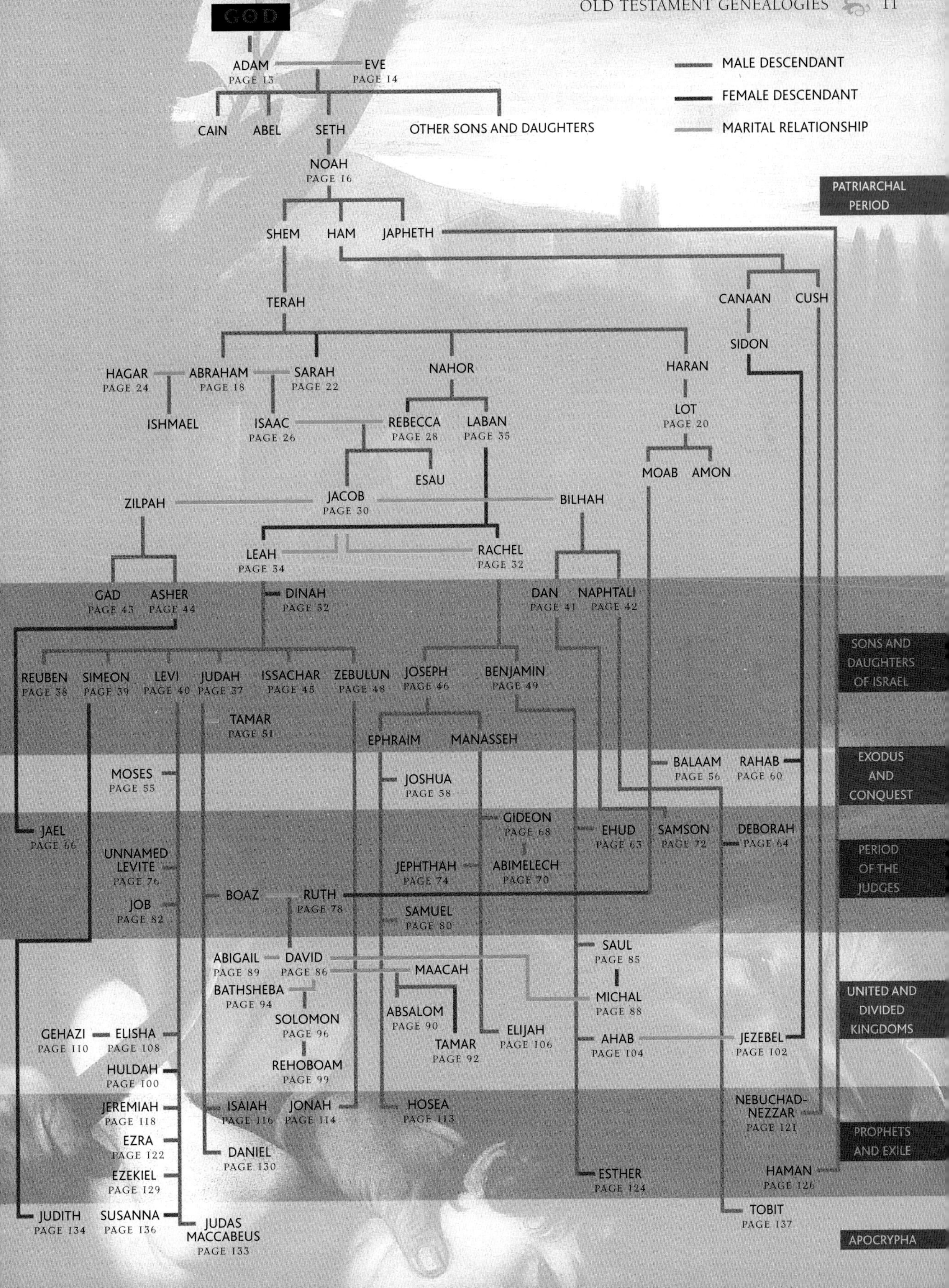

GOD

ADAM
PAGE 13

EVE
PAGE 14

CAIN   ABEL   SETH   OTHER SONS AND DAUGHTERS

──── MALE DESCENDANT

──── FEMALE DESCENDANT

──── MARITAL RELATIONSHIP

NOAH
PAGE 16

PATRIARCHAL
PERIOD

SHEM   HAM   JAPHETH

CANAAN   CUSH

TERAH

SIDON

HAGAR
PAGE 24

ABRAHAM
PAGE 18

SARAH
PAGE 22

NAHOR

HARAN

ISHMAEL

ISAAC
PAGE 26

REBECCA
PAGE 28

LABAN
PAGE 35

LOT
PAGE 20

ESAU

MOAB   AMON

ZILPAH

JACOB
PAGE 30

BILHAH

LEAH
PAGE 34

RACHEL
PAGE 32

GAD
PAGE 43

ASHER
PAGE 44

DINAH
PAGE 52

DAN
PAGE 41

NAPHTALI
PAGE 42

SONS AND
DAUGHTERS
OF ISRAEL

REUBEN
PAGE 38

SIMEON
PAGE 39

LEVI
PAGE 40

JUDAH
PAGE 37

ISSACHAR
PAGE 45

ZEBULUN
PAGE 48

JOSEPH
PAGE 46

BENJAMIN
PAGE 49

TAMAR
PAGE 51

EPHRAIM   MANASSEH

MOSES
PAGE 55

JOSHUA
PAGE 58

BALAAM
PAGE 56

RAHAB
PAGE 60

EXODUS
AND
CONQUEST

JAEL
PAGE 66

GIDEON
PAGE 68

EHUD
PAGE 63

SAMSON
PAGE 72

DEBORAH
PAGE 64

PERIOD
OF THE
JUDGES

UNNAMED
LEVITE
PAGE 76

JEPHTHAH
PAGE 74

ABIMELECH
PAGE 70

BOAZ

RUTH
PAGE 78

JOB
PAGE 82

SAMUEL
PAGE 80

ABIGAIL
PAGE 89

DAVID
PAGE 86

MAACAH

SAUL
PAGE 85

BATHSHEBA
PAGE 94

MICHAL
PAGE 88

UNITED AND
DIVIDED
KINGDOMS

GEHAZI
PAGE 110

ELISHA
PAGE 108

SOLOMON
PAGE 96

ABSALOM
PAGE 90

ELIJAH
PAGE 106

AHAB
PAGE 104

JEZEBEL
PAGE 102

TAMAR
PAGE 92

HULDAH
PAGE 100

REHOBOAM
PAGE 99

JEREMIAH
PAGE 118

ISAIAH
PAGE 116

JONAH
PAGE 114

HOSEA
PAGE 113

NEBUCHAD-
NEZZAR
PAGE 121

PROPHETS
AND EXILE

EZRA
PAGE 122

DANIEL
PAGE 130

EZEKIEL
PAGE 129

ESTHER
PAGE 124

HAMAN
PAGE 126

JUDITH
PAGE 134

SUSANNA
PAGE 136

JUDAS
MACCABEUS
PAGE 133

TOBIT
PAGE 137

APOCRYPHA

PATRIARCHAL PERIOD

The Patriarchal Period is contained within the pages of Genesis, the first book of the Bible. Traditionally attributed to Moses, Genesis is in fact an anonymous work, like most of the books that make up the Old Testament. Beginning with the story of the creation of the universe, Genesis moves quickly from fratricide to the Great Flood. Biblical genealogies show ten generations from Adam to Noah, and ten between Noah and Abraham. In the seventeenth century, Bishop Ussher, a religious scholar and Primate of All Ireland, published a chronology that attempted to pin the creation to 4004 B.C.E. by adding up the patriarchs' life spans. However, the selective nature of these genealogies, along with the biblical authors' general disinterest in chronology, demonstrate that time-span calculations were not likely their purpose.

The Condemnation of Adam by God
God condemned Adam and his descendants to a life of hard physical labor and banished him from the Garden of Eden. (Jacopo Bassano, c. 1510–92)

ADAM

Adam, the first human being, was given the world's first job: to tend the Garden of Eden.

GOD
ADAM ———— EVE

CAIN   ABEL   SETH   OTHER SONS AND DAUGHTERS

NOAH

ANCESTRY

Primary appearance in the Bible:
Genesis 1–5

—— MALE
—— FEMALE
—— MARRIED

The author of Genesis writes that God created the first man, Adam, from dust. In Hebrew, the name Adam simply means "of the earth." God says that he made the first man and woman as a pair "in the image of God" (Genesis 1:27). Thus, the image of God is reflected in men and women as a unity.

Just as all parts of our bodies are important and the lack of any part is missed, so every human being is vital, and needed to reflect the fullness of the divine. Human beings were designed to be like God. The contrast between the biblical concept of humanity versus that of the surrounding Near Eastern cultures is striking. Where Babylonians thought of human beings as slaves of the gods, human beings are pictured as lords of creation in the Bible. God tells Adam and his wife, **Eve,** "Be fruitful and increase in number; fill the earth and subdue it. Rule over the fish of the sea and the birds of the air and over every living creature that moves on the ground" (Genesis 1:28).

In the Garden of Eden, God lets Adam name all the animals, before putting him to sleep and building a woman from his rib. Two trees in the Garden are special: the Tree of Life and the Tree of the Knowledge of Good and Evil. Adam may eat from every tree, except those. If he eats from the Tree of the Knowledge of Good and Evil, God says he will die.

Unfortunately, Adam eats that Forbidden Fruit, bringing mortality upon himself and the human race. In the fifth century, St. Augustine described this as original sin, which has afflicted humanity ever since, explaining thereby the presence of evil in our lives. Since God allowed Adam and Eve freedom of choice to obey or not, we may conclude from the story that God believes freedom is very important—perhaps more important than making us behave. The unfortunate consequence of human freedom is that people can make poor choices, but God would rather have that than robots.

Following the disobedience of Adam, God cursed him and his descendants with hard physical labor that would often be unrewarding. Every human being will, some day, return to the dust from which he was created. Thanks to Adam, humans became mortal.

Adam was expelled from the Garden of Eden with his wife. The way to the Tree of Life was blocked by sword-wielding angels to prevent humanity from gaining immortality by eating its fruit. In Christian thought, the barring from the Tree of Life is considered a blessing, because it made redemption possible. The immortal God became a mortal human being: **Jesus.** Had Adam and Eve eaten from the Tree of Life and gained immortality for humanity, Jesus, like any human being in that case, would have been unable to die. Without his death, humanity would have remained forever cursed, with no hope of salvation.

Another clear purpose of the creation narrative in Genesis was to argue for the universalism of God: Yahweh was not a deity belonging only to the Jewish people. Rather, all human beings were his offspring.

EVE

Eve, the first woman, was created by God from one of Adam's ribs, and she became Adam's wife.

God created Eve to be a "helper suitable for him [**Adam**]" (Genesis 2:18). Early translations rendered this concept into English as "an help meet for him," in which "meet" meant a "suitable" partner to help Adam, compared to the animals in the garden. Eve's name (Havvah in Hebrew) means "life." According to the author of Genesis, Adam gave her this name because she would become "the mother of all the living" (Genesis 3:20). Since humanity is descended from Eve, all humans are essentially one family, according to the Bible.

In Genesis, a talking serpent approached Eve one day as she was walking about the Garden of Eden. The serpent told Eve that God was withholding something good by forbidding her to eat fruit from the Tree of the Knowledge of Good and Evil. Believing the serpent's lie, Eve went ahead and ate the fruit, then shared it with her husband Adam. Why did Adam eat fruit from the tree, when God had previously warned him that should he eat from it, he would most certainly die?

Perhaps he ate out of fear of being separated from Eve, the woman he loved. Some scholars suggest that, out of pride, he may have thought that eating the Forbidden Fruit would give him enough knowledge and power to raise him, a created human being, up to a level that would be equal to God. On the other hand, the biblical text clearly says that humanity was created to be like God: It was designed to rule over the world and all its creatures (Genesis 1:26–27). This portrayal of humanity as dominant is in sharp contrast to the Babylonian creation epic, *Enuma Elish*, where humans are created in order to serve the gods. In any case, as soon as Adam and Eve disobeyed God's warning and ate the Forbidden Fruit, they realized they had done a "bad" thing. Then God sent them out of the Garden of Eden.

God cursed the serpent for its role in tempting Eve, telling the beast that it would, from that day on, crawl on its belly and eat dust. Likewise, God told Eve that she would henceforth hate the serpent, and the serpent would strike at the feet of human beings—but human beings would crush the serpent's head. Many later Christian theologians interpreted the serpent as Satan, or somehow possessed by Satan, and believed that God figuratively spoke of the future, when **Jesus** would be victorious over the devil.

Following the condemnation of the talking serpent, God turned to Eve and pronounced two punishments upon her. First, God promised that childbirth would be a painful experience, and second, that her husband would now rule over her. God decreed mortality and hard, unrewarding physical labor to Adam. Humanity has ever since resisted and sought to overcome these hardships, with varying degrees of success.

In the New Testament, Jesus' sacrifice is believed to have vanquished these curses, especially that of death. The author of Revelation expresses that in the Kingdom of God, "No longer will there be any curse" (Revelation 22:3). Since one of the curses was that Eve

CAIN, ABEL, AND SETH

Adam and Eve's sons, Cain and Abel, brought God offerings, but God rejected Cain's because of his bad attitude, demonstrated when he murdered his brother Abel. Cain then married. Where did he get his wife? Genesis 5 explains that Adam and Eve had "many sons and daughters." So he married one of his sisters. Eve then gave birth to Seth, an ancestor of **Noah**.

GOD

ADAM — EVE

CAIN ABEL SETH OTHER SONS AND DAUGHTERS

NOAH

MALE

FEMALE

MARRIED

Primary
appearance in
the Bible:
Genesis 1–5

would be "subject" to her husband, it is not surprising that **Paul** writes about equality in the New Testament, "There is neither Jew nor Greek, slave nor free, male nor female, for you are all one in Christ Jesus" (Galatians 3:28).

A late Jewish text called the *Alphabet of Ben Sira*, written between the eighth and eleventh centuries C.E., relates that Lilith, not Eve, was Adam's first wife. According to this legend, Lilith was created from dust at the same time as Adam. Claiming to be his equal, she refused to sleep with Adam or serve "under him." When Adam tried to force her, she fled and ended up among demons. After conceiving hundreds of children with demons, God sent three angels after her, who threatened to kill a hundred of her children each day that she refused to return to Adam. She responded by threatening to kill the children of Adam and Eve and thus never returned to Adam.

Adam and Eve
Expelled from Paradise

Adam and Eve were expelled from the Garden to keep them from eating from the Tree of Life. Their future redemption would only be possible if they remained mortal. (Juan Correa, 1646–1716)

NOAH

At God's command, Noah built a large ship, loaded it with
animals, and survived the Great Flood that destroyed all life.

The story of Noah demonstrates that God, for all his love, is willing to punish people for evil they do, just as the most loving parents must discipline children. The story of the Great Flood is the first time in the Bible that rain is mentioned; weather simply played no role in earlier stories.

The world was full of violence and Noah alone found favor with God. God instructed Noah to build an ark, a large ship measuring about 450 feet long, 75 feet wide, and 45 feet high (137 x 23 x 13.5 meters). God told Noah to load two pairs of each species of sacrificial animal and seven pairs of every other animal species. The only humans spared from the flood were four pairs: Noah and his wife, and his three sons and their wives.

After 40 days and nights of rain, the world was covered with water. Nearly a year later, Noah released a variety of birds to determine whether it was safe to leave the ark. After Noah offered a sacrifice to thank God for everyone's survival, God promised Noah and every living thing that he would never again destroy the world by such a flood. The rainbow would serve as a reminder of God's promise. God told Noah and his family to repopulate the world. Although people had subsisted only on vegetation before the flood, now God told them that they could also eat meat. In addition, whereas **Adam** and **Eve**'s son Cain had been banished for murdering his brother Abel, now murder was to be punished by death. Noah also planted a vineyard, made wine, and got drunk. Noah died at the extreme age of 950.

Noah's Ark

"For forty days the flood kept coming on the earth, and as the waters increased they lifted the ark high above the earth."
Genesis 7:17 *(School of Raphael, mid-sixteenth century)*

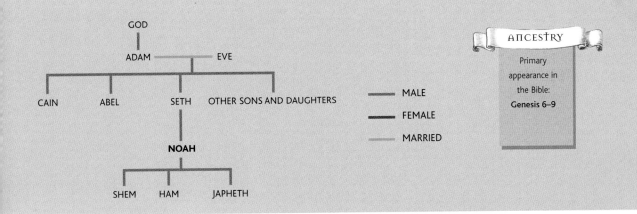

GOD

ADAM ——— EVE

CAIN   ABEL   SETH   OTHER SONS AND DAUGHTERS

NOAH

SHEM   HAM   JAPHETH

—— MALE

—— FEMALE

—— MARRIED

ANCESTRY

Primary appearance in the Bible:
Genesis 6–9

The story of Noah is not unique to the Bible. In the *Epic of Gilgamesh*, the Babylonians relate the story of a man named Utnapishtim who survived a great flood. Tired of people, the gods decided to destroy them. One god, however, disagreed with the planned extermination and warned Utnapishtim, who built a cubical ship and rode out a devastating flood. Afterward, the gods swarmed around Utnapishtim's sacrificial offering "like flies." They were thankful that their plan to exterminate the human race had failed because they had forgotten about their need to be fed by regular sacrifice and had become very hungry during the deluge.

Another Babylonian account of the flood shows up in what is called the *Atrahasis Epic*. Where the Bible says that God brought on the flood due to humanity's wickedness, the *Atrahasis Epic* explains that the god Enlil was finding it hard to sleep because of a noisy and ever-growing human population. He turned to the divine assembly for help. They sent a series of disasters in an attempt to reduce the human population and thereby still the noise. Following each attack, there was a temporary respite, but nothing solved the problem permanently because humans were so fertile. Eventually the gods decided on a final solution: just kill everyone with a great flood. However, one of the gods, Enki, had moral objections to this plan and revealed the gods' intentions to Atrahasis, who built a ship to rescue himself and his family from the impending calamity. To prevent the other gods from bringing such a disaster ever again, Enki found ways to reduce the tendency for human overpopulation by creating women who never married, infertility, miscarriages, and infant mortality.

Despite some similarities in details between the stories, the Babylonian versions contrast significantly with the biblical account on a fundamental point: The Bible is rooted in a strict belief in only one God. Some scholars believe that the biblical and other flood stories may derive from common memories of an ancient cataclysm.

Noah Cursing Canaan
"Cursed be Canaan! The lowest of slaves will he be to his brothers."
Genesis 9:25 *(Gustave Doré, 1832–83)*

SHEM, HAM, AND JAPHETH

Noah's three children who survived the flood with him were Shem, Ham, and Japheth. While Noah blessed Shem and Japheth, he cursed Canaan, one of Ham's children, who was the father of the Canaanites. According to Genesis 9:21–27, Noah got drunk and lay naked on the ground. His son Ham saw his father and, instead of helping him, told his siblings. They covered their senseless father without looking at him. A sober Noah later cursed Ham's son Canaan with enslavement by Ham's two brothers. Later in the Old Testament, God ordered the Israelites—descendants of Shem—to displace and exterminate the Canaanites for their wickedness, such as their practice of child sacrifice. Rather than killing all the Canaanites, the Israelites simply enslaved many of them (Joshua 9:25–27).

ABRAHAM

Abraham, married to his half-sister Sarah, was the father of the Jewish people and founder of monotheism.

Abraham, also called Abram, was born in Ur near the Persian Gulf in what is today Iraq. As a young man, he married his beautiful half-sister, Sarai (whose name was later changed to **Sarah**). God told him to leave his homeland and "go to the land I will show you" (Genesis 12:1) that turned out to be Ancient Palestine. God made an agreement with him, promising him the land of Ancient Palestine, prosperity, fame, and offspring who would become a blessing to humanity. God promised to keep him and his descendants safe: "I will bless those who bless you, and whoever curses you I will curse; and all peoples on earth will be blessed through you" (Genesis 12:3).

In making this contract with Abraham, God first performed what appears to modern readers to be a very odd ceremony: God had Abraham take a heifer, a goat, and a ram and cut them in half. Late that night, God appeared as a flaming fire pot and walked between the halves of the animals. Why? In the ancient Near East, when kings signed a contract, they would perform this very ritual, walking side by side between the split animals. The image implied that should either signatory to the contract renege, then what had happened to the animals would

happen to him. Thus by using a custom from Abraham's culture, God reassured Abraham that his promise to him was certain: He would have children. In addition, God ordered that Abraham, his servants, and all male children of Abraham from that day forward should be circumcised, as a sign of the contract God had made with Abraham and his descendants.

Abraham and his wife Sarah were old and childless. Following the customs of the day, Abraham first designated a servant as his heir. Later, at Sarah's urging, Sarah's servant **Hagar** became Abraham's secondary wife. Hagar gave birth to Ishmael, but God told Abraham that Ishmael would not be the promised heir. Instead, Sarah herself finally became pregnant in her extreme old age and gave birth to **Isaac.**

So, Ishmael and his mother Hagar were driven into exile. Later, God told Abraham to sacrifice Isaac as a burnt offering. At the last minute, God stopped Abraham and told him to sacrifice a ram instead. Later Jewish and Christian commentators suggest that the purpose of this very odd exercise was to teach something about the nature of sacrifice: The sacrificial animal took the place of the sinner. Some argue that the story may also be designed

to discourage the Israelites from sacrificing their children, a common practice in many neighboring cultures.

Abraham's nephew **Lot,** who traveled with him for a time, settled near Sodom and Gomorrah. When Sodom and Gomorrah were attacked by raiders, they carried off Lot. Abraham pursued the raiders and defeated them, rescuing Lot, his family, and all his belongings. Years later, Abraham would bargain with God over the fate of Sodom and Gomorrah. God promised he would spare the notorious cities if he could find ten righteous people in them. Unfortunately, God could not find anyone who fit the criteria except for Lot, his wife, and his two daughters. God agreed to spare their lives, destroying those two cities only after angels sent Lot and his family away.

After Sarah's death at the age of 127, Abraham remarried and had other children by his wives and concubines. He died at the age of 180.

The Sacrifice of Isaac
"Take your son, your only son, Isaac, whom you love, and go to the region of Moriah. Sacrifice him there as a burnt offering on one of the mountains." Genesis 22:2 *(Caravaggio, 1571–1610)*

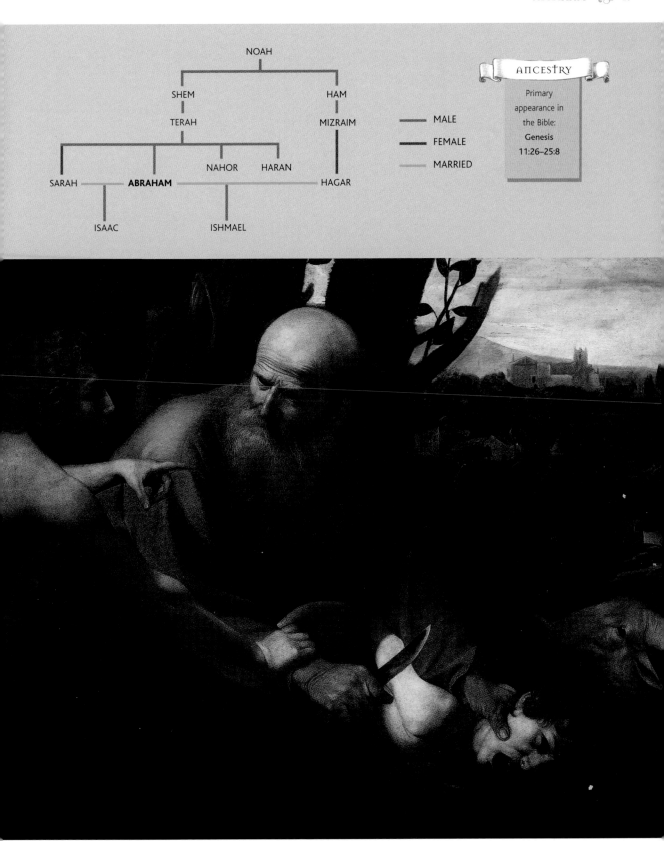

NOAH

SHEM | HAM

TERAH | MIZRAIM

NAHOR | HARAN

SARAH — ABRAHAM — HAGAR

ISAAC | ISHMAEL

—— MALE

—— FEMALE

—— MARRIED

ANCESTRY

Primary
appearance in
the Bible:
Genesis
11:26–25:8

LOT

Abraham's nephew Lot survived the destruction of Sodom and Gomorrah, together with his two daughters.

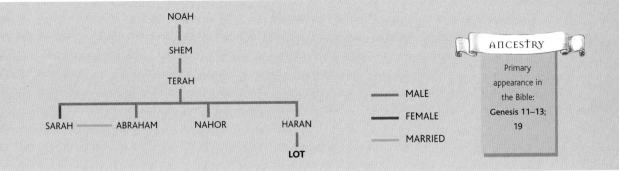

NOAH

SHEM

TERAH

SARAH —— ABRAHAM   NAHOR   HARAN

LOT

—— MALE

—— FEMALE

—— MARRIED

ANCESTRY

Primary appearance in the Bible: Genesis 11–13; 19

L ot was **Abraham**'s nephew and traveling companion. When their flocks got too large for their grazing lands, the men were forced to separate. Lot moved to a region near Sodom and Gomorrah and became a leader in the city of Sodom. Sodom's later rebellion against its Mesopotamian masters resulted in Lot and his family being taken prisoner. Abraham then managed to rescue him (Genesis 14).

After God decided to destroy Sodom and Gomorrah because of their inhabitants' wickedness, he revealed his plans to Abraham. Thinking of Lot, Abraham begged God to spare the cities if he could find ten righteous people there. God agreed and sent two angels to search for them.

Not recognizing the two angels as anything other than human travelers, Lot offered them lodging in his house. When a mob appeared at his door demanding that the two men be brought out to be raped, Lot refused, offering his two daughters instead. The mob rejected his counteroffer and

Lot's Family Leaving Sodom
"But Lot's wife looked back, and she became a pillar of salt."
Genesis 19:26 *(Juan Urruchi, 1828–92)*

attempted to break into his home. Why did the men of the town want to rape the visitors? Although the story is sometimes used to condemn homosexuality, it is unlikely that homosexuality actually had much to do with what was happening there. Rather, the mob viewed the angels as a threat that needed to be subdued. By engaging in intercourse with them, they hoped to demonstrate their dominance over the visitors.

The angels intervened, blinded the mob, and forcibly removed a reluctant Lot, his wife, and two daughters from the city, warning them to flee from the place and not look back. Unfortunately, Lot's wife disobeyed, looked back, and turned into a pillar of salt.

Although the Bible does not give Lot's wife a name, Jewish tradition calls her Edith. As to the reason for her transformation, one thought is that her "looking back" was not out of curiosity, but rather out of wistfulness and a desire to be back in Sodom. Thus, it can be argued that God granted her desire to remain in Sodom and so she experienced what its wicked inhabitants experienced.

Lot and his two daughters escaped the destruction and wound up living in a cave, far from any city. Fearful of never having children of their own,

the daughters gave their father wine and slept with him. One daughter gave birth to a son named Moab and the other to a son named Amon. A descendant of Moab, **Ruth,** became the great-grandmother of **David,** king of Israel.

So the question becomes: If God destroyed Sodom and Gomorrah for their wickedness, how is it that Lot was spared? What made him "righteous" enough to be rescued?

While the New Testament describes Lot as a righteous man (2 Peter 2:7–8), it is clear that Lot is not considered righteous as a consequence of his behavior. Rather, his righteousness is understood to be a result of his relationship with God: Despite the fact he behaved abominably, he cared about God and apparently wanted to do what God wanted, even if most of the time he could not manage it. The story seems to serve as an illustration of the possibility of forgiveness, mercy, and grace, even in the face of deserved judgment.

In the New Testament, **Jesus** argues that the fate of Lot's wife also serves as a warning for those who are unprepared for his coming: "Remember Lot's wife! Whoever tries to keep his life will lose it, and whoever loses his life will preserve it" (Luke 17:32–33).

SARAH

Sarah, also called Sarai, was Abraham's wife and half-sister.
At the age of 90 she gave birth to her firstborn son, Isaac.

Abraham's wife and half-sister—they shared a father but had different mothers—the lovely Sarah was known as Sarai most of her life. When God made a contract with Abraham and changed his name, he also changed her name to Sarah.

The biblical text notes that Sarah was extremely beautiful. So beautiful, in fact, that when they entered a town Abraham was always worried that someone would steal Sarah away and murder him. So wherever they went, he had her tell people that she was his sister—a half-truth. As a consequence, at least twice in his life, other men took Sarah to become their wife. They both paid Abraham well for his "sister," and he seemed willing to go along with the transactions. In both instances, however, God intervened to prevent the marriages from being consummated when the truth of Abraham and Sarah's relationship was revealed. Remarkably, in both cases Abraham made a good profit and escaped unpunished by the men who had been fooled.

What Sarah thought of her husband's subterfuge is never revealed in the Bible. Her primary concern most of the time was that she was unable to conceive or bear children. Years later, when God arrived one day at their tent accompanied by two angels to inform Sarah that she was finally going to give birth, her response was laughter. She laughed, not only because she knew she was too old to bear children, but also because Abraham was too old to sire a child.

Miraculously, although she was 90 years of age and Abraham was 100, she gave birth to her firstborn son **Isaac** a year after God told her that it would happen. Isaac was not the first child in her extended family, however. Thirteen years before, Sarah had talked Abraham into taking her servant **Hagar** as a secondary wife. Sarah wanted Abraham to have an heir, and if Sarah could not provide an heir herself, she could claim a child by means of a surrogate. Such arrangements were not uncommon in the second millennium B.C.E. culture of the ancient Near East.

Hagar had got pregnant easily and had given birth to the one whom they thought would be heir: Ishmael. However, Sarah was jealous and made life so unpleasant for Hagar that Hagar had even run away for a while during her pregnancy. Now, having finally given birth to Isaac years later, Sarah decided she wanted to undo her first attempt at producing an heir, so she told Abraham to get rid of both Hagar and Ishmael for good.

Ordinarily, that would have been impossible. The law was clear: The firstborn was the firstborn, regardless of the status of the wife. Sarah could not easily get rid of Hagar and Ishmael simply because they stood in the way of Sarah's own flesh and blood getting the birthright. However, she was determined and eventually prevailed upon Abraham to grant her request. It helped that God finally told Abraham to listen to his wife, and so Abraham expelled Ishmael and his mother. Thus, Sarah's son, Isaac, could become the heir.

Sarah lived until she was 127 years old. After burying her in a cave near Hebron that Abraham had purchased from the local Hittites, he remarried and had other sons and daughters.

The Angel Appearing to Sarah

"Abraham and Sarah were already old and well advanced in years, and Sarah was past the age of childbearing. So Sarah laughed to herself as she thought, 'After I am worn out and my master is old, will I now have this pleasure?'" Genesis 18:11–12 *(Giambattista Tiepolo, 1696–1770)*

NOAH

SHEM HAM

TERAH MIZRAIM

SARAH ABRAHAM NAHOR HARAN HAGAR

ISAAC ISHMAEL

MALE

FEMALE

MARRIED

ANCESTRY

Primary
appearance in
the Bible:
Genesis 11–12;
16–23

HAGAR

Sarah's servant Hagar became Abraham's secondary wife and the mother of Ishmael, Abraham's firstborn son.

Hagar and Ishmael in the Desert Comforted by an Angel

"God heard the boy crying, and the angel of God called to Hagar from heaven and said to her, 'What is the matter, Hagar? Do not be afraid; God has heard the boy crying as he lies there. Lift the boy up and take him by the hand, for I will make him into a great nation.'" Genesis 21:17 (Francesco Solimena, 1657–1747)

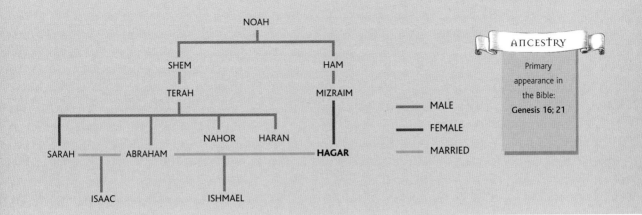

NOAH

SHEM | HAM

TERAH | MIZRAIM

NAHOR | HARAN

SARAH | ABRAHAM | HAGAR

ISAAC | ISHMAEL

—— MALE
—— FEMALE
—— MARRIED

ANCESTRY

Primary appearance in the Bible:
Genesis 16; 21

Hagar was an Egyptian woman who served as a slave in **Abraham**'s household. As **Sarah,** his first wife, grew older and older without conceiving a child, she began to think about using Hagar as a surrogate mother for their childless family. This might be the only way to have the son she had always wanted. Elevating a slave in this way as a secondary wife for her husband was a legally recognized practice in the ancient Near East. Finally, Sarah asked Abraham to take Hagar as a wife. He agreed. Once Hagar was pregnant, however, Sarah became jealous because of Hagar's change of status as well as her increasing arrogance. Sarah treated her so badly that the frightened Hagar ran away.

In the wilderness, the angel of Yahweh appeared and told Hagar that she would have a son whom she would name Ishmael. "I will

so increase your descendants that they will be too numerous to count" (Genesis 16:10) and Ishmael will be "a wild donkey of a man; his hand will be against everyone and everyone's hand against him, and he will live in hostility toward all his brothers" (Genesis 16:12).

Hagar responded by telling Yahweh: "You are the God who sees me," commenting "I have now seen the One who sees me" (Genesis 16:13). Abraham was 86 years old when Hagar gave birth to Ishmael.

Years later, Abraham drove both Hagar and Ishmael into exile, so that Sarah's son **Isaac** could become the heir. In the desert of Beersheba, Hagar ran out of water. Leaving Ishmael, she ran off to cry, but while she sobbed, God sent an angel who told her, "Do not be afraid; God has heard the boy crying as he

lies there. Lift the boy up and take him by the hand, for I will make him into a great nation" (Genesis 21:17–18). Then the angel showed her a well of water. When Ishmael was fully grown, he became an archer. Arranged marriages were common in that era, and so Hagar found a wife for him in Egypt.

When Abraham died, the author of Genesis explains that Isaac and Ishmael came together and saw to it that Abraham was buried next to his wife, Sarah (Genesis 25:9). Ishmael is said to have had twelve sons, who became the founders of twelve tribes (Genesis 25:13–16).

In the New Testament, **Paul** writes to the Christian community in Galatia (Galatians 4:21–31) that just as Abraham had two children, one by a free woman, his wife, Sarah, and one by a slave woman, Hagar, so also were there two covenants or contracts that God had made: one of slavery to the Law of Moses, and one of freedom by grace in Christ. Paul compares Hagar to the Law given to Moses on Mount Sinai, and Sarah to the grace given by **Jesus'** death on the cross and argues that Christians are, figuratively speaking, the children of Sarah.

ISHMAEL

Ishmael was the firstborn son of Abraham and Abraham's servant and secondary wife, Hagar. Ultimately rejected by Abraham and disinherited, Ishmael grew up to be an archer. Traditionally, he is believed to be the father of all the Arab people. In fact, the *Quran*, the sacred scripture of Islam, reverses the roles of Isaac and Ishmael (*Quran* 37:102), with Ishmael as the heir instead of Isaac.

ISAAC

Isaac was Abraham's son and heir, whom Abraham tried to sacrifice as a burnt offering. Isaac became the father of Jacob.

Isaac is a transition character. He spends his time on the biblical stage being acted upon, rather than acting. When Isaac was a teenager, his father **Abraham** tried to sacrifice him because God asked him to do it. Isaac was spared only when God told Abraham to stop and not kill his son after all. Abraham substituted a ram for the boy.

Isaac remained unmarried until he was 40 years old, far older than normal in that culture. He managed to get a wife only when his father arranged a marriage for him. Abraham sent his servant Eliezer under oath to return to Abraham's homeland to find a relative for Isaac to marry. The servant prayed that God would send him a sign so that he would know which girl to pick. The servant was not shy about asking for a very specific sign: He told God that the girl who offered to give both him and his camels water from a nearby well should be the one. **Rebecca,** the sister of **Laban,** a son of Abraham's nephew, first offered him water and after he drank, took water to his camels. The servant brought her back for Isaac, who married her.

Like his father before him, Isaac was not always truthful about his relationship with his wife. Once, while visiting the Philistines in Gerar, he told the men who asked him about Rebecca that she was his sister. He was afraid they might kill him if they knew she was his wife, because she was so beautiful. However, one day Abimelech, the king of the Philistines, looked out his window and saw Isaac and Rebecca hugging and kissing. He summoned Isaac and told him, "She is really your

Isaac and Jacob

Rebecca dressed Jacob in goat skins so that Isaac, who was nearly blind, would mistake him for his brother Esau, who was covered with hair. As a result, Isaac gave Jacob the blessing of the firstborn. (Jusepe de Ribera, 1591–1652)

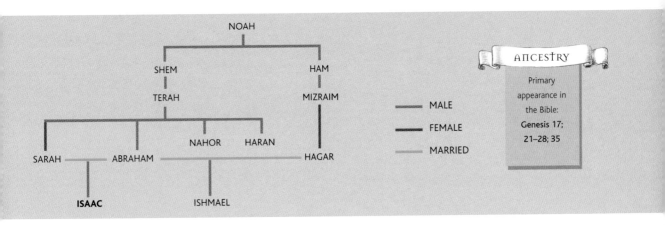

ANCESTRY

Primary
appearance in
the Bible:
Genesis 17;
21–28; 35

MALE

FEMALE

MARRIED

wife! Why did you say 'She is my sister'?" (Genesis 26:9). Isaac responded by telling the king how he feared for his life. The king yelled at him and said, "What is this you have done to us? One of the men might well have slept with your wife, and you would have brought guilt upon us" (Genesis 26:10). So, Abimelech issued a decree that anyone who harmed either Isaac or his wife would be executed.

Isaac's wife, Rebecca, later gave birth to fraternal twins: Esau and **Jacob.** Esau was his father's favorite. He was a good hunter and outdoorsman, noted for being covered head to foot with red hair. His younger brother Jacob liked to stay in camp and cook and became Rebecca's favorite. Rebecca was a conniving woman. Years later, when Isaac was old and suffering from poor eyesight, she helped Jacob to steal the blessing of the firstborn from his brother Esau.

Isaac died at the advanced age of 180.

REBECCA

Rebecca was Isaac's beautiful wife, the mother of the fraternal twins Jacob and Esau, and the sister of Laban.

It is not surprising that Rebecca agreed to an arranged marriage with **Abraham**'s son **Isaac,** sight unseen, because she knew that he was from a prominent and wealthy family. Isaac was still unmarried at the age of 40, so his father had sent his servant Eliezer to his homeland to seek a relative for his son to marry. When Eliezer arrived on the outskirts of Rebecca's village, he waited near the village well, praying that "May it be that when I say to a girl, 'Please let down your jar that I may have a drink,' and she says, 'Drink, and I'll water your camels, too'—let her be the one you have chosen for your servant Isaac. By this I will know that you have shown kindness to my master" (Genesis 24:14).

Rebecca came to the well, fulfilled his prayer, and so he gave her expensive jewelry. She invited Eliezer to her home, where he explained his purpose in coming. Once the family determined that Rebecca was willing to marry Isaac, they sent her off.

When she first saw Isaac, Rebecca fell off her camel, then quickly veiled herself. Although most suggest she veiled herself out of modesty, it may be that she was simply trying to hide herself from her future spouse. Given that she had been traveling for several weeks on camelback, it may be just that she wanted to bathe, change her clothes, and fix her hair before she revealed herself to Isaac.

Rebecca was infertile for the first twenty years of marriage. When she finally became pregnant, it was with twins: Esau and **Jacob.** They seemed to be fighting in her womb and so she asked God for an explanation. God informed her that her twins were going to become the founders of two nations who would be in conflict, and that the older son would serve the younger son. Some Jewish traditions explain that the older son was the progenitor of the Romans and that the prophecy therefore characterized the future relationship between Rome and the Jewish people. Most interpreters today believe the oldest son, Esau, was the father of the Edomites, a nation bordering Israel with whom they would battle for many years.

Rebecca thus gave birth to two sons. The firstborn, named Esau, apparently suffered from hypertrichosis, also called "werewolf syndrome"—he was born covered with red fur. Esau became a good hunter and was the favorite of his father Isaac. The second son, Jacob, born clutching Esau's heel, lacked both the excessive hair and any interest in hunting.

Jacob spent most of his time in camp with his mother. Rebecca doted on him and he was clearly her favorite.

One day Esau came home from a long day of hunting. Jacob was busy cooking a pot of stew. Esau wandered over and commented, "Quick, let me have some of that red stew! I'm famished!" Jacob responded, "First sell me your birthright" (Genesis 25:30–31). Esau agreed and accepted a bowl of stew in exchange for the birthright. What was the birthright? It imparted leadership in the family and granted double the inheritance.

A few years later, when the time came for his father Isaac to dispense the blessing of the firstborn, Rebecca conspired to ensure that it was given to Jacob instead of Esau. As with the other women mentioned in the patriarchal narratives, it seems that Rebecca was a very strong-willed individual, not afraid to stand up to the men around her.

Rebecca and Eliezer at the Well
Rebecca became Isaac's wife when he was 40, and later gave birth to fraternal twins, Esau and Jacob. Like her mother-in-law Sarah, she was noted as being strikingly beautiful. (Bartolomé Estebán Murillo, 1618–82)

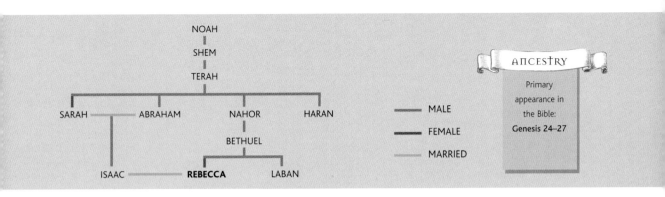

NOAH
SHEM
TERAH

SARAH — ABRAHAM   NAHOR   HARAN

BETHUEL

ISAAC — **REBECCA**   LABAN

— MALE

— FEMALE

— MARRIED

ANCESTRY

Primary appearance in the Bible: **Genesis 24–27**

JACOB

Jacob got into a wrestling match with an angel, had his name changed to Israel, and his twelve sons became the founding patriarchs of the Twelve Tribes of Israel.

The second-born twin son of **Rebecca** and **Isaac,** Jacob was a homebody and his mother's favorite. She conspired with him to steal his brother Esau's birthright—a blessing from their father and a larger part of the inheritance. Esau is described as a hunter, and he is also said to have been covered head to foot with hair. Isaac had asked Esau to go hunt down his favorite game and cook it for him; afterward, Isaac said, he would give Esau the blessing of the firstborn son. Esau left.

While Esau was gone, Jacob's mother helped Jacob dress up in goat skins in order to convince his nearly blind father Isaac that Jacob was his furry sibling. She also took two young goats and cooked them just the way Isaac liked. Then she sent Jacob in to see Isaac. Jacob was successful in convincing his father that he was Esau, and so Isaac gave Jacob the blessing he had promised Esau. Esau was furious when he found out his brother had stolen his blessing, so Jacob left home out of fear that his swindled brother might kill him. Jacob went to live with **Laban,** his mother's brother. Jacob quickly fell in love with his uncle's daughter, his cousin **Rachel.**

Laban consented to a marriage between Jacob and Rachel on the condition that Jacob would first work as his slave for seven years. The seven years sped by because of Jacob's love for Rachel, but at the wedding feast Jacob drank so much that he consummated the marriage later that night with Rachel's older sister, **Leah,** instead of the woman he loved.

Laban had tricked Jacob. During the festivities, he had switched daughters, explaining later that the older daughter must marry first. Jacob could also have Rachel, if he would agree to another seven years of servitude—and he could have her within a week, immediately following Leah's honeymoon. He would not have to wait until the agreed years of servitude had been fulfilled this time.

Once Jacob finally married his true love Rachel, it turned out that she had trouble getting pregnant. Her sister and Jacob's other wife, Leah, was having no such difficulty. So Rachel was miserable. Following the customs of the day, Jacob agreed to take Rachel's maidservant, Bilhah, as a third wife, so that she could serve as a surrogate to bear children for Rachel. Almost at once, Leah also became infertile, so by the time all was said and done, Jacob wound up with a fourth wife, Zilpah, to do the same for Leah as he was doing for Rachel. Leah, Bilhah, and Zilpah gave birth to Jacob's first ten sons, as well as his only daughter mentioned in the Bible. Through all this, his true love remained childless.

In the course of time, however, Rachel finally gave birth to a son, **Joseph.** Some while later, she gave birth to **Benjamin,** but she died in childbirth. This happened as Jacob was returning home to face Esau. Twenty years had passed and his brother finally forgave him. Besides losing Rachel, Jacob also had the odd experience of wrestling with an angel all night, so that God changed his name from Jacob to Israel, a name that means "he struggles with God." Some take this name and the wrestling match with the angel as a sort of prophecy that indicates the nature of the relationship the Jewish people would ever after have with their God.

Jacob showed favoritism to Joseph, the firstborn son of the one woman out of the four whom he had actually loved. Joseph's brothers hated him as a result, sold him into slavery, and then told Jacob that Joseph had been killed by wild animals. A heartbroken Jacob mourned Joseph for twenty years, before finally discovering him alive and prosperous as a ruler in Egypt. Jacob died at the age of 120.

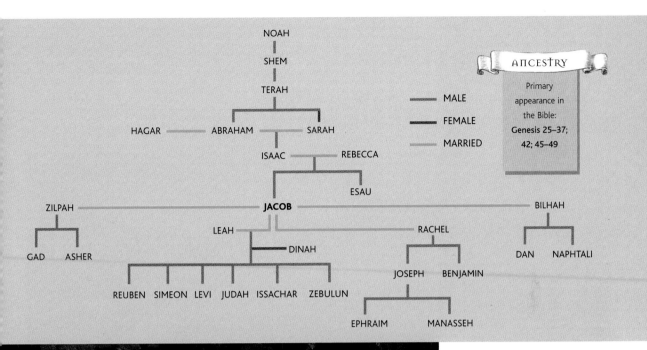

NOAH

SHEM

TERAH

HAGAR — ABRAHAM — SARAH

—— MALE
—— FEMALE
—— MARRIED

ISAAC — REBECCA

ESAU

JACOB

ZILPAH — JACOB — BILHAH

GAD   ASHER

LEAH

DINAH

RACHEL

DAN   NAPHTALI

REUBEN SIMEON LEVI JUDAH ISSACHAR ZEBULUN

JOSEPH BENJAMIN

EPHRAIM   MANASSEH

ANCESTRY

Primary appearance in the Bible: **Genesis 25–37; 42; 45–49**

ESAU

Esau was Jacob's brother, noted for being covered with red fur. He received an alternate name, Edom, explained in the Bible both as a reference to the "red stew" that he bought from his brother in exchange for the birthright and because of the red hair that covered his body. The Edomites are said to have descended from him. King Herod, ruling Judea as a puppet king set up by the Roman Empire when **Jesus** was born, was an Edomite.

Jacob Wrestling with the Angel

"Your name will no longer be Jacob, but Israel, because you have struggled with God and with men and have overcome." Genesis 32:28 *(Eugène Delacroix, 1798–1863)*

RACHEL

Rachel was Jacob's true love and his second of ultimately four wives.
She became the mother of Joseph and Benjamin.

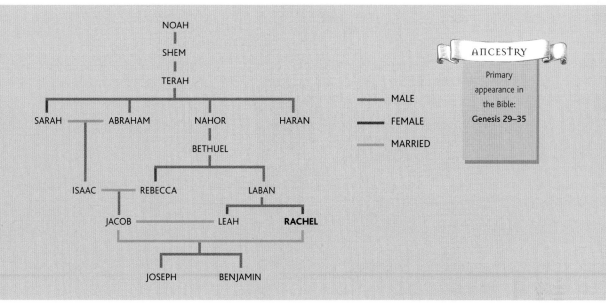

ANCESTRY

Primary appearance in the Bible: Genesis 29–35

MALE
FEMALE
MARRIED

When **Jacob** fled from his older twin brother Esau, he was in fear of his life. He had just tricked their aging father **Isaac** into giving him—instead of his older brother Esau—the blessing of the firstborn. His mother **Rebecca** suggested that he seek shelter with her family.

Upon arriving on the outskirts of their village, Jacob saw Rachel approaching the village well with a flock of sheep. Impressed by her beauty, he dashed to the well and rolled its covering stone out of the way. Then he drew water from the well and watered her sheep. After finishing the job, he kissed Rachel and burst into tears, announcing that he was her cousin. She immediately went and told her father **Laban,** who invited Jacob to come and stay with them.

The Meeting of Jacob and Rachel at the Well

"But Rachel was lovely in form, and beautiful." Genesis 29:17 *(School of Raphael, mid-sixteenth century)*

After Jacob had been there a month, Laban said to him: "Just because you are a relative of mine, should you work for me for nothing? Tell me what your wages should be" (Genesis 29:15). Jacob agreed to become his uncle's slave for seven years in exchange for the privilege of marrying Rachel, with whom he had already fallen desperately in love. The biblical text explains that he loved her so much that his seven years of servitude seemed like "only a few days" (Genesis 29:20).

Unfortunately, Laban had another daughter, **Leah,** and he thought Jacob was the perfect man for her, too. On the night of Jacob's wedding with Rachel, Laban got Jacob so drunk that when Jacob went to consummate the marriage, he was unaware that Laban had switched Rachel for the older daughter. Given the culture and laws of the time, the fact that he had slept with her following a formal wedding party meant that they were married. Laban told Jacob that if he would indenture himself

for another seven years, he could have Rachel after he had spent a week's honeymoon with Leah. Jacob agreed and wound up with Rachel as his second wife.

Rachel's relationship with her sister was contentious and full of jealousy, not least because she went for many years without being able to conceive a child. After her sister had given birth several times, Rachel finally got pregnant and gave birth to **Joseph,** who became Jacob's favorite son.

Twenty years later, when Jacob finally left Laban's servitude to return to his homeland, Rachel stole her family's household idols from her father and hid them. She did this because the one who held the idols would become the rightful heir to her father's property. Of course, Laban was angry and chased after Jacob in order to recover them, but was unable to locate them because Rachel hid them by sitting on them. A few months later during the journey she died giving birth to **Benjamin** and Jacob buried her along a road near Bethlehem.

LEAH

Leah was Jacob's first of ultimately four wives.
She gave birth to Jacob's firstborn son, Reuben.

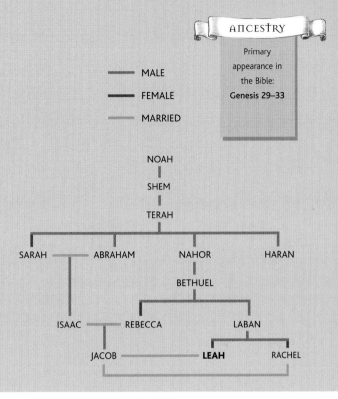

ANCESTRY

Primary
appearance in
the Bible:
Genesis 29–33

— MALE
— FEMALE
— MARRIED

NOAH
SHEM
TERAH

SARAH — ABRAHAM   NAHOR   HARAN

BETHUEL

ISAAC — REBECCA   LABAN

JACOB — **LEAH**   RACHEL

Dante's Vision of Rachel and Leah

Leah was not as beautiful as her sister Rachel. Her father had to trick Jacob into marrying her. (Dante Gabriel Rossetti, 1828–82)

Leah became **Jacob**'s wife through her father **Laban**'s trickery. On the wedding night of Jacob's marriage to her sister **Rachel,** Laban put Leah in the wedding tent in place of Rachel. Jacob, somewhat inebriated from the festivities, failed to recognize the switch and consummated his wedding with Leah. Jacob was furious, because it was Rachel he truly loved. Laban promised him Rachel as a second wife later.

The unloved Leah, ironically, was far the more fertile sister. She had at least seven pregnancies and gave birth to the founders of half the Twelve Tribes of Israel.

There was a considerable amount of jealousy between the two sisters. Although never outlawing polygamy, later Mosaic legislation prohibited men from marrying women who were sisters, perhaps as a consequence of Jacob's experiences.

One day, Leah's firstborn son **Reuben** found some mandrake roots, which were considered an aphrodisiac. Rachel asked for some of them. Leah commented, "Wasn't it enough that you took away my husband? Will you take my son's mandrakes too?" Rachel replied, "He can sleep with you tonight in return for your son's mandrakes" (Genesis 30:15).

Leah agreed, and told Jacob when he returned home from work that she had exchanged some mandrakes with Rachel so that he would spend the night with Leah. She became pregnant with the fifth of her six sons: **Issachar.** At his birth she expressed a belief that she had been granted that son because God was pleased with her decision to give her servant Zilpah to Jacob as another wife.

BILHAH AND ZILPAH

When Rachel discovered that she could not get pregnant, she gave Jacob her servant girl Bilhah as a wife to have children in her name. Later, when Leah became temporarily infertile, she gave Jacob Zilpah for the same reason. Both surrogates each gave birth to two boys. Bilhah had **Dan** and **Naphtali,** while Zilpah had **Gad** and **Asher.** It was not an uncommon practice in the ancient Near East for servant women to become surrogates for infertile primary wives.

LABAN

Laban was Jacob's uncle. He tricked Jacob into marrying his daughter Leah first, instead of Jacob's true love, Laban's other daughter Rachel.

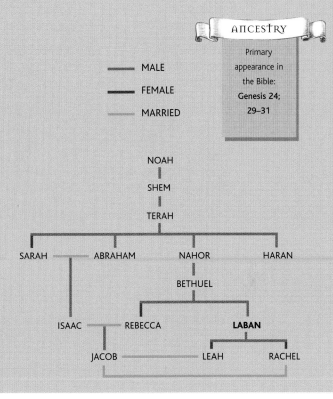

ANCESTRY

Primary appearance in the Bible: Genesis 24; 29–31

— MALE
— FEMALE
— MARRIED

NOAH
SHEM
TERAH
SARAH — ABRAHAM — NAHOR — HARAN
BETHUEL
ISAAC — REBECCA — **LABAN**
JACOB — LEAH — RACHEL

Rachel Hiding the Idols from Laban

Rachel, Laban's daughter and one of Jacob's wives, sat on the household idols to hide them from her father and save Jacob's inheritance. (Giambattista Tiepolo, 1696–1770)

aban lived in Mesopotamia. He was a speaker of Aramaic, a Semitic language similar to that spoken by **Abraham** and his descendants who had moved into Canaan. Laban was the brother of **Rebecca,** who agreed to send his sister with Abraham's servant to marry Abraham's son, **Isaac,** in the land of Canaan. Later, when his nephew **Jacob** arrived at his door, Laban was happy to put Jacob to work in exchange for marrying his youngest daughter, **Rachel.** Despite the fact that Aramaic was spoken by both his mother and his uncle, Jacob was primarily a speaker of a Canaanite dialect that would ultimately come to be known as Hebrew.

Laban was more concerned with maximizing his profits than doing what was right by his family. He repeatedly cheated his nephew, culminating in the switch on his wedding night when Jacob was tricked into marrying the older daughter, **Leah,** first. Laban continued to mistreat his nephew, so much so that when Jacob had finally had enough of him after twenty years and ran away with his wives and accumulated cattle wealth, Laban's daughter Rachel stole the household idols to make certain that her husband Jacob would not be cheated out of a proper inheritance. In the end, Laban accepted the separation of Jacob and his wives, and agreed to a treaty of peace, vowing never to enter armed conflict against his son-in-law. Obviously, his relationship with his daughters and son-in-law could never be described as harmonious.

During Passover ceremonies, the youngest child asks a question: "Why is this night different from all other nights?" The prescribed answer begins "An Aramean destroyed my father." Tradition argues that the Aramean referred to was Laban. Although Rachel was the woman whom God wanted Jacob to marry, Laban had tried to thwart God's will, and his trickery nearly led to the destruction of the Jews. If events had gone the way God originally intended, then Rachel's firstborn son **Joseph** would not have had jealous older brothers to sell him into Egyptian slavery. With no Egyptian bondage for the Jews, there would have been no pharaoh attempting to slay all their baby boys, no plagues, and no wandering in the desert for forty years. Laban thus gets blamed for all the early suffering of the Jewish people.

The Twelve Sons of Israel

The nation of Israel was composed of twelve marginally connected tribes descended from the twelve sons of Jacob. Jacob had been renamed Israel by God, a name that means "he struggles with God," after an all-night wrestling match with an angel. When the land of Canaan was divided among the tribes of Israel during the time of Joshua, the Levites received no land because they had been made priests. The Bible explains that their land or "inheritance" was God alone, and they had no need to farm for themselves. They received a tenth of the produce of each of the other tribes instead. To maintain the original number of twelve tribal units, Joshua split the tribe of Joseph into two, based on his two sons: Ephraim and Manasseh.

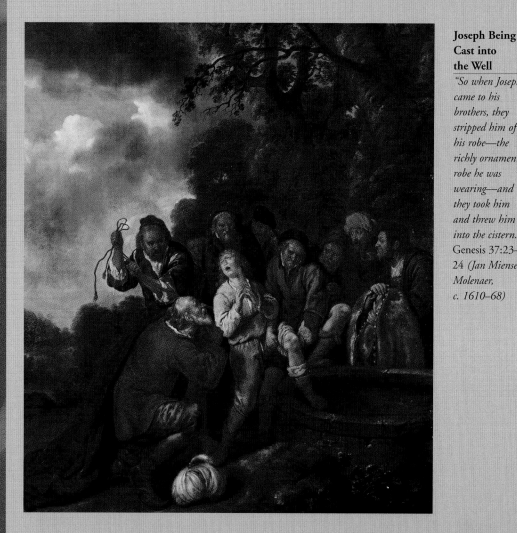

Joseph Being Cast into the Well

"So when Joseph came to his brothers, they stripped him of his robe—the richly ornamented robe he was wearing—and they took him and threw him into the cistern." Genesis 37:23–24 *(Jan Miense Molenaer, c. 1610–68)*

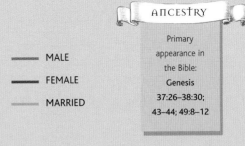

JUDAH

Judah was the fourth son of Jacob born to his first wife, Leah. He became the ancestor of the largest of the Twelve Tribes of Israel.

ANCESTRY

Primary appearance in the Bible: Genesis 37:26–38:30; 43–44; 49:8–12

MALE
FEMALE
MARRIED

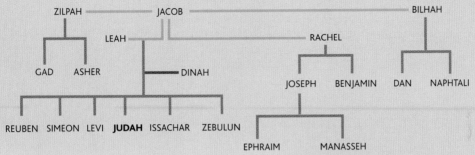

udah played a role in saving the life of his brother **Joseph.** When his older brothers plotted to leave Joseph in a cistern to die, Judah convinced his siblings to sell Joseph into slavery instead (Genesis 37:26–28).

Judah had trouble with his own sons. His firstborn, Er, displeased Yahweh and Yahweh killed him. In ancient Israelite custom, later codified in Deuteronomy 25:5–10, if a man died, his brother was supposed to marry his widow. The first son born from that union was then supposed to carry on the dead brother's name and inherit his property. Therefore, Er's brother Onan properly married Er's widow, **Tamar,** but "whenever he lay with his brother's wife, he spilled his semen on the ground to keep from producing offspring for his brother" (Genesis 38:9). This prompted God to kill him, too.

Oddly, Onan's name has entered the English language as a synonym for masturbation. Clearly, however, Onan was not masturbating. Motivated by a greedy desire to keep his brother's inheritance for himself, he was performing a sort of birth control. If his brother had no children, then his brother's property would belong to Onan instead. God killed Onan as a consequence of greed, not because of his sexual activity.

Although Judah promised Tamar that she could marry his third-born son when he came of age, he instead married his son off to someone else. After having two of his sons die in her arms, he was fearful of losing another.

However, following the death of Judah's wife, Tamar tricked Judah into impregnating her when she disguised herself as a prostitute. She had merely tricked Judah into doing what had been his legal duty as the next nearest male relative to her dead husband. Thus, Judah ultimately praised Tamar for her righteousness.

Jacob's Blessing of Judah

"You are a lion's cub, O Judah; you return from the prey, my son." Genesis 49:9 *(Johann Christoph Weigel, 1654–1726)*

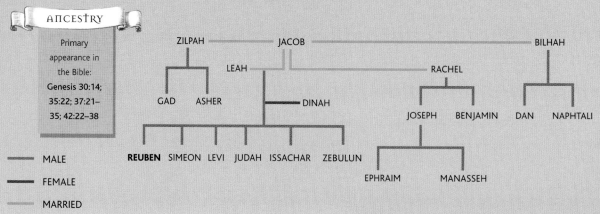

ANCESTRY

Primary appearance in the Bible: Genesis 30:14; 35:22; 37:21–35; 42:22–38

— MALE
— FEMALE
— MARRIED

ZILPAH — JACOB — BILHAH
LEAH — RACHEL
GAD   ASHER   DINAH   JOSEPH   BENJAMIN   DAN   NAPHTALI
REUBEN   SIMEON   LEVI   JUDAH   ISSACHAR   ZEBULUN
EPHRAIM   MANASSEH

REUBEN

Reuben was the firstborn son of Jacob's first wife, Leah. He became the ancestor of one of the Twelve Tribes of Israel.

With her firstborn son Reuben, his mother **Leah** thought she might win her husband's love at last. Reuben's name resembles a Hebrew phrase that means, "He saw my misery." She picked that name because she believed God intended to end her unloved status. The name also resembles the Hebrew phrase, "See, a son."

As an adult, this eldest of **Joseph**'s brothers talked his siblings into putting Joseph into a cistern rather than killing him. Behind Reuben's back, however, **Judah** sold Joseph into slavery. Although Reuben had no great love for Joseph, he did love his father, **Jacob,** and understood how much it would hurt him to lose his beloved Joseph.

Reuben later had an affair with Bilhah, one of his father's secondary wives. Jacob became aware of the liaison, and, as a consequence, Reuben lost the privileges of the firstborn. He received a curse from his father in place of a blessing.

When famine struck their land, Reuben and nine of his brothers went to Egypt to purchase grain. There they met Joseph, but did not recognize him now that he was a governor in Egypt. Joseph recognized them, but did not reveal that fact and treated them badly, locking one brother, **Simeon,** in a dungeon. Joseph informed them that he would release Simeon only on the condition that they return to Egypt with their youngest brother, **Benjamin.**

When informed of this condition, Jacob was distraught. He was reluctant to let Benjamin make the journey, even if it meant the loss of Simeon. Reuben offered his own sons to Jacob as collateral against the life of Benjamin, and so Jacob finally let them travel back to Egypt to secure the release of Simeon.

Following the Exodus from Egypt, the tribe that bore Reuben's name settled east of the Jordan River in what is today the nation of Jordan.

Jacob's Blessing of Reuben
"Reuben, you are my firstborn, my might, the first sign of my strength, excelling in honor, excelling in power. Turbulent as the waters, you will no longer excel, for you went up onto your father's bed, onto my couch and defiled it." Genesis 49:3–4 (Johann Christoph Weigel, 1654–1726)

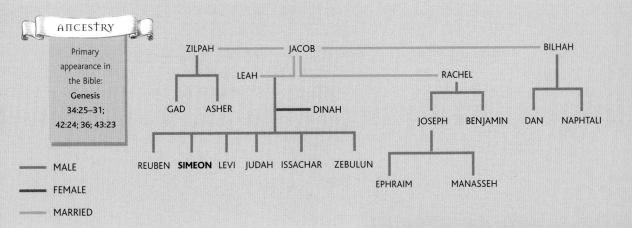

ANCESTRY

Primary appearance in the Bible:
Genesis 34:25–31; 42:24; 36; 43:23

ZILPAH — JACOB — BILHAH

LEAH

RACHEL

GAD ASHER DINAH

JOSEPH BENJAMIN DAN NAPHTALI

REUBEN **SIMEON** LEVI JUDAH ISSACHAR ZEBULUN

EPHRAIM MANASSEH

— MALE
— FEMALE
— MARRIED

SIMEON

Simeon was the second son of Jacob's first wife, Leah. He became the ancestor of one of the Twelve Tribes of Israel.

Simeon was the hot head among **Jacob**'s sons. When Shechem, a local prince, kidnapped Simeon's sister **Dinah** and raped her, then asked her father Jacob for her hand in marriage, Simeon was furious. Together with his brother **Levi,** he convinced Shechem that the marriage could proceed only if both Shechem and all his people would agree to be circumcised.

Three days after everyone was circumcised, Simeon and Levi avenged the rape of Dinah by killing Shechem and every man in the village. They also stole the villagers' possessions and enslaved the women and children. Jacob was terrified by his sons' actions, fearing retribution from other villages in the area, but nothing ever came of it.

Several years later, Simeon participated in selling **Joseph,** his half-brother, into slavery in Egypt. Two decades later, when the brothers went to buy food from Egypt during a famine, they met with Joseph, who had been elevated to the governorship. Although they did not recognize him, Joseph recognized them. Joseph asked how the family was doing and learned that **Benjamin,** the other son born to **Rachel,** his mother, was alive and well. Joseph expressed doubt about the truthfulness of his brothers' tale and accused them of spying.

Joseph ordered Simeon to be imprisoned until the rest of the brothers returned with Benjamin from Canaan, thereby proving the truthfulness of their story. Simeon's father Jacob was unhappy with the terms needed to secure Simeon's release and only begrudgingly agreed. As it was, they did not return with Benjamin until after they had run out of food again, leaving Simeon to suffer in the dungeon.

The Israelite tribe that bore Simeon's name settled in southern Canaan following the Exodus from Egypt. Simeon, along with his brother Levi, were later cursed by their father Jacob for their violent tempers.

Jacob's Blessing of Simeon
"Simeon and Levi are brothers—their swords are weapons of violence. Let me not enter their council, let me not join their assembly, for they have killed men in their anger and hamstrung oxen as they pleased."
Genesis 49:5–6 (Johann Christoph Weigel, 1654–1726)

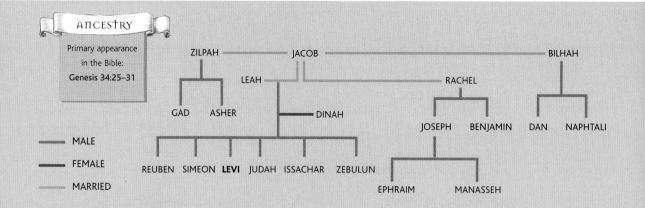

ZILPAH   JACOB   BILHAH

LEAH   RACHEL

GAD   ASHER   DINAH   JOSEPH   BENJAMIN   DAN   NAPHTALI

—— MALE

—— FEMALE

—— MARRIED

REUBEN   SIMEON   **LEVI**   JUDAH   ISSACHAR   ZEBULUN

EPHRAIM   MANASSEH

Jacob's Blessing of Levi
*"Cursed be their anger, so fierce, and their fury, so cruel!
I will scatter them in Jacob and disperse them in Israel."*
Genesis 49:7 *(Johann Christoph Weigel, 1654–1726)*

LEVI

*Levi was the third son of Jacob born to his first wife, Leah.
He became the ancestor of one of the Twelve Tribes of Israel,
the tribe devoted to priestly duties.*

Levi helped his brother **Simeon** to avenge the rape of their sister **Dinah.** Beyond his participation in the slaughter of a Canaanite village, little else is known of Levi.

Levi's descendants include both **Moses** and his brother Aaron. While Moses was on Mount Sinai receiving the Ten Commandments from God, the Israelites convinced Aaron to construct an idol of gold shaped like a calf. They worshiped it and began celebrating, convinced that Moses was gone for good. When Moses returned with stone tablets bearing the Ten Commandments, he was so angry that he smashed them on the ground. He then ordered the Levites to go through the Israelite camp and kill as many of the revelers as possible. In the end, over 3,000 people died.

The tribe of Levi ultimately became devoted to performing the rites associated with the worship of Yahweh. Those of the tribe descended from Aaron served as priests. The rest of the tribe served a variety of functions within the temple. Because of their priestly status, the Levites received no lands or property within the borders of Israel, aside from the cities that were designated as their homes. Since they did not practice agriculture or other trades, their sole source of income was the tithe paid to the temple by the rest of the Israelites, along with the animals they brought for sacrifice. Given that the tribe of Levi made up only about eight percent of the Israelite population, this income meant that most of the Levites, especially the descendants of Aaron, lived well. In fact, the Levites generally became the wealthiest people in Israelite society, next to the royal family. When the prophets arose later, the bulk of their criticism, both religious and social, was directed at the wealthy in Israelite society: that is, the priests, the Levites, and the royal family.

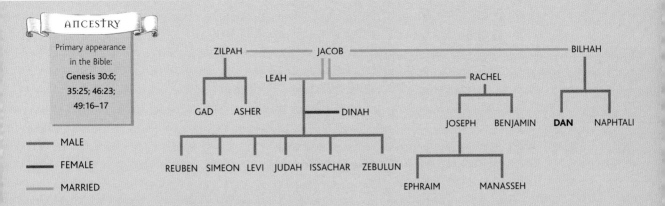

Primary appearance
in the Bible:
Genesis 30:6;
35:25; 46:23;
49:16–17

—— MALE

—— FEMALE

—— MARRIED

ZILPAH — JACOB — BILHAH

LEAH — RACHEL

GAD   ASHER   DINAH   JOSEPH   BENJAMIN   **DAN**   NAPHTALI

REUBEN   SIMEON   LEVI   JUDAH   ISSACHAR   ZEBULUN   EPHRAIM   MANASSEH

Jacob's Blessing of Dan

"Dan will provide justice for his people as one of the tribes of Israel. Dan will be a serpent by the roadside, a viper along the path, that bites the horse's heels so that its rider tumbles backward." Genesis 49:16–17 (Johann Christoph Weigel, 1654–1726)

DAN

Dan was the fifth son of Jacob, and the firstborn to his third wife, Bilhah. He became the ancestor of one of the Twelve Tribes of Israel.

Although Dan's mother was Bilhah, **Rachel** considered him her own. Discouraged after many barren years that she might never have a child, she had given her servant Bilhah to **Jacob** to serve as a surrogate mother. Dan's birth made Rachel exclaim, "God has vindicated me; he has listened to my plea and given me a son" (Genesis 30:6).

The name Dan means "judge" in Hebrew. His father seems to have named him with that in mind. Near death after being reunited with his son **Joseph** in Egypt, Jacob gave each of his twelve sons a blessing. Such blessings were important to the ancients who viewed them as prophecies. Part of Jacob's blessing for Dan was that Dan would judge his people. **Samson,** one of the better known judges of ancient Israel, was a descendant of Dan.

Following the conquest of Canaan by **Joshua,** the tribe of Dan was the last to receive territory when the land was partitioned among the tribes. The territory of Dan extended west from Ephraim and Benjamin to the sea. It was a small but fertile territory. The modern city of Tel Aviv is located in the region assigned to Dan. The tribe had difficulty conquering this area, so it sent five spies north to the source of the Jordan River above the Sea of Galilee. They brought back a favorable report that led 600 members of the tribe to march north and capture the town of Leshem from the Sidonians. They renamed the conquered town Dan. Ever after, Israel's length north to south was denoted by the expression "from Dan to Beersheba," a distance of only about 144 miles (230 km). The New Testament author of Revelation lists the Twelve Tribes of Israel, but without explanation substitutes Manasseh for the tribe of Dan.

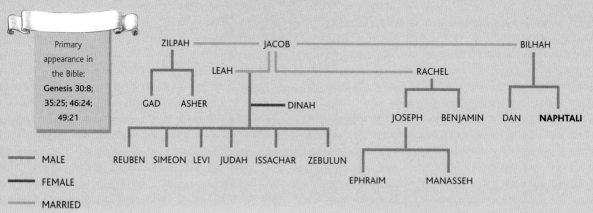

Primary appearance in the Bible: Genesis 30:8; 35:25; 46:24; 49:21

— MALE
— FEMALE
— MARRIED

NAPHTALI

Naphtali was the sixth son of Jacob, and the second born to his third wife, Bilhah. He became the ancestor of one of the Twelve Tribes of Israel.

Naphtali means "my wrestling" and he must have been named by **Rachel,** who considered him her son—his mother was Rachel's servant and surrogate mother to two sons. Rachel wrestled to come up with two sons in competition with her sister **Leah,** who was **Jacob**'s first wife and mother of six sons. At Naphtali's birth Rachel said, "I have had a great struggle with my sister, and I have won" (Genesis 30:8), meaning that she could claim to have another child as her own. Her jealousy would also have derived from the fact that she had to share her husband with Leah.

Decades later, when Jacob and his children went down into Egypt at the invitation of his son **Joseph,** who had become the governor of Egypt, the Bible tells us that Naphtali had four sons. Little else is known of him.

At the time of the Exodus the tribe of Naphtali numbered 53,400 adult males, but by the close of their wanderings they numbered only 45,400. When the land of Canaan was split up among the tribes in the time of **Joshua,** the tribe of Naphtali received territory in the northeastern corner of Canaan, bounded on the east by the Jordan River and the lakes of Merom and Galilee. It extended northward as far as Syria, covering about 800 square miles (2,070 sq km).

The region around Kedesh, one of its towns, was originally called Galil, a name given later to the whole northern region of Ancient Palestine: Galilee. Since a large number of foreigners settled there, it was referred to as "Galilee of the Gentiles" in the New Testament. This area was the home of **Jesus,** and is where he spoke most of his parables and where he also performed most of his miracles. The cities of Tiberius and Nazareth are both located in the region that was assigned to Naphtali.

Jacob's Blessing of Naphtali
"Naphtali is a doe set free that bears beautiful fawns."
Genesis 49:21 *(Johann Christoph Weigel, 1654–1726)*

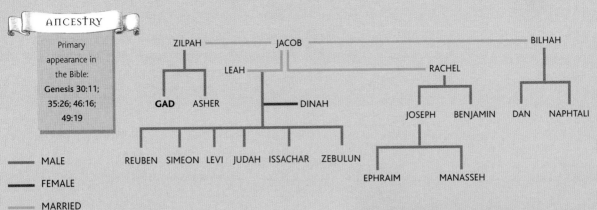

ANCESTRY

Primary
appearance in
the Bible:
Genesis 30:11;
35:26; 46:16;
49:19

ZILPAH — JACOB — BILHAH

LEAH — RACHEL

GAD ASHER — DINAH

JOSEPH BENJAMIN DAN NAPHTALI

REUBEN SIMEON LEVI JUDAH ISSACHAR ZEBULUN

EPHRAIM MANASSEH

—— MALE

—— FEMALE

—— MARRIED

GAD

Gad was the seventh son of Jacob, and the first born to his fourth wife, Zilpah. He became the ancestor of one of the Twelve Tribes of Israel.

Gad's name means "fortune" or "good luck." Gad was the firstborn son of Zilpah, the servant and surrogate of **Jacob**'s first wife, **Leah.** Leah had little fondness for her younger sister **Rachel,** feeling jealous over the fact that Jacob favored Rachel above her. Her only satisfaction and sense of worth came from her own fertility and the sons she had been able to give her husband. So when Leah found herself unable to bear any more children, she gave one of her servant girls to her husband Jacob as a surrogate, to bear more children in Leah's name. Upon the birth of Zilpah's first son, Leah commented, "What good fortune!" (Genesis 30:11) and named him Gad. The surrogate Zilpah would later have one other son, Gad's brother **Asher.**

The blessing that Jacob later bestowed on his son Gad sounds more like a curse, perhaps because he was one of **Joseph**'s half-brothers who participated in selling Joseph into slavery.

During the time of **Joshua,** the portion of the land of Canaan allotted to the tribe of Gad was made up of about half of the region of Gilead. It was bounded on the east by the Arabian Desert, on the west by the Jordan River, and on the north by the Jabbok River. It thus included the Jordan Valley as far north as the Sea of Galilee.

Gad was also the name of the Semitic god of fortune. He appears in the ancient records of Aram and Arabia, besides being mentioned by the prophet **Isaiah** (Isaiah 65:11). Apparently, he was worshiped by a number of Jews during the Babylonian captivity. Many scholars have suggested that when Leah named her son after exclaiming "What good fortune!" (Hebrew, *Gad*), both her exclamation and her son's name were actually a reference to this deity.

Jacob's Blessing of Gad
"Gad will be attacked by a band of raiders, but he will attack them at their heels." Genesis 49:19 *(Johann Christoph Weigel, 1654–1726)*

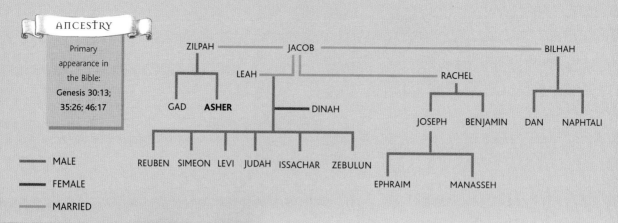

ANCESTRY

Primary appearance in the Bible: Genesis 30:13; 35:26; 46:17

—— MALE

—— FEMALE

—— MARRIED

Jacob's Blessing of Asher

"Asher's food will be rich; he will provide delicacies fit for a king." Genesis 49:20 (*Johann Christoph Weigel, 1654–1726*)

ASHER

Asher was the eighth son of Jacob and the second born to his fourth wife, Zilpah. He became the ancestor of one of the Twelve Tribes of Israel.

When Asher was born, **Leah,** who considered him her own son, exclaimed "How happy I am! The women will call me happy" (Genesis 30:13). She named him Asher, which means "happy" in Hebrew. Leah's success in producing more children for her husband through the surrogate Zilpah alleviated her feelings of jealousy for her sister **Rachel, Jacob**'s second and favorite wife. Asher's daughter, Serah, is the only granddaughter of Jacob mentioned in the Bible.

Like all the tribes except Levi, the people of Asher were mainly farmers and herdsmen. The boundaries of their inheritance and the names of their towns are recorded in Joshua 19:24–31. They were granted a region west of the Jordan River in central Ancient Palestine. **Jael,** the woman who put a tent peg through the head of Sisera in Judges, appears to be one of Asher's descendants. In the New Testament, the prophetess **Anna** is described as a member of this tribe (Luke 2:36).

Some have speculated that the tribe of Asher may be the same as the *Weshesh*, mentioned in Egyptian accounts, who were part of a tribal confederation known as the Sea Peoples. The Sea Peoples also included *Peleset* (Philistines), *Danua* (possibly the tribe of **Dan**), *Tjekker* (perhaps meaning *of Acco* and a reference to the tribe of Manasseh, one of **Joseph**'s sons), and *Shekelesh* (perhaps meaning *men of Sheker*, referring to the tribe of **Issachar**).

Most modern scholars think that the Sea Peoples (apart from the *Peleset*, which all believe are the Philistines) were mainly of Mediterranean origin. The question remains, however, as to why the Egyptians show the Sea Peoples as having Semitic names and being circumcised. The issue is one of many unresolved matters of ancient Near Eastern history.

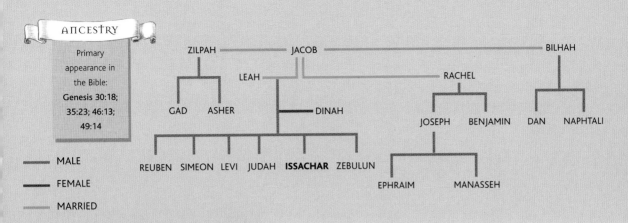

ANCESTRY

Primary
appearance in
the Bible:
Genesis 30:18;
35:23; 46:13;
49:14

ZILPAH — JACOB — BILHAH

LEAH — RACHEL

GAD ASHER — DINAH

JOSEPH BENJAMIN DAN NAPHTALI

REUBEN SIMEON LEVI JUDAH **ISSACHAR** ZEBULUN

EPHRAIM MANASSEH

—— MALE

—— FEMALE

—— MARRIED

Jacob's Blessing of Issachar

*"Issachar is a rawboned donkey lying down between
two saddlebags. When he sees how good is his resting
place and how pleasant is his land, he will bend his
shoulder to the burden and submit to forced labor."*
Genesis 49:14–15 (*Johann Christoph Weigel,
1654–1726*)

ISSACHAR

*Thanks to some mandrake roots, Issachar was the ninth son
of Jacob and the fifth born to his first wife, Leah. Issachar
became the ancestor of one of the Twelve Tribes of Israel.*

Issachar got his name—
Hebrew for "hired"—from
the way his mother hired
his father, **Jacob,** to sleep with
her. One day **Leah**'s first son
Reuben was out in the fields
during the wheat harvest and he
came upon some mandrake roots.
These were an ancient folk remedy
used as an aphrodisiac and fertility
drug. He gave the roots to his
mother, but Jacob's second wife,
Leah's sister **Rachel,** found out
and asked for some of them. Leah
responded, "Wasn't it enough
that you took away my husband?
Will you take my son's mandrakes
too?" "Very well," Rachel said,
"he can sleep with you tonight in
return for your son's mandrakes."
So when Jacob came home from
the fields that night, Leah told
him, "You must sleep with me.
I have hired you with my son's
mandrakes" (Genesis 30:15–16).

The consequence of her night
with Jacob was the birth of
Issachar. She had been infertile
for some time, and had already

given Jacob her servant Zilpah
as a surrogate. Leah interpreted
her pregnancy as a sign that
God was pleased with her for
having given Zilpah to Jacob.
At Issachar's birth, Leah
exclaimed, "God has rewarded
me for giving my maidservant
to my husband" (Genesis 30:18).

Issachar had four sons by
the time he and his brothers
and father went down into
Egypt at the invitation of
his brother **Joseph,** who had
become the governor of Egypt
by then. The prophetic blessing
Jacob pronounced on Issachar
corresponds with that **Moses**
later gives to the tribe as a
whole. As with many of the
blessings Jacob pronounced
on his sons, it sounds more
like a curse.

One of Issachar's descendants,
Baasha, the son of Ahijah,
assassinated Nadab, an evil king
of the Northern Kingdom of
Israel around 909 B.C.E. and
became king in his place.

JOSEPH

As the firstborn son of his father's favorite wife, Rachel, Joseph enjoyed every advantage—until his resentful brothers sold him into slavery.

ANCESTRY

Primary appearance in the Bible: Genesis 30–50

Joseph's mother **Rachel** had spent years childless. Such barrenness was considered a sign of divine disfavor in the ancient world, but having given up hope, she unexpectedly became pregnant. Upon the joyful occasion of the birth of her firstborn son, she commented, "God has taken away my disgrace" (Genesis 30:23). When it came time to name the boy, she said, "May the Lord add to me another son" (Genesis 30:24). Then she called him Joseph, a name that sounds like the Hebrew word "to add."

Joseph was the eleventh of the twelve sons born to the patriarch **Jacob.** Upon his birth, Jacob left the employ of his father-in-law **Laban** and moved back to Bethlehem. Sadly, Rachel would die along the way when she gave birth to Joseph's brother, **Benjamin.** Jacob and his remaining three wives raised his twelve sons. As the firstborn of his beloved Rachel, and as Jacob's favorite, Joseph was spoiled and placed in charge of his older brothers. Jacob gave him a special coat that signified his status. Although the Hebrew term is traditionally translated as a coat of "many colors," the actual meaning is uncertain.

Predictably, Joseph's older brothers came to hate him. They tossed him into a cistern one day and planned to murder him, but wandering traders appeared, causing a quick change in plans. Selling him into slavery at a discount, they took his special coat, dipped it in goat's blood, and convinced their father that Joseph had been killed by wild animals.

Meanwhile in Egypt, Joseph became a slave. His new master Potiphar placed him in charge of his household affairs. Potiphar's wife tried to seduce him, but Joseph rejected her advances. Furious, she accused Joseph of attempted rape. Consequently, Potiphar threw him into prison. In prison, Joseph interpreted the dreams of two of his fellow prisoners, a cook and a cupbearer, both out-of-favor employees of the Egyptian pharaoh. Joseph predicted that the cook would be executed but that the cupbearer would be restored to his former job.

Joseph's prophecies came true. Three years later, the pharaoh had a bad dream, but none of his advisors could interpret it for him. The cupbearer, recalling Joseph's accurate interpretations, told the pharaoh about Joseph. The pharaoh sent for Joseph who interpreted the monarch's dream as a warning that seven good seasons would be followed by seven years of drought and famine. Joseph warned the pharaoh that he should prepare for this disaster by appointing someone to oversee emergency preparations. The grateful pharaoh placed Joseph in charge of storing food for the coming famine, making him second only to the pharaoh in power.

When the predicted famine arrived, not only was there enough food for Egypt but also enough extra to sell to the surrounding starving nations. Suffering famine back in Ancient Palestine, Joseph's brothers made their way to Egypt. It had been twenty years since they sold him as a slave, so they failed to recognize their now powerful brother. However, Joseph recognized his brothers, accused them of espionage, and locked one of them, **Simeon,** into the dungeon. He then demanded they bring their youngest brother **Benjamin** next time if they ever hoped to see Simeon again.

When they returned a year later, Joseph planted his favorite cup of divination in Benjamin's bag, then accused him of stealing it, and threatened to enslave him. When his brother **Judah** offered to take Benjamin's punishment, Joseph at last revealed his identity. Reconciled

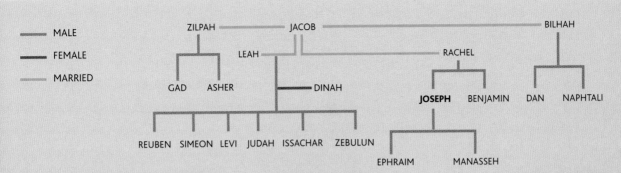

- MALE
- FEMALE
- MARRIED

ZILPAH — JACOB — BILHAH

LEAH — RACHEL

GAD ASHER — DINAH JOSEPH BENJAMIN DAN NAPHTALI

REUBEN SIMEON LEVI JUDAH ISSACHAR ZEBULUN EPHRAIM MANASSEH

to his brothers and subsequently reunited with his father, Joseph resettled them in Egypt's Goshen region where they prospered. Just before he died, Jacob bestowed a blessing of great prosperity on Joseph (Genesis 49: 22–26).

Joseph Recognized by his Brothers

"And he kissed all his brothers and wept over them. Afterward his brothers talked with him." Genesis 45:15 (*Lithograph from French catechism, late eighteenth century*)

MANASSEH AND EPHRAIM

Near death, Joseph's father, Jacob, pronounced a blessing upon Joseph's two sons, a standard practice in the ancient Near East. Although Ephraim was born second, Jacob imparted the firstborn's traditional blessing upon him instead of upon his older brother, Manasseh. When the Israelites left Egypt, the tribe of **Levi** were made priests and given no land. To keep the tribal count at twelve, the descendants of Manasseh and Ephraim were made into tribes in the Levites' place. In later poetry, the name Ephraim came to be used as a synonym for Israel as a whole.

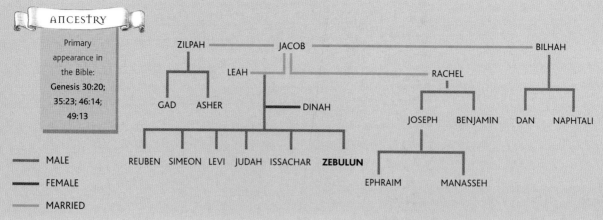

ANCESTRY

Primary appearance in the Bible: Genesis 30:20; 35:23; 46:14; 49:13

ZILPAH — JACOB — BILHAH

LEAH — RACHEL

GAD — ASHER — DINAH

JOSEPH — BENJAMIN — DAN — NAPHTALI

REUBEN — SIMEON — LEVI — JUDAH — ISSACHAR — **ZEBULUN**

EPHRAIM — MANASSEH

— MALE
— FEMALE
— MARRIED

ZEBULUN

Zebulun was the sixth son of Jacob's first wife, Leah. He became the ancestor of one of the Twelve Tribes of Israel.

Zebulun was **Jacob**'s tenth son and the last of **Leah**'s six natural children. He was the second born to her after having given Zilpah, her servant, to her husband as a surrogate. Upon his birth, Leah commented, "God has presented me with a precious gift. This time my husband will treat me with honor, because I have borne him six sons" (Genesis 30:20). Zebulun's name resembles the Hebrew word meaning "honor."

Little is known of Zebulun's personal life, beyond that he married and had three sons with him when he followed his father and brothers to Egypt at **Joseph**'s invitation (Genesis 46:14). Jacob's blessing on him was somewhat enigmatic, suggesting a life near water.

Sidon is a city in what is today the country of Lebanon, but when the Twelve Tribes conquered Canaan following the Exodus from Egypt, Zebulun was given territory that did not match Jacob's blessing. The tribe was landlocked between the tribes of **Asher** on the west and **Issachar** on the east and held no territory anywhere near Sidon.

Moses' blessing upon the tribe is recorded in the book of Deuteronomy; it is a blessing not just for Zebulun, but also for Issachar, perhaps because they are so closely linked in the original stories of their births to Leah: "Rejoice, Zebulun, in your going out, and you, Issachar, in your tents. They will summon peoples to the mountain and there offer sacrifices of righteousness; they will feast on the abundance of the seas, on the treasures hidden in the sand" (Deuteronomy 33: 18–19). Although Zebulun would never border the Mediterranean, Issachar did border the lake called "the Sea of Galilee." Some scholars have speculated that Issachar may have been one of the Sea Peoples (the *Shekelesh*, perhaps meaning *men of Sheker*) mentioned in ancient Near Eastern literature.

Jacob's Blessing of Zebulun
"Zebulun will live by the seashore and become a haven for ships; his border will extend toward Sidon." Genesis 49:13 *(Johann Christoph Weigel, 1654–1726)*

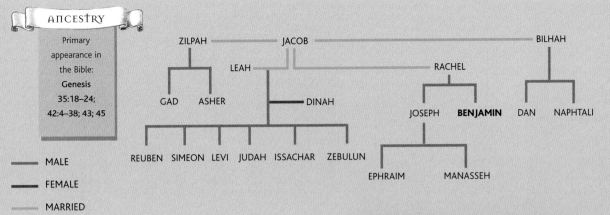

ANCESTRY

Primary appearance in the Bible: Genesis 35:18–24; 42:4–38; 43; 45

ZILPAH — JACOB — BILHAH

LEAH — RACHEL

GAD ASHER — DINAH

JOSEPH **BENJAMIN** DAN NAPHTALI

— MALE

— FEMALE

— MARRIED

REUBEN SIMEON LEVI JUDAH ISSACHAR ZEBULUN

EPHRAIM MANASSEH

BENJAMIN

Benjamin was the second son of Jacob's true love, Rachel. He was the last of Jacob's twelve sons and the youngest child.

Jacob and his family returned to his homeland in Ancient Palestine after **Laban**'s sons grew old enough to help their father. On the road to Bethlehem, **Rachel** went into a difficult labor with what would be Jacob's last-born son. As she was dying, she named him "Ben-Oni," which means "son of my sorrow." After her death, Jacob changed the boy's name to Benjamin, which means "son of the right hand" (Genesis 35:18).

Jacob doted on Benjamin, though not to the extent that he had on **Joseph,** Benjamin's older brother and the firstborn son of Rachel. Nevertheless, after famine struck their land, Jacob was willing to sacrifice **Simeon,** a son of his first wife, **Leah,** in exchange for keeping Benjamin safe at home. Jacob was reluctant to let Benjamin travel to Egypt to face the ruler there who seemed bent on causing ever more suffering for Jacob. Jacob of course did not know that the man in question was his son

Joseph, whom he had assumed was long dead, but who had instead become the governor of Egypt. When Benjamin finally arrived in Egypt, Joseph gave him a double portion of food at the banquet where he revealed himself to his family.

The most famous descendants of Benjamin were both named Saul. One **Saul** was the first and failed king of Israel who died in battle and whose dynasty was replaced by **David,** a descendant of **Judah.** The other, who appears in the New Testament, is better known as the apostle **Paul.** Saul was his Hebrew name.

The tribe of Benjamin was bordered on the south by Judah and included the cities of Jericho and Jerusalem. The tribe was nearly exterminated in a civil war during the period of the Judges. When Israel split into two kingdoms, the tribe of Benjamin, together with the tribe of **Simeon,** remained loyal to the dynasty of David in the Southern Kingdom of Judah.

The Discovery of the Stolen Cup
"Then the steward proceeded to search, beginning with the oldest and ending with the youngest. And the cup was found in Benjamin's sack." Genesis 44:12 (Francesco Bacchiacca, 1494–1557)

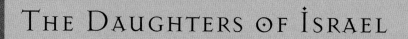

THE DAUGHTERS OF ISRAEL

Women did not have an easy time in the ancient world, where they were treated as chattel more often than not. However, women of the Bible are portrayed as strong-willed and able to surmount the limitations their culture imposed. Here is the tale of two of them who suffered at the hands of men but overcame terrible odds to triumph. Dinah was Jacob's daughter and Tamar was married to two of Judah's sons. Their stories illustrate the growing status of women in Jewish society far beyond that enjoyed by women anywhere else in the Near East at that time. The Law of Moses that came afterward would finally grant women some protections and privileges, and the future history of Israel even saw a few women become rulers, prophets, and military commanders.

Landscape with Judah and Tamar
"Not realizing that she was his daughter-in-law, he went over to her by the roadside and said, 'Come now, let me sleep with you.'"
Genesis 38:16 *(Lucas Gassel, c. 1500–c. 1570)*

TAMAR, JUDAH'S DAUGHTER-IN-LAW

Tamar married two sons of Judah and lost both husbands. Disguised as a prostitute, she seduced her father-in-law and bore him twin sons.

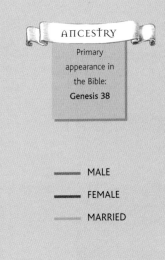

ANCESTRY

Primary appearance in the Bible: Genesis 38

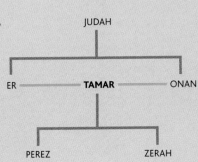

JUDAH

ER — **TAMAR** — ONAN

PEREZ — ZERAH

— MALE
— FEMALE
— MARRIED

Tamar first married Er, **Judah**'s oldest son, but God killed him because he was wicked. Custom demanded that Tamar next marry her dead husband's brother, Onan, so that she would become pregnant and her firstborn son would continue Er's name and inherit his property. Onan was unwilling to do this and "whenever he lay with his brother's wife, he spilled his semen on the ground" (Genesis 38:9), so God killed him. Why? Because of his greed: Rather than see his brother's property passed on to a son who would carry his brother's name, Onan had hoped to keep it for himself and his own children.

After being widowed for the second time, Tamar's father-in-law Judah promised Tamar that when his third son, Shelah, got old enough, he would give her to him in marriage. When Shelah came of age, however, Judah married him to someone else. This was a breach both of promise and of law. Frustrated, Tamar took matters into her own hands to make sure that she

would have a son to inherit her first husband's property.

Judah's wife had recently died. Dressing up as a prostitute, Tamar stationed herself along a road where she knew that her father-in-law would be traveling. Not recognizing her, he agreed to pay the price of a goat from his flock for her services. He left his seal, its cord, and a staff as pledge that he would pay. Afterward, Tamar went back home, removed her disguise, and went about her business.

A few days later, Judah sent his servant to pay the prostitute, but she could not be found. When Tamar's pregnancy was revealed about three months later, a furious Judah, still

unaware of his daughter-in-law's subterfuge, ordered her execution. She then sent him his seal, its cord, and his staff, saying that she was pregnant by the owner of these items.

Judah quickly canceled the execution, commenting that "She is more righteous than I, since I wouldn't give her to my son Shelah" (Genesis 38:26). She had, in fact, behaved entirely properly: If there were no brothers left to marry her, then the next closest male relative had that responsibility. In this case, that relative was Judah, so she had merely tricked him into doing what he was supposed to do anyhow. Tamar gave birth to twin boys.

PEREZ AND ZERAH

Tamar gave birth to twins: Perez and Zerah. Zerah stuck his hand out from the birth canal first, and so the midwife put a scarlet thread around his wrist. Then the hand disappeared and his brother Perez was born first; his name means "he broke out." Zerah was born next, but because he got his hand out first and got that thread around his wrist, he was counted as the firstborn. Perez was an ancestor of **David,** the king of Israel, who was also an ancestor of **Jesus.**

DINAH

Dinah was a daughter of Jacob by his first wife, Leah. She was raped by Shechem, a prince who thought he could get away with anything. Her brothers thought otherwise.

JACOB ——————— LEAH

—— MALE

—— FEMALE

—— MARRIED

REUBEN SIMEON LEVI JUDAH ISSACHAR ZEBULUN **DINAH**

D inah was the younger sibling of **Leah**'s six sons and as far as we know the only daughter **Jacob** ever had. One day she went out to visit women friends in another village when she caught the eye of the king's son, Shechem, who kidnapped and raped her. Some have speculated that Dinah had deliberately run off to town to meet Shechem, that they were, in fact, secret lovers involved in a "forbidden" relationship. Nothing in the text supports such a romantic interpretation, however. Shechem was a child of privilege. His father was a king who ran the village where the two met. The story, therefore, is exactly what it appears to be: an abuse of power. In most ancient Near Eastern cultures, since women had few rights and royal privilege was unchecked, Shechem's behavior was not unusual. Shechem had no reason to fear any negative consequences for his actions. After raping her,

The Rape of Dinah

Jacob's daughter Dinah was raped by a prince who expected to get away with his crime, but her brothers, Simeon and Levi, took revenge. (Started by Fra Bartolomeo, 1472–1517; finished by Giuliano Bugiardini, 1475–1554)

he expressed his love and asked her to marry him. Shechem's father, Hamor, then went to talk to Dinah's father, Jacob, to make the formal arrangements, as was the custom.

While they were negotiating the marriage, Jacob's sons learned what had happened. Furious, they took control of the negotiations. Hamor begged them, "My son Shechem has his heart set on your daughter. Please give her to him as his wife. Intermarry with us; give us your daughters and take our daughters for yourselves. You can settle among us; the land is open to you. Live in it, trade in it, and acquire property in it" (Genesis 34:8–10). Shechem, the rapist, then let Jacob and his sons know that he was willing to pay any price they asked for Dinah.

So, they explained that they would be happy to let him marry their sister, but on one condition: Shechem and all the other men in his town must be willing to get circumcised. Shechem agreed, and both he and all the men in the village suffered the procedure. Three days later, while they were still in pain from the operation, two of Jacob's sons, **Simeon** and **Levi,** attacked the village and slaughtered all the men,

including both Hamor and Shechem. They took the women and children as slaves, plundered all their property, and returned home with their sister, Dinah. Dinah is mentioned only one more time in the Bible, in Genesis 46:15, where she appears in the list of family members who accompanied Jacob into Egypt to join **Joseph.**

Jacob was terrified of possible reprisals from the surrounding villages and told his two sons, "You have brought trouble on me by making me a stench to the Canaanites and Perizzites, the people living in this land. We are few in number, and if they join forces against me and attack me, I and my household will be destroyed" (Genesis 34:30).

Simeon and Levi were not worried and told Jacob, "Should he have treated our sister like a prostitute?" (Genesis 34:31). Rather than seeking retribution, the surrounding villages lived in fear of Jacob and his sons from that day forward. Levi and Simeon were subsequently criticized for their violent ways, a character flaw that seems to have been passed on. **Moses,** a descendant of Levi, is noted for his nasty temper, which led him to disobey God. As punishment, God did not allow him to enter the Promised Land.

Exodus and Conquest

The children of Jacob moved to Egypt to escape drought and famine. They prospered there for many years, but after a change of pharaohs, the Egyptians put the descendants of Jacob into slavery. Four hundred years of bondage passed before God intervened. He sent ten plagues against the Egyptians before the pharaoh decided to let the Israelites go off to worship God for three days. When they did not return, he pursued them to the shores of the "Sea of Reeds," traditionally called the Red Sea. Moses led Israel through this sea to freedom, while the Egyptian army perished in its waters. After 40 years of wandering in the wilderness, Moses died. His general, Joshua, took his place and led the Israelites in successful conquest against the Canaanite inhabitants of Ancient Palestine. The most widely accepted date for the Exodus events puts them in the thirteenth century B.C.E.

Moses Holding the Tablets of the Law
"Moses was there with the Lord forty days and forty nights without eating bread or drinking water. And he wrote on the tablets the words of the covenant—the Ten Commandments." Exodus 34:28 *(Guido Reni, 1575–1642)*

MOSES

Moses led the people of Israel out of Egyptian bondage, through the Red Sea, and delivered the Ten Commandments to them on two stone tablets.

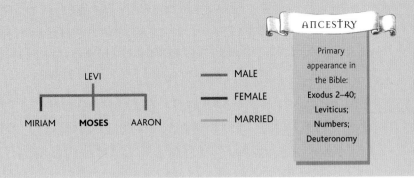

ANCESTRY

LEVI

MIRIAM   **MOSES**   AARON

———— MALE

———— FEMALE

———— MARRIED

Primary appearance in the Bible:

Exodus 2–40; Leviticus; Numbers; Deuteronomy

When the Egyptian pharaoh wanted to stem the rising Jewish population in his country, he ordered the murder of all Jewish baby boys. Therefore, Moses' parents placed him in a reed basket near the place where the pharaoh's daughter regularly bathed. They left his sister Miriam to watch over him. When the pharaoh's daughter found Moses, she fell in love with the baby boy. Thanks to Miriam's intervention, the princess hired Moses' own mother to act as his wet nurse.

Moses' story has parallels in other ancient Near Eastern literature. Sargon the Great, the king of the Babylonians, was said to have been placed into a floating reed basket, where he was scooped up by the daughter of a king.

Moses' name in Hebrew means "drawn out," a reference to how the princess pulled him from the Nile. In Egyptian, "Moses" means simply "son of" and is a common ending attached to Egyptian names. Moses, therefore, may be a shortened form of his longer Egyptian name.

Moses grew up in the palace of the pharaoh of Egypt. However, he knew his own story, understood his own background, and so as a young man, he killed an Egyptian overseer whom he saw beating a Hebrew slave. Fearing for his life, Moses fled and spent the next 40 years herding sheep in the Midianite desert, marrying a local girl named Zipporah. Resigned to his life as a shepherd, he was startled one day by a burning bush. Approaching it, he met God, who ordered him to return to Egypt to rescue his people from slavery.

Reluctantly, Moses obeyed. His success followed after ten devastating plagues against the Egyptians. The final blow, the death of every firstborn in the land of Egypt, convinced the pharaoh to let the people leave for three days of worshiping Yahweh—the cover story God concocted for Moses to tell the king. When the people failed to return after three days, pharaoh's suspicions that it had all been a ruse were confirmed. He ordered his army out to bring the fleeing slaves back.

Unfortunately for the pharaoh, his army was wiped out when they followed the Israelites through the parted "Sea of Reeds" (traditionally, the Red Sea) and so the Israelites made good their escape. When the Israelites balked at the initial attempt to conquer the land of the Canaanites, God sent them back into the desert to wait for the cowardly people to die, so that their children could do what he wanted instead. During their 40 years of waiting and wandering in the desert, God gave Moses the Ten Commandments, along with other regulations for the people to follow once they established themselves as a nation. The Mosaic legislation resembles laws found elsewhere in the ancient Near East. However, it was more egalitarian, with the king made equal under the law to those he ruled (Deuteronomy 17:14–20).

Over the course of the 40 years, Moses led purges and encouraged the slaughter of various enemies, both foreigners and Israelites. Moses' bad temper led him to disobey God. The people were complaining that they were thirsty and, instead of following God's orders and telling a rock to bring forth water, Moses hit it with his staff and shouted at the people. God told him that his punishment would be never to enter the Promised Land nor lead the people in their second attempt to conquer it.

Instead, Moses died at the age of 120 and was buried in an unknown grave by God himself. Moses' right-hand man, **Joshua,** got the job of leading the Israelites into the Promised Land.

BALAAM

Balaam, a prophet famous for his divinations, blessed the Israelites after his life was saved by a talking donkey.

When the Israelites began wandering into his territory, the king of Moab immediately sent for Balaam, a prophet from Mesopotamia. He wanted the prophet to curse the Israelites. He would pay much more than his standard prophet's fee. God told Balaam not to curse them under any circumstances. When the king continued offering ever more money, Balaam begged God to let him go anyhow. God relented, but solemnly warned him again not to curse them.

Balaam saddled up his donkey and headed off to do the job. Given what happened next, it appears obvious that Balaam had no intention of obeying God's command. The Bible explains that God was angry when Balaam set off on his journey, and so he sent an angel armed with a sword to stand in the road to oppose him. When Balaam's donkey saw the angel, it ran off the road and into a field. Angry and unaware of the angel, Balaam beat the donkey to get it back on the road.

When the angel stood in the narrow path between two walled vineyards, the donkey pressed close to one of the walls, crushing Balaam's foot against it. Balaam beat it again. Finally, the angel moved on ahead and stood in a narrow spot where there was no place left to pass through. At this point, the donkey just lay down on the ground. Furious, Balaam pounded on the animal with his staff.

The donkey looked at him and asked him a question, "What have I done to you to make you beat me these three times?" Oddly, Balaam did not seem startled that his donkey was talking to him. Instead, he simply answered the question: "You have made a fool of me! If I had a sword in my hand, I would kill you right now." The donkey responded with another question: "Have I been in the habit of doing this to you?" "No," Balaam replied (Numbers 22:28–30).

At that point, the angel materialized so that Balaam could finally see him. The angel informed Balaam that the donkey had just saved his life; if she had not refused to go where Balaam wanted, the angel would have killed Balaam, but spared the donkey, in order to stop him from cursing the Israelites.

Chastised, Balaam traveled on to meet the king. When the king ordered Balaam to curse the Israelites, Balaam instead uttered repeated blessings. An enraged monarch threatened not to pay him, saying "I summoned you to curse my enemies, but you have blessed them these three times. Now leave at once and go home! I said I would reward you handsomely, but the Lord has kept you from being rewarded" (Numbers 24:10–11).

Shortly after Balaam had returned home, Moabite women began seducing Israelite men and encouraging them to worship the Moabite gods. Yahweh told **Moses** to kill all those who were guilty of such idolatry. The New Testament author of Revelation suggests that Balaam was responsible: He had taught the Moabite king "to entice the Israelites to sin by eating food sacrificed to idols and by committing sexual immorality" (Revelation 2:14).

Later, the Israelites went to war against the Moabites. They defeated the Moabite army in battle and they executed both the king and Balaam.

Balaam and the Angel of God
"When the donkey saw the angel of the Lord standing in the road with a drawn sword in his hand, she turned off the road into a field. Balaam beat her to get her back on the road." Numbers 22:23 *(German etching, c. 1500–1699)*

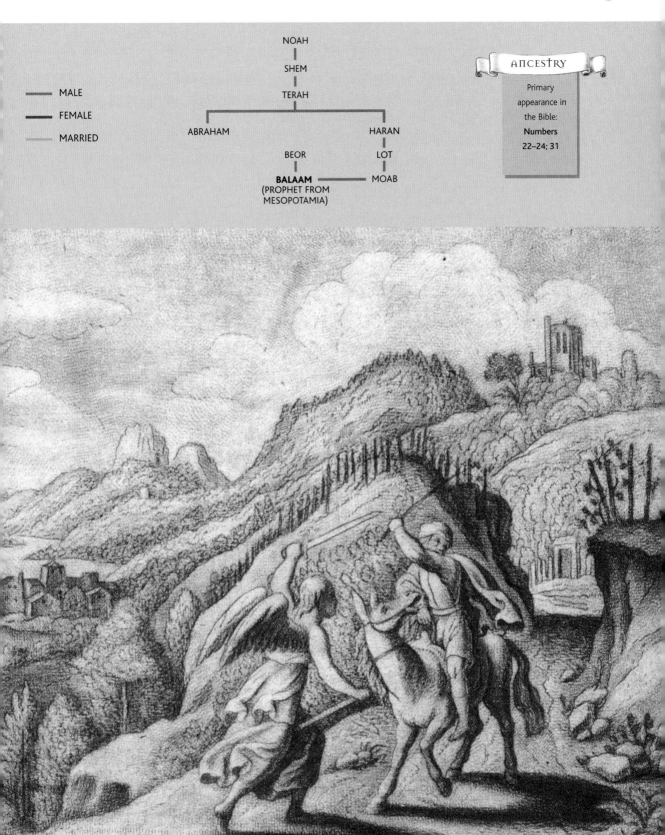

NOAH

SHEM

TERAH

ABRAHAM   HARAN

BEOR   LOT

BALAAM ——— MOAB
(PROPHET FROM
MESOPOTAMIA)

—— MALE

—— FEMALE

—— MARRIED

ANCESTRY

Primary
appearance in
the Bible:
**Numbers
22–24; 31**

JOSHUA

*Joshua led the people of Israel to victory against the
Canaanites and conquered the Promised Land.*

Shortly after leaving Egypt, the Israelites stood on the border of Canaan. **Moses** sent twelve spies, one from each of the Twelve Tribes, into Canaan to find out what the land was like. All twelve returned with glowing stories about the wealth and beauty of the land: a land "flowing with milk and honey" (Exodus 3:8). However, ten of the twelve spies said that the obstacles to victory were insurmountable and recommended that they should give up.

Two of the spies disagreed: Joshua and Caleb. God decided that those who were afraid to enter the land would get their wish and die in the desert. For 40 years they wandered, until all those who thought conquest was impossible had died. Even Moses died, leaving Joshua in charge.

Joshua led the new generation of Israelites into the land of Canaan. He sent out spies, like Moses had done 40 years earlier. The results were different this time around, and both the spies and the people accepted the opportunity to invade.

Overlooking the Jordan River and waiting for the moment to attack, Joshua met an angel with a drawn sword in his hand.

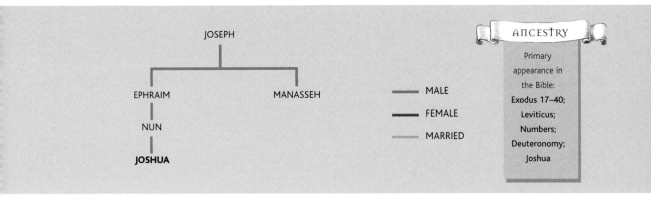

JOSEPH

EPHRAIM   MANASSEH

NUN

JOSHUA

——— MALE
——— FEMALE
——— MARRIED

ANCESTRY

Primary
appearance in
the Bible:
Exodus 17–40;
Leviticus;
Numbers;
Deuteronomy;
Joshua

Startled, Joshua asked, "Are you for us or for our enemies?" "Neither," the angel replied, "but as commander of the army of the Lord I have now come" (Joshua 5:13–14). God affirmed that he had his own plans, and that he was not on anyone's side. The issue for Joshua and the Israelites was to figure out whether they were on God's side. When the Israelites are described as "the Chosen People," it possibly means that they chose God as much as God chose them.

The first obstacle for Joshua was getting the Israelites across the Jordan River. Just as when Moses faced the problem of getting the people across the Sea of Reeds (traditionally, the Red Sea), God intervened once again. Where the Sea of Reeds had been parted by a strong wind, this time the Jordan was stopped by the collapse of its bank several miles upstream. Once across the dry riverbed, the Israelites first targeted Jericho. God's instructions on how to conquer the city were odd: The entire Israelite army was simply to march around the city walls for seven days, once each day. They obeyed. On the seventh day, God told them to walk around Jericho seven times, after which the city's walls would fall down. They did and, at God's command, the Israelites killed all the inhabitants of Jericho except for a prostitute, **Rahab,** and her family. Such wholesale slaughter would be a practice that they followed with intermittent completeness against the other Canaanite cities from then on.

During a battle against the Amorites, Joshua asked God to make the sun and moon stand still in the sky. God granted his request, giving the Israelites a day lasting twice as long as normal, ensuring the Israelites' victory over their enemy (Joshua 10:1–14).

At the end of his life, Joshua told the Israelites that they needed to decide which god or gods they were going to serve. Having come as slaves from the polytheistic nation of Egypt, and having now moved into the polytheistic nation of Canaan, the temptation for idolatry was strong for the Israelites. Many worshiped other gods in addition to Yahweh. Joshua told the people of Israel that "as for me and my household, we will serve the Lord" (Joshua 24:15). Although the nation agreed, the majority of Israelites continued to practice idolatry and polytheism from Joshua's time until the Babylonian captivity nearly 700 years later.

Joshua at the Battle of Jericho

After the Israelites walked around the city of Jericho for seven days, the city walls fell down and Joshua was finally able to lead them into the Promised Land. (Lithograph from French catechism, late eighteenth century)

RAHAB

Rahab was a Canaanite prostitute who hid
Israelite spies from the king of Jericho.

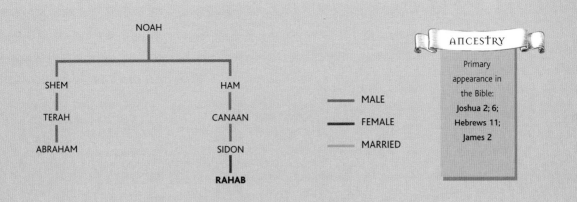

NOAH

SHEM   HAM

TERAH   CANAAN

ABRAHAM   SIDON

RAHAB

— MALE

— FEMALE

— MARRIED

ANCESTRY

Primary
appearance in
the Bible:
Joshua 2; 6;
Hebrews 11;
James 2

Rahab the prostitute was a descendant of Canaan, Ham's son. She lived in Jericho, a major city in Canaan. During this ancient period, the cities of Canaan were nominally under the protection of the Egyptians, but they operated independently, each city ruled by its own king. The various city-states of Canaan often quarreled with one another. It was into this disunited mix that the Israelites were arriving.

As they approached their Promised Land, the Israelite leader **Joshua** sent spies into Jericho. The soldiers soon arrived in the home of a prostitute. Her name was Rahab, and she lived on the city walls of Jericho. According to tradition, Rahab was one of the most beautiful women in the world. Although some biblical commentators have suggested that Rahab was merely an innkeeper, the Hebrew word used to describe her job would

Joshua Spares Rahab

"But Joshua spared Rahab the prostitute, with her family and all who belonged to her, because she hid the men Joshua had sent as spies to Jericho." Joshua 6:25 *(Gustave Doré, 1832–83)*

suggest that she was, in fact, a prostitute. The spies did not find themselves under her roof just because they were weary and in need of a place to slumber, but chances are they were not just after sex, either. An establishment like Rahab's was also likely to be a good source for information.

The government of Jericho knew that the Israelites were just on the other side of the Jordan River, and they knew of the devastating plagues that had befallen the Egyptians because of the Egyptians' enslavement of the Israelites. They also knew what the Israelites had accomplished since leaving Egypt: their successful conquests of the small kingdoms on the eastern side of the Jordan River. With the Israelites now practically on their doorstep, the king of Jericho knew that he was the target of Israelite spies and he was scared. Before long, his officials realized that spies had entered the city, and they were quickly traced to Rahab.

Confronted by soldiers pounding on her door, Rahab acknowledged that some Israelite spies had indeed shown up, but she lied and explained that they had already left and were headed

back the way they had come. Perhaps, she suggested, if the king's soldiers hurried, they could catch the spies. In reality, Rahab had hidden the spies in her well. Once the soldiers had departed, she pulled them out of the well and extracted an oath from them: If she kept their secrets, then they must spare both her and her family when the inevitable siege came.

Grateful for the fact that she had not revealed their presence, the spies agreed to her request. When Jericho fell, Rahab and her family were spared and welcomed into the Israelite camp. In the New Testament, the author of Hebrews lists Rahab as a great example of faith, praising her for protecting the Israelite spies (Hebrews 11:31). James points out that her behavior was proof of her righteousness (James 2:25).

Some Jewish traditions (Megillah 14b) have asserted that Rahab married Joshua and became the ancestor of eight famous prophets, including **Jeremiah** and **Huldah.** But the New Testament author of Matthew names her as the mother of Boaz, who was the great-grandfather of King **David,** an ancestor of **Jesus** (Matthew 1:5).

PERIOD OF THE JUDGES

After Joshua died, near-anarchy overtook the Twelve Tribes of Israel. Tribal leaders called *shophtim*—translated as the "judges"—arose to lead the people in battle against their foes. The book of Judges is their story. A phrase repeated three times in Judges, "in those days, Israel had no king" indicates that the book's purpose is to serve as a justification for the later monarchy that arose in Israel under Saul and David. These ancient judges did more than simply settle disputes between litigants. They also led armies into battle, performed perilous feats, and even used guerrilla tactics against the enemies of the Israelites. Sometimes they were little more than assassins. Most scholars fit the stories of the judges into the period between about 1200 B.C.E. and 1000 B.C.E.

Ehud Kills Eglon

"Ehud reached with his left hand, drew the sword from his right thigh and plunged it into the king's belly." Judges 3:21 *(Johann Christoph Weigel, 1654–1726)*

EHUD

Ehud was one of the early judges of Israel, before Israel had a monarchy. He killed an oppressive and fat Moabite king named Eglon.

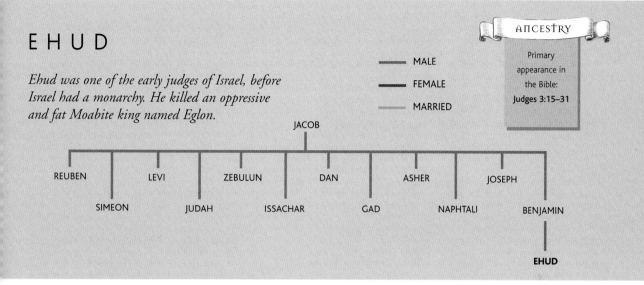

—— MALE
—— FEMALE
—— MARRIED

ANCESTRY

Primary appearance in the Bible:
Judges 3:15–31

The temptation to worship gods other than Yahweh remained a serious issue for the Israelites throughout their history, at least until the time of the Babylonian Exile in the sixth century B.C.E.

The Israelites believed in a single deity, which was unique since other peoples in the ancient world believed in many gods. It was easy for them to slip into idolatry—worshiping gods other than Yahweh. This did not replace worship of Yahwah, however, but was simply an addition to their original belief.

As a result, the Israelites repeatedly adopted Canaanite religious practices such as the worship of Asherah, the fertility goddess. They often thought of Asherah as Yahweh's wife, and worshiping her was a way to ensure good crops, fertile animals, and their wives' ability to bear children. Worshiping Asherah also involved having intercourse with temple prostitutes—a practice that doubtless added to her popularity.

This tendency to worship Canaanite gods in addition to Yahweh influenced later Hebrew prophets to compare Israelites with adulterers, and they frequently used "adultery" as a metaphor for "idolatry."

God sent trouble, followed by prophets to explain the meaning of the trouble, in his attempts to get the Israelites to abandon the worship of other gods. During their early history, whenever the Israelites repented of this sort of idolatry, God sent judges to rescue them from their troubles. Ehud, who was a descendant of **Benjamin,** was one of the judges.

The early Israelites sent Ehud with an annual tribute to Eglon, the king of Moab, who was an unusually fat man. Ehud, a left-hander, strapped a double-edged sword to his right thigh, allowing him to enter the king's presence armed, since the lazy guards only checked his left thigh.

Once in the king's presence, Ehud informed the king that he bore a secret message for him alone. Eglon quickly sent his servants away. Alone with the king in the upper chamber of his summer palace, Ehud announced, "I have a message for you from God" (Judges 3:20). Then Ehud plunged the sword into Eglon's fat belly, which wrapped itself around the hilt while the blade poked out his back. Eglon struggled to pull the sword out, but died while his intestines dripped their contents all over the floor.

Ehud escaped out the back door. Meanwhile, the king's attendants were puzzled by their sovereign's long silence, but the stench from his leaking intestines convinced them that he was simply spending a long time relieving himself. After far too long a time had passed to make sense of anything that he might reasonably be doing on his chamber pot, the guards eventually opened the door and discovered the king's corpse. Meanwhile, Ehud had made good his escape. He quickly rallied the Israelites and led an army that ultimately conquered Moab and made it subject to Israel, thus reversing the Israelites' status from subjugated to subjugators.

DEBORAH

Deborah was a prophetess, a judge, and a general. She was the model for the "powerful woman" described in Proverbs.

ANCESTRY

Primary
appearance in
the Bible:
Judges 4–5

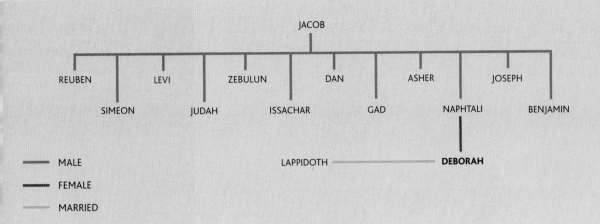

JACOB

REUBEN — LEVI — ZEBULUN — DAN — ASHER — JOSEPH

SIMEON — JUDAH — ISSACHAR — GAD — NAPHTALI — BENJAMIN

LAPPIDOTH ——— **DEBORAH**

— MALE

— FEMALE

— MARRIED

Deborah was a prophetess and a judge who lived and worked at a time when Jabin, a Canaanite king in Hazor, ruled the land of Israel. She solved disputes that arose where she lived, in the villages of Ramah and Bethel. Her name means "honeybee" and she is described as "a mother in Israel," not because of any children she may have borne, but as an honorific—just as Americans might refer to George Washington as the "father" of their country.

One day Deborah announced to Barak, an Israelite general, that God wanted him to lead an army of 10,000 men from the tribes of **Naphtali** and **Zebulun** against Jabin's forces. Meanwhile, Deborah explained, she planned to lure Jabin's general Sisera to the Kishon River, where Barak could ambush both him and his army. She predicted, however, that Barak would get no glory from the battle because it would be a woman, not he, who would kill

Deborah

"The Israelites came to her to have their disputes decided." Judges 4:5 *(Gustave Doré, 1832–83)*

Sisera, thus freeing Israel from foreign domination.

Deborah accompanied Barak, who succeeded in defeating Sisera's army despite his overwhelming numerical and technological advantages: Sisera had 900 chariots made of iron. At this period in history, using iron weapons was a new technology and a closely guarded secret. The Israelites did not discover how to make iron implements until the time of King **David,** centuries later. Victories of this sort led the author of Proverbs to write, "There is no wisdom, no insight, no plan that can succeed against the Lord. The horse is made ready for the day of battle, but victory rests with the Lord" (Proverbs 21:30–31). The narrator of the story of Deborah explains that "At Barak's advance, the Lord routed Sisera and all his chariots and army by the sword" (Judges 4:15). Fleeing the carnage, Sisera was killed by **Jael.**

The Bible tells Deborah's story twice, first in prose, then in poetry. The poetic form of the story is thought to have been composed in the second half of the twelfth century B.C.E., soon after the events it describes.

Some have even suggested that Deborah herself was the author. If that is the case, then this *Song of Deborah* is one of the oldest passages in the Bible and the oldest sample of Hebrew poetry still in existence. Hebrew poetry, unlike the poetry most people might think of, does not rhyme sounds. Instead it uses ideas that repeat, stating the same thing twice using synonymous terms. That is why so much Hebrew poetry, such as one finds in Psalms, sounds repetitious. The story of Deborah is also significant because it is one of the earliest biblical passages portraying women in ways other than as victim or villain.

Proverbs ends with a poem that describes the "powerful woman," explaining that such an individual is as rare and as valuable as the finest ruby (Proverbs 31:10). Early translators described this woman as merely a "virtuous woman." Perhaps they were uncomfortable with what the Hebrew phrase actually meant. Elsewhere they translated the descriptive word as "power," "strength," "efficiency," or even "army." There is no reason to render it as something different when applying it to women.

JAEL

*Jael became famous for killing Sisera, an enemy
general intent on maintaining the domination
of Israel by Jabin, the Canaanite king.*

ANCESTRY

Primary
appearance in
the Bible:
Judges 4–5

The prophetess **Deborah** was not the only woman who helped General Barak defeat Israel's enemies commanded by Sisera, general of the Canaanite king Jabin. After his defeat Sisera took refuge with Heber, the Kenite leader, only to be murdered by Heber's wife Jael.

Her story is told in two versions in Judges—one in prose and one in poetry. Comparing the twin accounts in Judges 4 and 5 gives the reader a lesson in the differences between a prosaic and poetic description of an event.

In common with all poetry in all cultures, the primary goal of Hebrew poetry is the expression of emotion rather than the imparting of facts and information. One would no more expect a history text to be written in poetry than one would expect people in real life to burst suddenly into song, unlike what we experience in musicals or operas. The poetic description of Jael's actions in the Bible are more intense, more vibrant, more emotion-laden than the corresponding dry recitation of events in the prose narrative that precedes it. In essence, the poetry gives us the heart and soul of the matter, as a complement to the facts of the narrative that are laid out clearly in the earlier chapter.

Sisera, the general of Jabin, the king of Hazor, suffered defeat at the hands of Deborah and Barak, despite having superior forces. Fleeing in terror, he made his way to the tent of Heber, a descendant of **Asher,** who is described as a Kenite. **Moses'** father-in-law Jethro is described as a Kenite in Exodus, which also says that Jethro helped Moses to establish the early Israelite court system. Since Jethro is also described as a Midianite, it is thought that the Kenites may have formed a part of the Midianite tribal grouping. Kenites were noted metalsmiths living in the southern region of Ancient Palestine.

In any case, Sisera thought he had found a safe haven when he found the Kenites, since his king had an alliance with Heber's clan. Heber's wife Jael welcomed him warmly: "Come right in. Don't be afraid" (Judges 4:18). She gave him some milk to drink and it may have been fermented. Then she covered him up so he could rest. Some have suggested that the poetic account of the story in Judges 5 uses double entendres and may indicate that Jael seduced Sisera. Others disagree. Once Sisera had fallen soundly asleep, Jael quietly approached him and pounded a tent peg right through his skull. When

the pursuing Barak arrived at her tent soon afterward, she proudly showed him the body.

The ancient *Song of Deborah* in Judges 5, thought to have been composed in the second half of the twelfth century B.C.E., honors Jael for her action against Sisera, the general of Israel's oppressor, Jabin. The biblical author similarly writes in prose that "On that day God subdued Jabin, the Canaanite king, before the Israelites. And the hand of the Israelites grew stronger and stronger against Jabin, the Canaanite king, until they destroyed him" (Judges 4:23–24).

JUDGES 5:24–27

Most blessed of women be Jael,
the wife of Heber the Kenite,
most blessed of tent-dwelling women.

He asked for water, and she gave him milk;
in a bowl fit for nobles she brought him
curdled milk.

Her hand reached for the tent peg,
her right hand for the workman's hammer.
She struck Sisera, she crushed his head,
she shattered and pierced his temple.

At her feet he sank,
he fell; there he lay.
At her feet he sank, he fell;
where he sank, there he fell—dead.

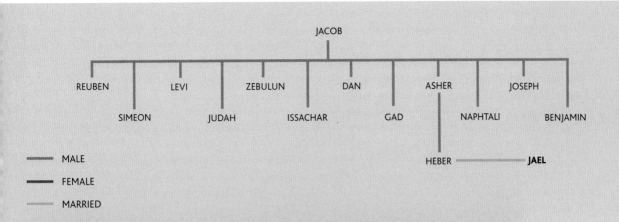

JACOB

REUBEN — LEVI — ZEBULUN — DAN — ASHER — JOSEPH

SIMEON — JUDAH — ISSACHAR — GAD — NAPHTALI — BENJAMIN

HEBER ——— **JAEL**

—— MALE

—— FEMALE

—— MARRIED

**The Death
of Sisera**

*"But Jael, Heber's
wife, picked up a
tent peg and a
hammer and went
quietly to him while
he lay fast asleep,
exhausted. She drove
the peg through his
temple into the
ground, and he
died."* Judges 4:21
*(Palma Il Giovane,
c. 1548–1628)*

GIDEON

Gideon, also known as Jerub-Baal, was a judge who led a 300-man Israelite army into successful battle against a much larger Midianite force.

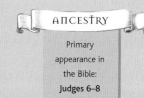

ANCESTRY

Primary appearance in the Bible: Judges 6–8

The Miracle of Gideon's Fleece

"Look, I will place a wool fleece on the threshing floor. If there is dew only on the fleece and all the ground is dry, then I will know that you will save Israel by my hand, as you said."
Judges 6:37
(School of Avignon, c. 1490)

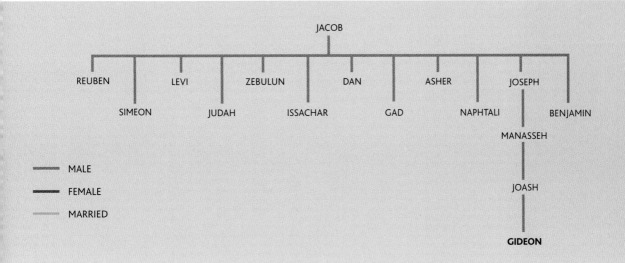

JACOB

REUBEN   LEVI   ZEBULUN   DAN   ASHER   JOSEPH

SIMEON   JUDAH   ISSACHAR   GAD   NAPHTALI   BENJAMIN

MANASSEH

JOASH

GIDEON

— MALE

— FEMALE

— MARRIED

For seven years the Midianites had oppressed the children of Israel. Things were so bad that Gideon, a descendant of **Joseph,** hid deep in a winepress to thresh his grain so that the oppressors would not steal his crops as was their custom. Years ago Midianite traders had taken Joseph to Egypt and now they were at it again.

While he was hiding, an angel appeared and announced, "The Lord is with you, mighty warrior" (Judges 6:12). Gideon protested: "If the Lord is with us, why has all this happened to us? Where are all his wonders that our fathers told us about when they said, 'Did not the Lord bring us up out of Egypt?' But now the Lord has abandoned us and put us into the hand of Midian" (Judges 6:13).

The angel explained that God had chosen Gideon to lead the Israelites to victory against the Midianites. Gideon objected that he belonged to a small clan within the tribe of Manasseh that lacked both influence and power. The angel insisted, so Gideon begged for a sign. Thus, when Gideon offered a sacrifice

not long after, the angel touched it with his staff. Fire burst forth from the altar of rocks, consuming the offering in a puff. Then the angel vanished.

That night, following God's command, Gideon tore down his father's altar to Baal, a Canaanite deity, and built one altar for Yahweh in its place. He even sacrificed one of his father's bulls on it, using the Asherah pole (probably a phallic symbol) as wood for the fire. In the morning, the townspeople were furious and demanded that Gideon's father kill him for the desecration. Gideon's father asked them if Baal were such a mighty god, could he not take care of himself? Surely they did not need to help him out. So Gideon survived and garnered the nickname Jerub-Baal, meaning "Baal's contender."

When God told him to amass an army to fight Midian, Gideon begged God for two more signs: first, that a fleece he left on the ground overnight would be damp with dew, but that the ground would be dry; second, that the request be reversed on the next night, dry fleece on wet ground.

Satisfied at last that God was really helping him, Gideon gathered an army of nearly 32,000 men from his tribe and the tribes of **Zebulun, Asher, and Naphtali.** God told him this was too many soldiers, so Gideon gave a speech saying that any men who were afraid should go home; 22,000 of them fled. God still thought there were too many, and so Gideon had the men gather near a stream to get a drink of water. Based on how they chose to drink, Gideon finally whittled his fighting force down to only 300 men.

Surrounding the Midianites that night, each of the 300 blew trumpets, then broke a jar to reveal a burning torch hidden inside. The Midianites panicked, fought among themselves, and then fled. Gideon regathered a large army and wiped out the remaining forces. Midian was utterly defeated. Although offered the kingship for this magnificent military success, Gideon declined the offer. He subsequently had 70 sons by several wives and concubines and died of old age.

ABIMELECH

Abimelech was one of Gideon's sons, born to a slave girl. After murdering 70 of his half-brothers, he tried to set himself up as the first king of Israel.

ANCESTRY

Primary appearance in the Bible:
Judges 8:31–9:57

The Death of Abimelech

"*Abimelech went to the tower and stormed it. But as he approached the entrance to the tower to set it on fire, a woman dropped an upper millstone on his head and cracked his skull. Hurriedly he called to his armor-bearer, 'Draw your sword and kill me.'*"
Judges 9:52–54
(*Gustave Doré, 1832–83*)

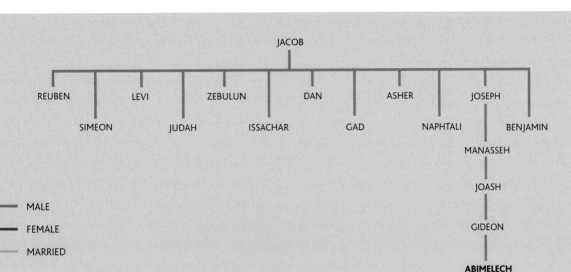

JACOB

REUBEN — SIMEON — LEVI — JUDAH — ZEBULUN — ISSACHAR — DAN — GAD — ASHER — NAPHTALI — JOSEPH — BENJAMIN

MANASSEH

JOASH

GIDEON

ABIMELECH

— MALE

— FEMALE

— MARRIED

After defeating the Midianites, **Gideon** led a prosperous and respected life. His many wives bore him more than 70 sons, among them Abimelech, the child of a slave girl. While Gideon lived the Israelites honored him and worshiped only one God, Yahweh. However, after he died they went back to their old habits of adhering to the Canaanite gods.

Abimelech led an unhappy childhood. Rejected by his half-brothers because of his mother, when he grew up, he went to live in his mother's hometown of Shechem. Shechem was a city in Samaria, located in the valley between Mounts Gerazim and Ebal. When **Abraham** had first entered Ancient Palestine, this was where he lived, and it was here that God first promised Abraham that he and his descendants would own the land (Genesis 12:6–7).

One day, Abimelech approached his mother's family and asked them to support his bid to become king over all of Israel. "Ask all the citizens of Shechem, 'Which is better for you: to have all seventy of Jerub-Baal's sons rule over you, or just one man?' Remember, I am your flesh and blood" (Judges 9:2). After his family repeated his words to the citizens of Shechem, they decided to follow Abimelech. After all, they commented, "He is our brother" (Judges 9:3).

They paid him 70 shekels of silver. Abimilech used the money to hire mercenaries. As his first act, he attempted to eliminate potential opposition by murdering 70 of his half-brothers—the brothers who had made his life so miserable growing up. However, one of them escaped his rage: Jotham.

On the day the people of Shechem crowned Abimelech as their king, Jotham stood on Mount Gerazim overlooking the city and shouted a warning against following Abimelech. He told them a fable about trees that sought a king, only to pick a thornbush. When the flames consumed the thornbush, it also consumed the trees. As soon as he finished his fable,

Jotham fled, never to be seen again. Abimelech reigned for three years, but his people began plotting against him almost at once. When he learned of the plot, Abimelech destroyed Shechem, killed thousands of its inhabitants, and poured salt over the ruins.

Abimelech's attempts at pacifying the region continued. He next successfully attacked the nearby city of Thebez. Only a tower inside the city remained; several of its defenders had holed up inside. He grabbed some branches and ordered his men to follow his example by piling up kindling at its base. He had burned people out of a similar tower at Shechem and planned on doing the same here. However, a woman on top of the tower in Thebez dropped a millstone on his head, injuring him so severely that he ordered a servant to stab him with his sword so that he could be spared the humiliation of having been killed by a woman. The death of Abimelech ended the first attempt at establishing an Israelite monarchy.

SAMSON

Samson was a judge who led Israel. Reputed to have had super strength, he lost it when his favorite prostitute, Delilah, cut off his hair.

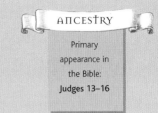

ANCESTRY

Primary
appearance in
the Bible:
Judges 13–16

Before he was born, an angel told Samson's parents to raise him as a Nazarite from birth. The Nazarite vow was ordinarily voluntary and usually only for a short length of time. Among other requirements, a Nazarite had to abstain from wine and grapes, avoid touching anything dead, and must never cut his hair (Numbers 6). Others who were Nazarites their whole lives were the prophets **Samuel** in the Old Testament and **John the Baptist** in the New Testament. Samson did not take his vow too seriously. At a young age, for instance, he scooped honey from a dead lion's carcass and shared it with his parents.

As a young man, Samson married a Philistine woman, much to his parents' dismay. At the wedding feast, he gave an unfair riddle to 30 of his guests, promising them new clothes if they could solve it. Unable to come up with the answer, they extracted it from his new bride after threatening her life. Samson paid off the debt by

Samson and Delilah

"Having put him to sleep on her lap, she called a man to shave off the seven braids of his hair, and so began to subdue him." Judges 16:19
(José Pina, 1830–1909)

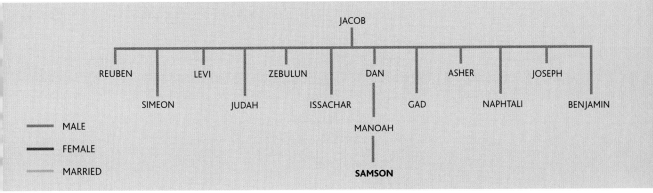

JACOB

REUBEN | LEVI | ZEBULUN | DAN | ASHER | JOSEPH

SIMEON | JUDAH | ISSACHAR | GAD | NAPHTALI | BENJAMIN

MANOAH

SAMSON

──── MALE
──── FEMALE
──── MARRIED

killing 30 Philistines and giving their clothing to the guests who had made the bet with him.

Still angry, Samson went back home without his new bride. His father-in-law, thinking Samson was gone for good, married off his daughter to another man. However, Samson soon came back looking for his new bride. Furious when he learned what had happened, Samson caught some foxes, tied torches to their tails, and released them among the Philistine grain fields. In response to the loss of their crops, the Philistines burned Samson's ex-wife and father-in-law to death. The conflict grew, with Samson wreaking havoc among the Philistines, thanks to his abnormal physical strength. He slaughtered a thousand of them, using nothing but a donkey's jaw bone for a weapon.

One day Samson visited the Philistine city of Gaza. While there, he spent the night with a prostitute. When the leaders of Gaza realized Samson was there, they set an ambush for him near the city gate, planning to kill him at dawn when he left town. However, Samson got up in the middle of the night, took hold of the doors of the city gate, together with the two posts, and tore them loose. He lifted them onto his shoulders and carried them to the top of a nearby hill, terrifying his would-be attackers, who decided to leave him alone.

Some time later, Samson fell in love with a prostitute named Delilah, who lived in the Sorek Valley in the Judean foothills. After he had been sleeping with her for some time, the Philistine leaders asked her to find out the secret to Samson's great strength. After lying to her for days, Samson finally got tired of her constant questions and revealed the truth: If his hair were cut off, he would lose his strength.

One night while Samson was sleeping, Delilah conspired to shave his head. The Philistines then captured him, poked out his eyes, and turned him into a slave—but his hair grew back. One day, while the Philistine leaders were celebrating his capture with Samson on display like a trophy, he pushed over the support pillars for their temple. The building collapsed, killing both Samson and a large number of Philistines.

Delilah Pressing Samson for his Secret
"With such nagging she prodded him day after day until he was tired to death." Judges 16:16 *(Gustave Doré, 1832–83)*

DELILAH

Delilah was a prostitute who had caught the eye of Samson. Her name has become synonymous with seductress as a consequence of her successful wooing of Samson's secret. Prostitution in the ancient world often had religious overtones. Asherah, Astarte, Ishtar, Aphrodite, and Venus were related deities, most popularly worshiped by going to their temples, paying a fee, and engaging in sex with the temple prostitutes. This was an example of sympathetic magic: the fertility of crops, farm animals, and wives was thought to be assured by this "sacrifice" to the goddess. Such goddess worship generally degraded the status of women in the ancient world.

JEPHTHAH

Jephthah was a judge who led Israel successfully against its enemies. He sacrificed his only daughter as a burnt offering to Yahweh.

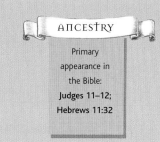

ANCESTRY

Primary appearance in the Bible:
Judges 11–12;
Hebrews 11:32

A descendant of **Joseph**, Jephthah was the son of Gilead and a prostitute and was not well received within his family. When he grew up, his half-brothers chased him away, denying him any inheritance. Settling in the land of Tob, he gathered bandits around him and conducted raids. Some years later, when the Ammonites began attacking Israel, his half-brothers and the leaders of Gilead begged Jephthah to return and become Israel's commander against the Ammonites. Jephthah was reluctant, but finally agreed, after extracting formal promises from them.

He wrote a letter to the Ammonites, attempting to resolve the conflict by outlining the history of the Israelites and explaining that just as the god Chemosh had given the Ammonites their land, so Yahweh had given land to the Israelites, the very land that the Ammonites were now trying to take. It is interesting to notice Jephthah's explicit acceptance of a polytheistic world view; he had no trouble acknowledging the god of the Ammonites, and in fact placed their god on an equal status with Yahweh.

The Ammonites rejected Jephthah's overture of peace. Facing inevitable war, Jephthah made a vow to Yahweh, promising: "If you give the Ammonites into my hands, whatever comes out of the door of my house to meet me when I return in triumph from the Ammonites will be the Lord's, and I will sacrifice it as a burnt offering" (Judges 11:31).

Jephthah's battle against the Ammonites was successful. Upon his return, the first person out of his house was his only daughter. Grief stricken, he informed her of his vow. "'My father,' she replied, 'you have given your word to the Lord. Do to me just as you promised, now that the Lord has avenged you of your enemies, the Ammonites. But grant me this one request,' she said. 'Give me two months to roam the hills and weep with my friends, because I will never marry'" (Judges 11:36–37). When she returned, Jephthah fulfilled his vow and sacrificed her as a burnt offering.

Although some scholars wish to mitigate the horror of the story and suggest that his daughter was not actually sacrificed, but merely became a virgin for life, the wording of the story suggests otherwise. The motivation in reinterpreting the sad story is admirable: such scholars are justly horrified by what Jephthah did and would like to change the outcome.

However, human sacrifice, especially of children, was not uncommon among the Canaanite inhabitants of Ancient Palestine. Given Jephthah's acceptance of the different religious beliefs and practices of neighboring peoples such as the Ammonites, there is no reason to suspect that he would not have killed his daughter.

The reader's horror at Jephthah's action is the primary purpose of the story. The author of Judges wishes the reader to understand just how far the inhabitants of Israel have fallen without proper leadership and how destructive the acceptance of Canaanite religious practices was. The author of the New Testament epistle Hebrews praises Jephthah as one of the heroes of faith (Hebrews 11:32). Later Christian commentators explain that Jephthah's life illustrates that acceptance by God is determined by the individual's relationship with him, not the purity of that individual's doctrine or the perfection of his life.

The Homecoming of Jephthah

"When Jephthah returned to his home in Mizpah, who should come out to meet him but his daughter." Judges 11:34 *(Pieter Schoubroeck, 1570–1607)*

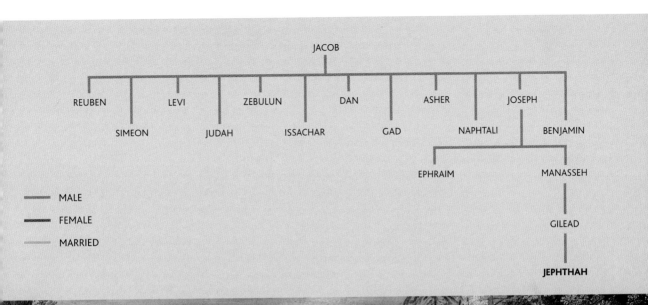

JACOB

REUBEN · SIMEON · LEVI · JUDAH · ZEBULUN · ISSACHAR · DAN · GAD · ASHER · NAPHTALI · JOSEPH · BENJAMIN

EPHRAIM · MANASSEH

GILEAD

JEPHTHAH

—— MALE
—— FEMALE
—— MARRIED

UNNAMED LEVITE

The story of the unnamed Levite echoes that of Jephthah, but with a much less happy ending: He allows his concubine to be raped and murdered by the mob.

ANCESTRY

Primary appearance in the Bible: Judges 19–20

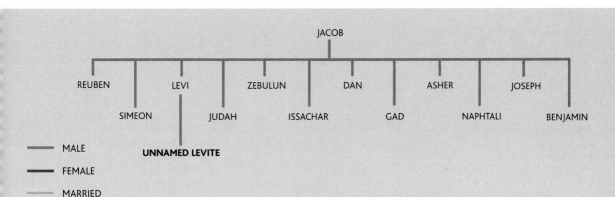

JACOB

REUBEN · LEVI · ZEBULUN · DAN · ASHER · JOSEPH

SIMEON · JUDAH · ISSACHAR · GAD · NAPHTALI · BENJAMIN

UNNAMED LEVITE

——— MALE
——— FEMALE
——— MARRIED

A Levite from the remote hill country of Ephraim had an unfaithful concubine who left him and went back to her father in Bethlehem. Four months later, the Levite took one of his servants and went to persuade her to return. Her father was happy to see the Levite and persuaded him to stay for three days and nights, eating and drinking.

On the fourth day, the Levite got up to go, but the woman's father suggested that he refresh himself with more food before leaving. The two of them sat down to eat and drink together. Later, when the Levite once again tried to depart, her father prevailed upon him to stay and enjoy himself for another night. The same thing happened on the fifth day, but as evening approached, the Levite finally refused to stay any longer and at

The Levite Finding the Woman's Corpse

"When her master got up in the morning and opened the door of the house and stepped out to continue on his way, there lay his concubine, fallen in the doorway of the house, with her hands on the threshold."
Judges 19:27 *(Gustave Doré, 1832–83)*

last took off with the woman to begin their journey to Ephraim.

On their way home, they neared the city of Jerusalem. At that time, the city was still occupied by Jebusites, a tribe of Canaanites. The Levite's servant suggested that they find lodging there for the night. The Levite refused, saying, "No. We won't go into an alien city, whose people are not Israelites" (Judges 19:12). So they traveled on until they reached the city of Gibeah, in the tribal lands of **Benjamin,** where they accepted the hospitality of an old man. During the night, a mob assembled at the old man's door and demanded that the old man send the Levite outside so they could have sex with him. The old man refused, and the Levite tossed his concubine outside instead. The mob raped her all night until dawn.

In the morning, the Levite found his concubine dead on the doorstep. Loading her body onto one of his donkeys, he returned to the hill country of Ephraim. Once home, he chopped his concubine into twelve pieces. He sent the pieces by messenger to the leaders of each of the Twelve Tribes of Israel. Having got their attention, he then explained what had happened

to him in Gibeah. Furious, they approached the tribe of Benjamin and demanded that the guilty parties be punished. The tribe of Benjamin refused.

In the ensuing civil war, the tribe was exterminated except for 300 Benjamite men. Since the other tribes had vowed, prior to beginning the war, never to give their daughters or sisters in marriage to any Benjamite ever again, the survival of the tribe was in doubt. Not wishing to see the tribe utterly destroyed, but unwilling to break their vow, the other Israelites solved the problem by encouraging the remaining 300 Benjamites to kidnap some of the other tribes' women. Since the women were taken involuntarily, the Israelites thus avoided violating their vow.

Similar to the story of **Jephthah,** the story of the unnamed Levite was perhaps designed by the author of Judges to illustrate the overemphasis that the ancient Israelites placed on vows, since he may have wanted to demonstrate that although keeping one's word is normally an honorable thing, sometimes it can be the most dishonorable thing imaginable. Following rules, instead of doing the right thing, can be evil.

RUTH

Ruth was a Moabitess who converted to Judaism.
She was King David's great-grandmother.

NAOMI AND BOAZ

Naomi was Ruth's mother-in-law. Her name means "pleasant" or "sweet," but she changed it to "Mara," which means "bitterness," after she returned to Israel as a widow. The name Mara became very popular in Israel and comes into English as the name Mary. Boaz became the husband of Ruth, ostensibly to fulfill the duty of Levirate marriage, where a brother or close relative of the deceased husband marries the widow. This custom developed as a practical way to protect widows from poverty or prostitution. Boaz's motivation in marrying Ruth had little to do with social convention or a desire to take care of the impoverished, however. He was simply in love with Ruth.

Elimelech, belonging to the tribe of **Judah,** and his wife Naomi moved to Moab to escape a drought. His two sons married Moabite women, one of whom was Ruth. Elimelech soon died, as did both his sons, leaving his wife and daughters-in-law as widows. In a patriarchal society, being an unmarried woman was difficult. Starvation or prostitution were the only options if they were to remain in Moab.

Naomi decided to go back to her home in Bethlehem where she had family who might take her in. One daughter-in-law chose to remain in Moab, but Ruth refused to leave Naomi's side and returned to Bethlehem with her. Back in Israel, Ruth gleaned in the fields of Naomi's relative, Boaz. Boaz was attracted to Ruth. He instructed those harvesting his fields to make sure they dropped extra grain where Ruth could get it easily. He ordered his servants to watch out for her and show her kindness.

Naomi and her Daughters-in-law

"Don't urge me to leave you or to turn back from you. Where you go I will go, and where you stay I will stay. Your people will be my people and your God my God."
Ruth 1:16 *(Gustave Doré, 1832–83)*

He also warned them not to molest her in any way.

When Naomi found out how well Boaz was treating Ruth, she immediately began plotting. Ancient Israelite law stipulated that if a man died childless, his closest relative was obligated to marry the widow. Boaz was a close relative of Ruth's dead husband, though not quite the closest, and he was well-off; Naomi decided he was the man to marry Ruth. If that were to happen, not only would Ruth be provided for, but so would Naomi.

When the time for the harvest festival arrived, Naomi told Ruth of her plan, and Ruth happily followed it to the letter. Boaz celebrated exuberantly during the party that night, got drunk, and then found a quiet place to fall asleep. Ruth followed him to where he was snoring, crawled into bed with him, and snuggled up close. During the night, he woke up and discovered Ruth in bed with him. Given the circumstances and the fact that he had a great attraction to her, he leapt to the obvious conclusion. In the morning, he worked quickly to secure Ruth's hand in marriage. Naomi's plan had worked. Nine months later, Ruth gave birth to a son, Obed, who became the grandfather of **David,** the king of Israel.

LOT

MOAB   JUDAH

RUTH —————————— BOAZ

OBED

JESSE

DAVID

——— MALE

——— FEMALE

——— MARRIED

ANCESTRY

Primary
appearance in
the Bible:
Ruth

Ruth and Boaz

"And Ruth the Moabitess said to Naomi, 'Let me go to the fields and pick up the leftover grain behind anyone in whose eyes I find favor.'" Ruth 2:2 *(Nicolas Poussin, 1594–1665)*

SAMUEL

Samuel was the last of the judges and a prophet. He designated first Saul, and then David, as kings of Israel.

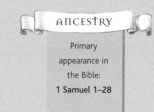

ANCESTRY

Primary appearance in the Bible: 1 Samuel 1–28

Samuel's father was Elkanah, a descendant of **Joseph**'s son Ephraim. His mother was Hannah, one of Elkanah's two wives. She had been unable to have children and suffered much verbal abuse from her husband's other wife as a consequence. She vowed that if God would let her get pregnant, the baby would serve Yahweh for the rest of his life as a Nazarite (see **Samson**) in the Tabernacle (1 Samuel 1:11).

God answered her vow and Samuel was born. Hannah said a poetic prayer of thanksgiving, in which she anachronistically refers to the king of Israel— perhaps a bit of foreshadowing by the author of the story, since Samuel would later play a vital role in establishing the monarchy in Israel (1 Samuel 2:10).

After he had been weaned, Hannah brought Samuel to the Israelite Tabernacle, then located

Hannah Presenting Samuel to the High Priest Eli

"And she said to him, 'As surely as you live, my lord, I am the woman who stood here beside you praying to the Lord. I prayed for this child, and the Lord has granted me what I asked of him. So now I give him to the Lord. For his whole life he will be given over to the Lord.' And he worshiped the Lord there." 1 Samuel 1:26–28 *(Lambert Doomer, 1624–1700)*

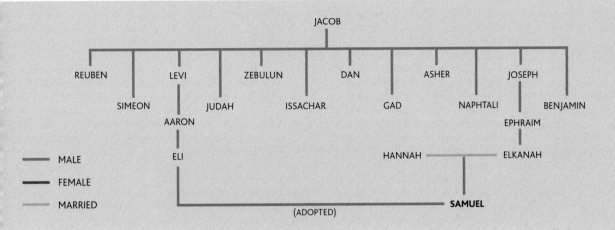

Family tree diagram:

JACOB

REUBEN — LEVI — ZEBULUN — DAN — ASHER — JOSEPH

SIMEON — JUDAH — ISSACHAR — GAD — NAPHTALI — BENJAMIN

AARON — EPHRAIM

——— MALE
——— FEMALE
——— MARRIED

ELI — HANNAH ——— ELKANAH

SAMUEL
(ADOPTED)

in Shiloh. The Tabernacle was a portable shrine dating from **Moses'** time; it housed the Ark of the Covenant and was moved about Israel from time to time. Hannah gave Samuel to the High Priest Eli.

Samuel thus entered the ranks of Levites and served in the Tabernacle. God appeared to Samuel one night while he was still a boy, in order to reveal to him the fate of the High Priest Eli and his two sons. The prophecy was fulfilled when they were all killed and the Ark of the Covenant was captured by the Philistines on a single day.

When he grew up, Samuel served as a judge, and was widely recognized and admired by the Israelites. When he was old, he appointed his sons to succeed him, but his children were dishonest and incompetent, so the people of Israel demanded that Samuel appoint a king to rule over them instead. Samuel warned the nation that a king would be oppressive, demanding taxes and the service of their children in his court and army, but the people insisted. God instructed Samuel to give them what they wanted.

A few days later, **Saul,** a young man from the tribe of **Benjamin,** came to Samuel in search of a lost donkey. Samuel informed a surprised Saul that he would be the new king. Quickly crowned, he was immediately acknowledged and accepted by the nation. Saul subsequently led Israel in a series of successful battles against the Philistines, but he became enamored of his power and prestige and within a few years refused to listen to God's instructions as given by Samuel.

As a result, God told Samuel to find a replacement for Saul in Bethlehem—someone who would be obedient to God. Samuel balked at the command, telling God, "How can I go? Saul will hear about it and kill me." God replied: "Take a heifer with you and say, 'I have come to sacrifice to the Lord'" (1 Samuel 16:2). The ruse worked, and Samuel made it safely to Bethlehem where God told him to anoint **David** as the next king.

Although Samuel died before David eventually took the throne from Saul, Samuel made one last brief appearance on the stage of scripture when a desperate Saul visited a medium in Endor. The medium successfully summoned Samuel back from the dead and then told Saul that he would die that very day by the hand of the Philistines. Civil war followed Saul's death, but David ultimately became king and unified the Twelve Tribes under his rule in Jerusalem.

HANNAH AND ELI, THE HIGH PRIEST

Hannah's desperation in her childlessness led her to make a drastic and ironic vow—when God fulfilled her request to have a child, she gave her son Samuel away to the High Priest Eli. As with so many other men in the Bible, Eli was a poor father. His own two sons, both priests, used religion merely for selfish gain: They were oppressors who stole from both their people and the God they claimed to serve. Moreover, they worshiped Asherah by frequently engaging in sex with her temple prostitutes in Yahweh's Tabernacle. Samuel later pronounced God's judgment on Eli and his two sons.

JOB

Job was a righteous man who suffered tragedy when Satan took a losing bet from God. His unfortunate experience answers the question, "Why serve God?"

ANCESTRY

Primary
appearance in
the Bible:
Job

**A Sick Job Visited
by his Wife**

*"His wife said to him,
'Are you still holding on to
your integrity? Curse God
and die!' He replied, 'You
are talking like a foolish
woman. Shall we accept
good from God, and not
trouble?' In all this, Job
did not sin in what he
said." Job 2:9–10 (Georges
de la Tour, 1593–1652)*

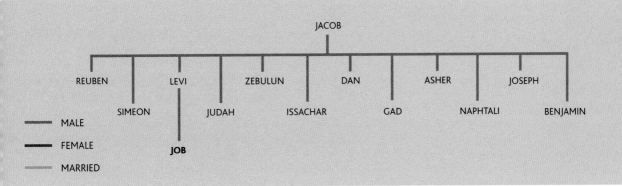

	MALE
	FEMALE
	MARRIED

Family tree showing JACOB at the top, with children: REUBEN, SIMEON, LEVI, JUDAH, ZEBULUN, ISSACHAR, DAN, GAD, ASHER, NAPHTALI, JOSEPH, BENJAMIN. JOB is shown connected to LEVI.

ob was a righteous man, whose story is one of unjust suffering. He deserves none of the bad things that happened to him. In fact, God assumes responsibility for Job's suffering and says that it is "without cause" (Job 2:3).

Satan bargained with God over Job's fate: " 'Does Job fear God for nothing?' Satan replied. 'Have you not put a hedge around him and his household and everything he has? You have blessed the work of his hands, so that his flocks and herds are spread throughout the land. But stretch out your hand and strike everything he has, and he will surely curse you to your face' " (Job 1:9–11).

God gave Satan permission to make Job suffer in any way that would not kill him. Satan proceeded to destroy Job's property, kill his children, and take away his health. Sick and impoverished, sitting on a pile of ashes, Job scraped his open sores with a piece of broken pottery. At that point, Job's wife told him that he should just "Curse God and die!" (Job 2:9). Job refused to curse God.

The question raised by Job's sufferings due to Satan's intervention might be: Was Job good only because he had good fortune? Job's friends, who came to comfort him, quickly moved from comfort to accusation. Their approach grew from a common belief among the Israelites of this period: God would reward good behavior with prosperity, and any evil people committed would incur punishment. Since Job's suffering had become almost unbearable, his friends were certain he must have been guilty of a crime, and they demanded that he confess and repent.

Job protested this wrong notion. His life served as prime evidence that they must be mistaken. He had done nothing wrong to deserve his agony, and through all his suffering, he refused to abandon trust in God. Even in dire circumstances, Job did not stop loving God. For him, leading a good life meant being faithful to God's law and covenant no matter what evil might befall. Loving God was the real reason for Job's righteousness. God sustained him throughout his grief, and, in the end, God restored Job's good fortune.

Job Hearing of His Ruin
Satan caused Job great suffering, but was only able to do so with God's permission. (Gustave Doré, 1832–83)

United Kingdom

Disgusted with their disunited tribal-based leadership system, the people of Israel demanded a king. The first, Saul, proved unsatisfactory, but the transition to the next, David, resulted in a bloody civil war. As with most monarchies, the transition from one ruler to the next was often messy. The United Kingdom was a very brief period in the history of the nation of Israel; it endured only through the reigns of three kings: Saul, David, and Solomon, from about 1050 B.C.E. until about 930 B.C.E. After the death of Saul, a civil war lasted for two years. Both David and Ishbosheth, Saul's son, laid claim to the throne. David was ultimately victorious. When Solomon's son, Rehoboam, took the throne after his father's death, the kingdom split almost at once into two nations; one retained the name Israel, while the other went by the name Judah.

Saul Attacking David

"Saul tried to pin him to the wall with his spear, but David eluded him as Saul drove the spear into the wall. That night David made good his escape."
1 Samuel 19:10 *(Guercino, 1591–1666)*

SAUL

Saul, the first king of Israel, lost his mind and God's favor, consorted with a medium in Endor, and finally committed suicide.

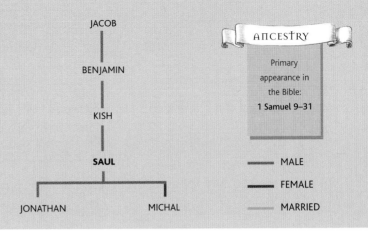

JACOB

BENJAMIN

KISH

SAUL

JONATHAN   MICHAL

ANCESTRY

Primary appearance in the Bible:
1 Samuel 9–31

━━ MALE
━━ FEMALE
━━ MARRIED

A head taller than the average Israelite, Saul was the son of Kish and a descendant of **Benjamin.** One day, his father's donkeys wandered off, and Saul was sent out to find them. His search eventually led him to the prophet and judge, **Samuel,** who told him that he would become the king of Israel. Samuel gave Saul a series of three signs to look for, to prove that what he was saying was true.

First, Samuel told him that he would meet two men near **Rachel**'s tomb; they would let him know that the donkeys had been found, but that Saul's father was worrying about him and his long absence.

Next, when Saul reached the great tree of Tabor, he would meet three men on their way to the Tabernacle in Bethel. One, said Samuel, would be carrying three young goats, the second three loaves of bread, and the third, a full skin of wine. Samuel told Saul that they would offer him two loaves of bread, which he would accept.

Finally, Saul would meet a procession of prophets coming down from the high place at Gibeah. People would be playing music as these men prophesied,

and God's spirit would come upon Saul and he would join them in prophesying.

After these things happened, Saul returned home and tried to pretend nothing had changed. Not long afterward, however, Samuel called the tribes of Israel together at Mizpeh to present the king that God had chosen. Saul arrived with his family and then hid himself among all the luggage until he was dragged out and Samuel proclaimed that he was the new king and poured oil on his head, thus anointing him as the new ruler.

Saul was at first a reluctant monarch, but grew into his role. As time passed, he became more concerned with maintaining his power and position. He demonstrated a lack of trust in Samuel as a prophet and in God. In the end, Saul's disobedience led God to reject him and to pick **David** as his replacement.

Saul began suffering from severe depression. David had entered Saul's service as a musician who played music for Saul whenever bouts of depression overwhelmed him. It seemed to help. David later became a leading general for Saul after David's success against Goliath.

As David's popularity with the people grew, Saul became increasingly paranoid, fearful that David would overthrow him. When Saul's daughter **Michal** fell in love with David, Saul decided this might be the perfect opportunity to get rid of him. He told the young man that he would consent to the marriage, but only if David brought him back the foreskins of 100 Philistines. He thought that David would die in the attempt, but David surprised him and returned with 200 foreskins. After David had become his son-in-law, Saul's paranoia only grew worse. Saul soon drove David out of his palace and spent the remaining years of his life hunting him down and trying unsuccessfully to kill him.

Later, facing a threat from the Philistines and unable to hear anything from God who abandoned him, Saul found a medium in Endor in order to contact the now dead Samuel. He hoped for advice, but instead received a message of doom. During the subsequent battle, he was severely wounded and committed suicide by throwing himself on his sword.

DAVID

David was the second king of Israel, noted for killing Goliath with a slingshot and for writing many of the Psalms.

David was the youngest of seven sons. Growing up, he served as a shepherd of his father's flock. In protecting the flock, he developed a good eye with the sling, but most of his time spent in the fields was quiet, allowing him to develop his musical abilities with playing the harp and singing.

While still a youth, **Samuel** came to Bethlehem and picked David to become the next king to replace **Saul.** Saul, suffering from severe depression, asked David to play music so that he could fall asleep at night. Later, during a standoff with the Philistine army, David heard the boasting of the giant Goliath, a champion in the Philistine army. Saul had offered his daughter in marriage to the man who could rid him of the giant. He also had promised to exempt the victor's family from taxes. David managed to kill Goliath with a well-aimed stone from his sling.

Impressed, Saul transferred David to his army, where he rose to become a general and the best friend of Saul's son and heir, Jonathan. After David killed 200 Philistines and delivered their foreskins to Saul, Saul consented to David's marriage to his daughter **Michal.** As Saul's depression increased and his mental stability deteriorated, he became ever more paranoid until

he was convinced that David was plotting to overthrow him and steal the throne from Jonathan, his heir. Despite Jonathan's attempts to protect David, David fled into exile, where he waged a guerrilla war against the Philistines while pretending to be their faithful servant.

When Saul died by suicide following a losing battle with the Philistines in which his son Jonathan was also killed, David became king over Judah, the southern part of Saul's kingdom. Some suggest the story of Saul's suicide was invented for David's political benefit, to help him consolidate his position and undermine that of his opponents who supported Saul's family. After two years of civil war, David unified all the Twelve Tribes under his rule. During his 40 years on the throne, he succeeded in destroying the Philistines. He also conquered the city of Jerusalem and converted it into the capital of his kingdom. In his personal life, however, things did not proceed so smoothly. He seduced **Bathsheba,** the wife of one of his generals, while the man was away fighting for David, then arranged for the general's death in battle to cover up the fact that Bathsheba was pregnant. The baby born from this liaison died (the baby is not named in the

Bible). Later, Bathsheba gave birth to a second son, **Solomon,** who became king after David.

Having gained several wives over the years, David had many children, but he was not a good father. His firstborn son Amnon, from one of the wives he married before Bathsheba, raped his half-sister **Tamar,** and then **Absalom,** David's third oldest son, murdered the rapist since David refused to do anything about the rape. Absalom escaped into exile for a time, but later returned and plotted against his father, finally rising in open revolt. Absalom drove David into exile for a time, until David eventually rallied his forces and put down his son's rebellion. Absalom was killed in the ensuing battle.

David was noted as a writer of poetry and music, producing about half of the Psalms in the Bible. Just before he died, David had Solomon crowned king of the United Kingdom in order to eliminate any questions regarding the succession.

David Holding Goliath's Head
"So David triumphed over the Philistine with a sling and a stone; without a sword in his hand he struck down the Philistine and killed him." 1 Samuel 17:50 *(Caravaggio, 1571–1610)*

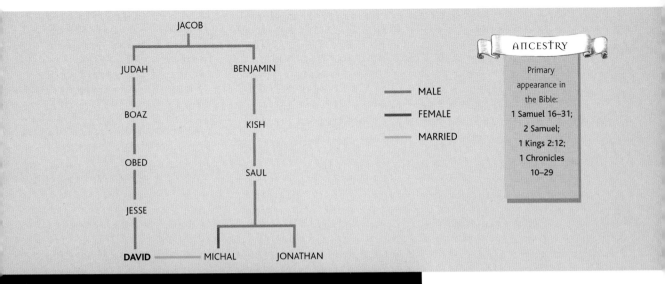

JACOB

JUDAH   BENJAMIN

BOAZ

KISH

OBED

SAUL

JESSE

DAVID ——— MICHAL   JONATHAN

——— MALE

——— FEMALE

——— MARRIED

ANCESTRY

Primary appearance in the Bible:
1 Samuel 16–31;
2 Samuel;
1 Kings 2:12;
1 Chronicles 10–29

JONATHAN

As Saul's firstborn son, Jonathan was the heir apparent to the throne of the United Kingdom. He became David's closest friend and worked hard at trying to keep his father's paranoia under control. Jonathan was a good soldier and had many successes against the Philistines on the battlefield. His relationship with his father Saul was troubled. Once, his father made his men take a vow that they would neither eat nor drink until the Philistines were all killed during one particular battle. Jonathan was unaware of the vow and ate some honey. When Saul discovered that his son had eaten, he ordered his execution. Only the protests of his soldiers prevented Saul from killing his own son. Later, as Saul's hatred of David grew, he became so angry at Jonathan's support for David that he grabbed a spear and hurled it at his son, who ducked and narrowly escaped death. Jonathan died in the same battle that killed his father. David vowed to support and protect Jonathan's children from that day on.

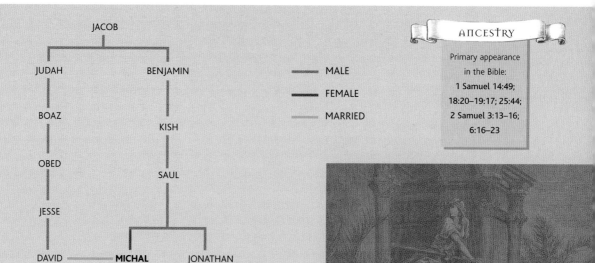

Ancestry tree:

- JACOB
  - JUDAH
    - BOAZ
      - OBED
        - JESSE
          - DAVID
  - BENJAMIN
    - KISH
      - SAUL
        - MICHAL
        - JONATHAN

DAVID — MICHAL — JONATHAN

— MALE
— FEMALE
— MARRIED

ANCESTRY

Primary appearance
in the Bible:
1 Samuel 14:49;
18:20–19:17; 25:44;
2 Samuel 3:13–16;
6:16–23

MICHAL

Michal, Saul's youngest daughter, became David's first wife. She eventually despised him.

Michal, the youngest daughter of **Saul,** Israel's first king, fell in love with **David.** Her father saw this as an opportunity to get rid of David. Paranoid, Saul believed that David intended to overthrow him, so he concocted what he thought would be a great plan to get rid of David for good. He told David that the price for marrying his daughter was for David to deliver 100 Philistine foreskins to him. He figured that David would die in the attempt. David, however, succeeded in delivering not 100, but 200 foreskins. As a result, Saul was forced to allow the marriage.

When Saul finally simply decided to execute David, he ordered his men to roust David from his home and bring him to Saul. Michal warned David that if he did not flee, her father would kill him. Michal helped David to escape, then took an idol and put it in his bed, telling the soldiers that David was sick. Saul ordered David to be hauled before him, sick or not. The ruse discovered, Saul confronted his daughter for helping his enemy, but she claimed that David had threatened to kill her if she did not help him.

The fact that Michal had an easily available idol to put into her husband's bed serves as an illustration of how widespread idolatry and the worship of gods other than Yahweh were in Israel. It raises questions about just how well either Saul or David understood the notion of monotheism if life-size statues of idols were a normal component of household furnishings.

While David was on the run, he married several other women. Meanwhile, Saul gave Michal to another man, Paltiel. When Saul finally died and David took the throne in Judah, the southern part of Saul's kingdom, he demanded that Michal be returned to him in exchange for an agreement between David and Saul's top general, Abner.

Years later, when David moved the Ark of the Covenant to Jerusalem, he danced naked in front of it. Michal berated him for his behavior. Although she remained his wife—as Saul's daughter, she helped legitimate his claim to the throne—he refused to sleep with her again.

Michal Helps David Escape
"So Michal let David down through a window, and he fled and escaped."
1 Samuel 19:12
(Gustave Doré, 1832–83)

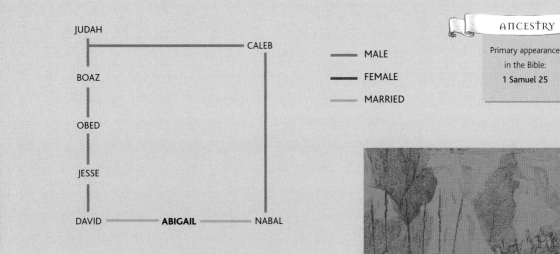

```
JUDAH ─────────────── CALEB
  │
BOAZ
  │
OBED
  │
JESSE
  │
DAVID ───── ABIGAIL ───── NABAL
```

──── MALE
──── FEMALE
──── MARRIED

ANCESTRY

Primary appearance
in the Bible:
1 Samuel 25

ABIGAIL

Abigail was David's second wife, whom he married after her previous husband died of fright and heavy drinking.

On the run from King **Saul** after the prophet and judge **Samuel** died, **David** and his band of followers made their way to the desert of Maon, located south of Hebron in southern Judah. They settled near the property of a man called Nabal (apparently a nickname since the word means "fool"). Nabal is described as "surly and mean in his dealings" (1 Samuel 25:3). David and his men helped Nabal's shepherds watch his sheep at night. One day, David sent his men to Nabal to ask for some food in payment for their efforts. Nabal refused and insulted them.

David was furious and he decided to kill Nabal. Nabal's wife, Abigail, who is described as "an intelligent and beautiful woman" (1 Samuel 25:3), recognized that Nabal was once again living up to his name. She prepared 200 loaves of bread, two skins of wine, five dressed sheep, a bushel (10 gallons or 37 liters) of roasted grain, 100 raisin cakes, and 200 fig cakes. She loaded them on donkeys and presented them to David, begging forgiveness for Nabal's folly.

David listened and accepted her gifts. When she got home, she found Nabal drunk once again, so she waited until the next day to let him know what David had been planning and how she had rescued him. The text tells us that "his heart failed him and he became like a stone" (1 Samuel 25:37) and ten days later he was dead. David asked Abigail to marry him and she agreed. She was the mother of his second son. In 2 Samuel 3:3, his name is given as Kileab in the Hebrew text, while the ancient Greek translation known as the Septuagint calls him Daluyah. In 1 Chronicles 3:1, he is called Daniel.

David and Abigail

"When Abigail saw David, she quickly got off her donkey and bowed down before David with her face to the ground. She fell at his feet and said: 'My lord, let the blame be on me alone. Please let your servant speak to you; hear what your servant has to say. May my lord pay no attention to that wicked man Nabal. He is just like his name—his name is Fool, and folly goes with him. But as for me, your servant, I did not see the men my master sent.'" 1 Samuel 25:23–25 (Johann Christoph Weigel, 1654–1726)

ABSALOM

Absalom was David's third son. He conspired to overthrow David and for a time drove his father from the kingdom before being killed in the ensuing civil war.

Absalom Pierced by Joab's Lance

"So he took three javelins in his hand and plunged them into Absalom's heart while Absalom was still alive in the oak tree. And ten of Joab's armor-bearers surrounded Absalom, struck him and killed him." 2 Samuel 18:14–15 (Giovanni Battista Viola, 1576–1622)

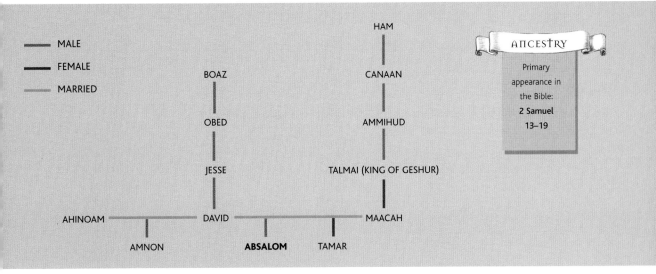

MALE
FEMALE
MARRIED

HAM

CANAAN

BOAZ

OBED

AMMIHUD

JESSE

TALMAI (KING OF GESHUR)

AHINOAM — DAVID — MAACAH

AMNON   **ABSALOM**   TAMAR

ANCESTRY

Primary appearance in the Bible:
2 Samuel 13–19

Absalom was handsome, popular, and noted for his long, flowing hair. He had three sons and a daughter who bore the same name as his sister, **Tamar.** When his half-brother Amnon raped his sister, Absalom was furious. After waiting two years for his father, King **David,** to do something, he took matters into his own hands and killed Amnon. Then he went into self-imposed exile for three years. At the insistence of David's general, Joab, David invited Absalom to return, but refused to talk to him.

Absalom's resentment and frustration with his father led him at last to plot his overthrow. Absalom provided himself with a chariot and horses, along with 50 men to run ahead of him. He got up early every day and stood by the side of the road leading to the city gate. As people approached with a case for his father to render a judgment upon, Absalom would listen to what they had to say and then comment, "Look, your claims are valid and proper, but there is no representative of the king to hear you." Then he would add,

"If only I were appointed judge in the land! Then everyone who has a complaint or case could come to me and I would see that he gets justice" (2 Samuel 15:4). Then, if anyone tried to bow down to him, he would grab them by their hand and kiss them instead, refusing the traditional honors of a prince.

Four years after returning from exile, Absalom asked his father if he could go to the city of Hebron in order to fulfill a vow he had made to Yahweh. David told him, "Go in peace" (2 Samuel 15:9). Absalom then sent secret messengers through the kingdom to say, "As soon as you hear the sound of trumpets, then say, 'Absalom is king in Hebron'" (2 Samuel 15:10). So Absalom headed off to Hebron, accompanied by 200 men whom he had invited as guests, without explaining to them what he was plotting. Once in Hebron, he proclaimed himself king in David's place and gathered several of David's closest advisors to join him in his coup.

When David learned what had happened, he fled his palace in panic for the countryside,

together with his remaining advisors and his top general, Joab. Absalom quickly captured Jerusalem without a fight and established himself as the new king. In order to humiliate David further and demonstrate his own power, one of his first acts as king was to set up a tent in the public square so he could engage in sex with his father's concubines who had been left behind in the palace.

One of David's advisors and friends, Hushai the Arkite, had remained behind in Jerusalem at David's request. He pretended to join Absalom, but worked tirelessly to subvert his cause by giving him bad advice. Hushai succeeded masterfully, allowing David the opportunity to rebuild his forces. In the ensuing civil war, Absalom got caught by his hair in a low hanging tree branch while riding a mule during a battle. Joab, David's general, found him hanging by his hair and threw three javelins into him, killing him instantly and ending the civil war. David returned to his throne victorious, but would forever mourn for his son Absalom.

TAMAR, KING DAVID'S DAUGHTER

Tamar was Absalom's sister. Her half-brother Amnon, David's firstborn son, raped her. Absalom avenged her by killing him.

Tamar was the sister of King **David**'s son, **Absalom.** Her mother, Maacah, was the daughter of Talmai, the king of Geshur. Tamar was very beautiful and she caught the eye of her half-brother Amnon, David's firstborn son and the heir to the throne. Amnon became so obsessed with his sister, and she seemed so out of reach to him, that he started to become ill with all his pent-up frustration. His friend and cousin Jonadab noticed that he seemed out of sorts and asked him about it. Amnon then confessed that he had fallen hopelessly in love with his sister but did not know what to do about it.

Jonadab had an idea, and told Amnon, "Go to bed and pretend to be ill. When your father comes to see you, say to him, 'I would like my sister Tamar to come and give me something to eat. Let her prepare the food in my sight so I may watch her and then eat it from her hand'" (2 Samuel 13:5).

Amnon did precisely as Jonadab suggested. David sent word to Tamar at the palace: "Go to the house of your brother Amnon and prepare some food for him" (2 Samuel 13:7). Tamar went to her brother's house, took some dough, kneaded it, made the bread in his sight, and baked it. When she took the pan and served him the bread, he refused to eat. "Send everyone out of here," Amnon demanded (2 Samuel 13:9). So everyone left but Tamar.

Then Amnon said to Tamar, "Bring the food here into my bedroom so I may eat from your hand" (2 Samuel 13:10). Once in his room alone with him, he attacked her. Pleading with him to let her go, she pointed out that if he were to request her hand in marriage from David, his request would doubtless be granted. Given that the Mosaic Law forbade such close relatives from marrying, despite the example of **Abraham** who was married to his half-sister **Sarah,** Tamar's words seem more likely to have been just a desperate attempt to escape Amnon's clutches. However, David might have authorized the marriage despite the Mosaic legislation, given Amnon's status as crown prince. Unfortunately, Amnon refused to listen to his sister and raped her.

Amnon's love evaporated and turned to intense hatred. He shouted at her to leave, but she protested that sending her away would be a greater wrongdoing than the rape itself. Amnon refused to listen to her. Instead, he called his personal servant and said, "Get this woman out of here and bolt the door after her" (2 Samuel 13:17).

Tamar put ashes on her head and tore the ornamented robe she was wearing. She put her hand on her head and went away, weeping.

Why did she say that sending her away was even a greater wrong than the rape? The Mosaic Law required a rapist to marry his victim and pay her father 50 shekels of silver (Deuteronomy 22:28–29). So Amnon was guilty not only of violating the commandments against rape and incest but also of abandonment.

Devastated by the attack, Tamar went into mourning. Her brother Absalom tried to comfort her, but with very little success. In fact, Tamar never recovered. She moved in with Absalom and then lived as a "desolate woman"—implying that she neither married nor had children her entire life. Absalom eventually killed Amnon.

The Expulsion of Tamar

"Then Amnon hated her with intense hatred. In fact, he hated her more than he had loved her. Amnon said to her, 'Get up and get out!' 'No!' she said to him. 'Sending me away would be a greater wrong than what you have already done to me.' But he refused to listen to her." 2 Samuel 13:15–16 (Guercino, 1591–1666)

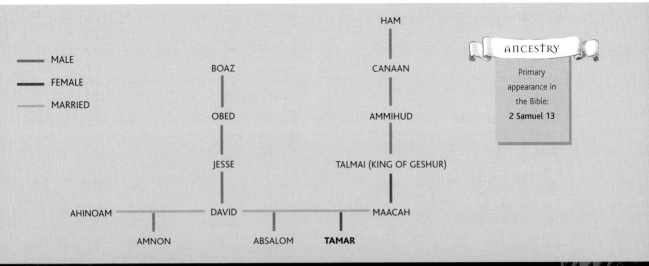

MALE

FEMALE

MARRIED

HAM

CANAAN

BOAZ

OBED

AMMIHUD

JESSE

TALMAI (KING OF GESHUR)

AHINOAM — DAVID — MAACAH

AMNON

ABSALOM

TAMAR

ANCESTRY

Primary
appearance in
the Bible:
2 Samuel 13

BATHSHEBA

Bathsheba committed adultery with David while her husband was at war. David then had her husband murdered so he could marry her.

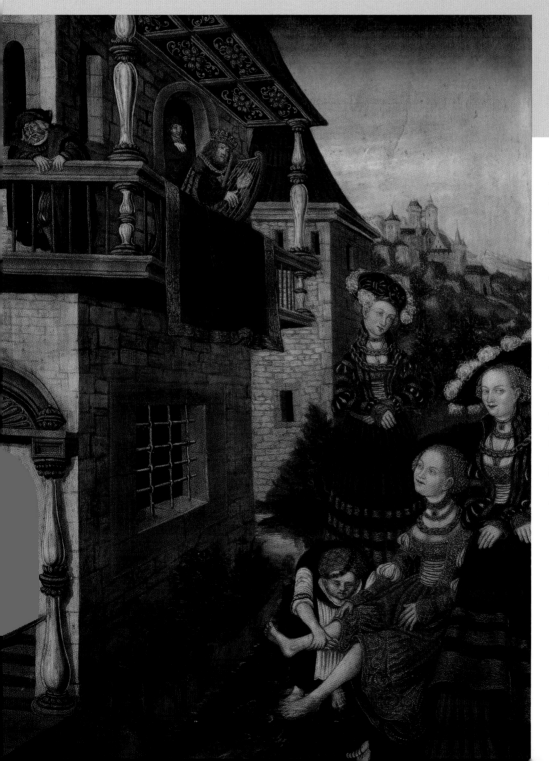

David and Bathsheba

"One evening David got up from his bed and walked around on the roof of the palace. From the roof he saw a woman bathing. The woman was very beautiful, and David sent someone to find out about her. The man said, 'Isn't this Bathsheba, the daughter of Eliam and the wife of Uriah the Hittite?'"
2 Samuel 11:2–3
(Wolfgang Krodel, c. 1500–61)

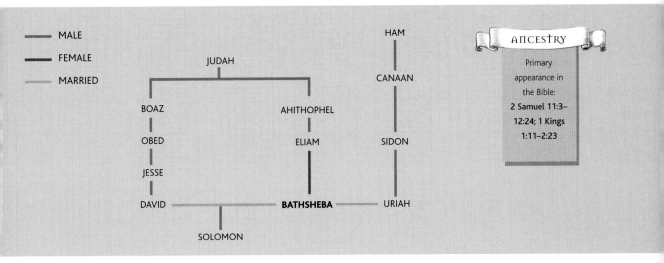

ANCESTRY

Primary
appearance in
the Bible:
2 Samuel 11:3–
12:24; 1 Kings
1:11–2:23

Bathsheba was the very beautiful, well-placed daughter of Eliam, one of David's "mighty men" (2 Samuel 23:8). Eliam was the son of Ahithophel, David's counselor who later backed David's son **Absalom** during his revolt. Bathsheba's husband, Uriah the Hittite, was also one of the "mighty men." While Uriah and the rest of the army were off fighting against the Ammonites, David remained in his palace. One night David watched from his balcony as Bathsheba bathed. David invited her to his palace to spend the night with him and she wound up pregnant.

Since her husband was still fighting in David's war, David had a problem, so he ordered her husband back from the front on the pretext of getting a report on the battle. After the report, David ordered Uriah home to his wife, but he refused so long as his comrades were still at war. Then David got him drunk, hoping that he would wind up back home with his wife, but that did not work either.

Frustrated, David gave Uriah a sealed message and sent him back to the front. The message instructed David's general, Joab, to make sure Uriah died in battle. "Put Uriah in the front line where the fighting is fiercest. Then withdraw from him so he will be struck down and die" (2 Samuel 11:15). Joab followed David's order.

After Uriah was killed, David married Bathsheba. He figured he had solved his problem, but God was displeased by David's behavior and sent the prophet Nathan to confront him. Nathan told David a story. "There were two men in a certain town, one rich and the other poor. The rich man had a very large number of sheep and cattle, but the poor man had nothing except one little ewe lamb he had bought. He raised it, and it grew up with him and his children. It shared his food, drank from his cup and even slept in his arms. It was like a daughter to him. Now a traveler came to the rich man, but the rich man refrained from taking one of his own sheep or cattle to prepare a meal for the traveler who had come to him. Instead, he took the ewe lamb that belonged to the poor man and prepared it for the one who had come to him" (2 Samuel 12:1–4).

David was furious and said that the man who had done this deserved to die. Then the prophet proclaimed, "You are the man!" (1 Samuel 12:7), and explained that conflict would never leave David's family because he had despised God and taken another man's wife to be his own. "This is what the Lord says: 'Out of your own household I am going to bring calamity upon you. Before your very eyes I will take your wives and give them to one who is close to you, and he will lie with your wives in broad daylight. You did it in secret, but I will do this thing in broad daylight before all Israel'" (2 Samuel 12:11–12).

Nathan told David that although God forgave him and would spare his life, the baby that Bathsheba had conceived would die. David comforted her following the child's death. Not long after, Bathsheba became pregnant again and had a second baby who lived. They named him **Solomon.** He became the next king of Israel. Bathsheba lived to see her son become king and died during his reign.

SOLOMON

Solomon was king of Israel after David. Noted for his wisdom, he wrote many of the Proverbs. He built the first Jewish Temple in Jerusalem.

Despite the adulterous affair that brought his parents together and the fact that he was hardly the firstborn son, Solomon became King **David**'s favorite very young. The king promised his mother, **Bathsheba,** that Solomon would become his successor.

When the time came to proclaim a new king, David's first son, Amnon, and his third son, **Absalom,** were both dead, so his fourth son, Adonijah, should have been the one to inherit the crown. (The reason David's second son, by **Abigail,** was not a contender for the throne is not explained.)

In fact, Adonijah remained so certain that he would become king that, as David lay on his deathbed, he crowned himself as his father's successor. However, David thwarted Adonijah and proclaimed Solomon king before he died. Afterward, Solomon executed Adonijah in order to eliminate any questions about his right to the throne. The transition from one king to the next, and even the survival of a king in power, was never smooth in the Israelite monarchy.

Solomon became noted for his great wisdom. God came to him in a dream one night and asked him to make a wish. Solomon requested wisdom, so that he could better rule a united kingdom. God granted his wish and, as a reward for his unselfishness, also gave Solomon great wealth, power, and long life.

Many stories were told to illustrate Solomon's wisdom. The most famous relates to a pair of prostitutes who came before him, both claiming to be the mother of a baby. Solomon listened to them carefully and then called for a sword to slice the baby in half so that he could give half a baby to each woman, since he could not tell which woman was telling him the truth. One woman immediately broke down in tears and begged Solomon to let the other woman have the baby. Solomon announced that this tearful woman was clearly the real mother and so turned the baby over to her, unharmed.

One day the queen of the south Arabian kingdom of Sheba visited Solomon, after she heard tales of his great wisdom. They lavished expensive gifts on each other and apparently concluded a trading pact. Legends suggest they became lovers.

Solomon built a permanent temple for Yahweh to replace the Tabernacle, a movable tent that housed the Ark of the Covenant. He hired builders from Tyre, in Lebanon, to construct it. The Temple survived until the Babylonian King **Nebuchadnezzar** destroyed it, about 400 years later, around 586 B.C.E.

The biblical account contains extreme criticism of Solomon because of his failure to obey God completely. The Mosaic Law established regulations regarding how the king of Israel should behave: He was supposed never to think himself better than any other Israelite; to write a copy of the Mosaic legislation for himself; not to accumulate a great number of wives; not to send the people back to Egypt to get horses; and not to accumulate excessive wealth (Deuteronomy 17:14–20).

In contrast, Solomon did everything a king was forbidden

WISDOM LITERATURE

Solomon's wisdom as described in the Bible was a reflection of a type of literature common throughout the ancient Near East: wisdom literature. Proverbs, Ecclesiastes, and the Song of Songs are examples. All three are traditionally ascribed to Solomon, but with some reservations. Many other examples of wisdom literature survive, both within the Bible and in other ancient Near Eastern texts. Such works were intended to be practical. Proverbs is designed to give wisdom to the young and to allow them to receive the experience of others, granting them the wisdom that they would otherwise only gain from age.

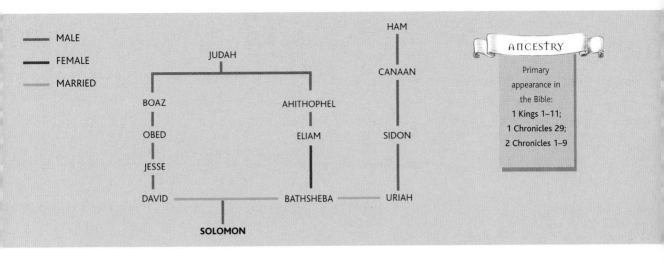

MALE

FEMALE

MARRIED

HAM

JUDAH

CANAAN

BOAZ — AHITHOPHEL

OBED — ELIAM — SIDON

JESSE

DAVID — BATHSHEBA — URIAH

SOLOMON

ANCESTRY

Primary
appearance in
the Bible:
1 Kings 1–11;
1 Chronicles 29;
2 Chronicles 1–9

to do: he had 300 wives and 700 concubines; he sent traders to bring horses from Egypt; he was described as wealthy beyond all measure; and he worshiped foreign gods and established temples and idols for them. God's anger was such that he promised Solomon that his kingdom would die with him: The house of David would retain only the tribe of **Judah** to rule over. The other tribes would form a new and separate kingdom. Solomon died after a 40-year reign as king.

The Judgment of Solomon
"Then the king said, 'Bring me a sword.' So they brought a sword for the king. He then gave an order: 'Cut the living child in two and give half to one and half to the other.'" 1 Kings 3:24–25 (Nicolas Poussin, 1594–1665)

Divided Kingdom

The Twelve Tribes remained united through the reigns of only three kings: Saul, David, and Solomon. Under the rule of the fourth king, Rehoboam, issues of taxation and military conscription resulted in splitting the kingdom: The Southern Kingdom, Judah, had Jerusalem as its capital; the Northern Kingdom, Israel, had the city of Samaria as its capital. Suffering numerous coups, civil wars, and shifts in ruling families, the new Northern Kingdom of Israel was politically less stable than the Southern Kingdom of Judah that continued under David's descendants. The Divided Kingdom only lasted about 200 years, from around 930 B.C.E. until the Northern Kingdom was destroyed by the Assyrian Empire, and its last royal family taken into exile around 722 B.C.E. The Southern Kingdom endured for a longer period until it was destroyed by the Babylonians around 586 B.C.E.

King Rehoboam
Rehoboam, the son of Solomon, was the last king to inherit a united kingdom of Israel and Judah. (Painted wooden ceiling in the Church of St. Martin, Zillis, Switzerland, c. 1150)

REHOBOAM

Rehoboam, son of Solomon, became king after his father. His policies led to the dissolution of the Kingdom of Israel into two new nations.

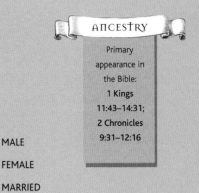

ANCESTRY

Primary appearance in the Bible: 1 Kings 11:43–14:31; 2 Chronicles 9:31–12:16

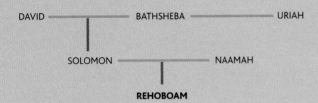

DAVID —————— BATHSHEBA —————————— URIAH

SOLOMON —————————— NAAMAH

REHOBOAM

———— MALE

———— FEMALE

———— MARRIED

Solomon's firstborn son and successor was Rehoboam. His mother was named Naamah; she was an Ammonite. Although the transition from Solomon to Rehoboam went smoothly, the actual reign started badly and got worse. Rehoboam became king of Israel when he was 41. At the beginning of his reign, a delegation representing each of the Twelve Tribes approached him. They complained that Solomon had been an oppressive ruler and that taxes were too high. They asked him to lighten the load. Rehoboam sent them away, promising to give them an answer in three days.

He consulted his advisors. The old advisors who had served his father counseled that he agree to the requests; the younger men, who were his friends and had been raised with him, told him that he should treat them even more harshly than his father Solomon: "Tell these people who have said to you, 'Your father put a heavy yoke on us, but make our yoke lighter'—tell them, 'My little finger is thicker than my father's waist. My father laid on you a heavy yoke; I will make it even heavier.

My father scourged you with whips; I will scourge you with scorpions'" (1 Kings 12:10–11).

Rehoboam, fool that he was, listened to the younger men. As a consequence, ten of the tribes declared their independence. Jeroboam became their king. Rehoboam planned to attack the rebels, but the prophet Shemaiah warned the king and people "Do not go up to fight against your brothers" (1 Kings 12:24). The rebellion split the nation between the Kingdom of Israel in the north and the Kingdom of Judah, ruled by Rehoboam (and his descendants), in the south.

Egypt attacked Judah during the fifth year of Rehoboam's reign and stripped the Temple in Jerusalem and the king's palace of all their gold. Rehoboam made replacements for the lost items out of bronze.

Besides splitting the kingdom that his father had given him, Rehoboam's reign was also noted for being a disaster religiously. During his reign the people of Judah built places of worship for the fertility goddess Asherah, raised sacred stones, and engaged in sacred prostitution. The biblical writer comments that "the people engaged in all the detestable practices of the nations the Lord had driven out before the Israelites" (1 Kings 14:24). He died at the relatively young age of 58, after only 17 years on the throne.

JEROBOAM

The Ephramite Jeroboam, one of Solomon's officials, had rebelled against Solomon and gone into exile in Egypt. After Solomon's death, he returned and became a leader in the rebellion against Rehoboam, Solomon's son. Afterward, Jeroboam was crowned king over the new Northern Kingdom of Israel. One of his first acts was to establish new centers of worship in the northern and southern portions of Israel, to prevent people from traveling to Jerusalem in the Southern Kingdom of Judah for religious pilgrimages and sacrifice. He established new temples and selected new, nonLevite priests of Yahweh for his kingdom. He set up golden calves in each of the two new temples to represent Yahweh, paralleling the Canaanite practice of picturing their god Baal as a bull. A prophet criticized his decision and told him that, as a consequence, his dynasty would not endure.

HULDAH

Huldah was a female prophet who explained the meaning of the lost book of Deuteronomy rediscovered during the reign of Josiah, king of Judah.

A rare female prophet, Huldah was a Levite married to the keeper of the wardrobe for the Temple in Jerusalem. She was clearly well respected in the community because men in high places sought her opinion on important issues and she spoke to them with ease and authority. She was a contemporary of the prophet **Jeremiah.** Her name means "weasel."

During the renovation of the Temple in Jerusalem while Josiah was king of Judah, the high priest, Hilkiah, came upon a copy of the "Book of the Law" (2 Kings 22:8), commonly understood to be Deuteronomy. After it was read to the king, he tore his clothes and told the high priest, "Go and inquire of the Lord for me and for the people and for all Judah about what is written in this book that has been found. Great is the Lord's anger that burns against us because our fathers have not obeyed the words of this book; they have not acted in accordance with all that is written there concerning us" (2 Kings 22:13).

So Hilkiah the priest, with several of the king's attendants, went to Huldah and asked her about the book they had found. Huldah was a prophetess accustomed to speaking the word of God directly to high priests and royal officials, and they believed that she had the authority to determine what was and was not the genuine law.

Huldah warned them of God's impending judgment against the Kingdom of Judah because of its idolatry. However, the judgment would be postponed until after Josiah's death, because of his faithfulness to Yahweh. So the high priest took the message back to Josiah, who publicly repented for the nation, read out loud from Deuteronomy to the assembled people, and renewed the covenant between Yahweh and Israel. He had the idols and articles of Baal and Asherah removed from Yahweh's Temple.

No more is heard from Huldah in the Bible. The rabbinic literature suggests that the reason the king sent his representatives to her rather than to Jeremiah was because he thought that women were more easily stirred to pity than men, and that Huldah would be more likely than Jeremiah to intercede with God on his behalf. Huldah is memorable because she is one of the rare female prophets mentioned by name in the Bible, and because the men were willing to defer to her judgment.

JOSIAH

Josiah was a descendant of **David** and a king of Judah. He was counted as a "righteous king" and during his reign he renovated the Temple and put several reforms in religious matters into effect after the "Book of the Law" was rediscovered. As a political leader, however, he made several mistakes, the worst of which was opposing Pharaoh Necho II of Egypt, who wanted to pass through Judah on his way to join the Assyrians in a battle against the Babylonians. Josiah tried to stop him and met him in battle at Megiddo (*Har Megiddo*, also known as Armageddon from the Greek form of Mount Megiddo; the author of Revelation connected his apocalyptic vision with this geographic location). Josiah died in that battle. Josiah's actions delayed and weakened the Egyptian army, so that at the subsequent battle of Carchemish on the Euphrates (about 605 B.C.E.) the Babylonians were victorious, destroying the Assyrians and so weakening Egypt that it was never again a world power. The now unopposed Babylonians attacked and destroyed Jerusalem only a few years later. They burned the Temple to the ground and took upper-class members of Judean society into captivity.

Hilkiah Inquiring of Huldah

Josiah sent the high priest Hilkiah and several other attendants to ask the prophetess Huldah about the rediscovered "Book of the Law." (Caspar Luiken, 1672–1708)

JACOB

LEVI

HARHAS

TIKVAH

HULDAH ——————— SHALLUM

——— MALE

——— FEMALE

——— MARRIED

ANCESTRY

Primary
appearance in
the Bible:
**2 Kings 22;
2 Chronicles 34**

JEZEBEL

Jezebel was the notorious wife of Ahab, the king of the Northern Kingdom of Israel.
She introduced the widespread worship of the Canaanite god Baal to Israel.

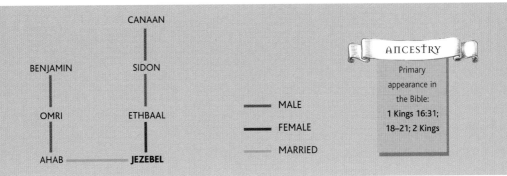

ANCESTRY

Primary
appearance in
the Bible:
1 Kings 16:31;
18–21; 2 Kings

CANAAN

BENJAMIN — SIDON

OMRI — ETHBAAL

AHAB ——— **JEZEBEL**

——— MALE
——— FEMALE
——— MARRIED

ezebel became the queen of the Northern Kingdom of Israel and the wife of King **Ahab.** Jezebel was not an Israelite; she was the daughter of Ethbaal, king of the Phoenician cities of Tyre and Sidon in Lebanon. Her name apparently means "no dung" or perhaps "unchaste" in Hebrew. In its original Phoenician, it probably meant something like "Where is the prince?" She introduced, or at least radically expanded, the worship of the Canaanite deity Baal-Melkart throughout her new homeland.

"Baal" is a term that in Hebrew and other northwest Semitic languages meant simply "lord" or "master," and it was on occasion used in reference to Yahweh. Several Canaanite deities received the title, and so it is not always clear which of these deities is being referenced in the Bible. The specific deity, Baal-Melkart, that Jezebel had introduced to Israel was the chief deity of Tyre, in Lebanon, and was also important in Tyre's colony, Carthage, in North Africa.

The Death of Jezebel

"'Throw her down!' Jehu said. So they threw her down, and some of her blood spattered the wall and the horses as they trampled her underfoot." 2 Kings 9:33
(Mozarabic Bible, tenth century)

Baal-Melkart was sometimes equated with the Babylonian deity known as Nergal, the god of the underworld and death, equivalent to the Roman god Pluto. According to the fifth-century B.C.E. Greek historian Herodotus, Baal-Melkart's temple in Tyre was the scene of annual winter and spring festivals. Some scholars believe that this temple was the model for **Solomon**'s Temple in Jerusalem.

Having replaced the worship of Yahweh with the worship of Baal-Melkart, and having established a priesthood for that deity, Jezebel persecuted and executed as many prophets of Yahweh as she could find. Several hundred of them managed to survive, however. One of them, **Elijah,** spoke repeated condemnations against Jezebel for her idolatry and her persecution of the followers of Yahweh. He thereby incurred her special disfavor.

When her husband Ahab, the king, sought to purchase a vineyard, and was rebuffed by the owner, her reaction illustrated both her lack of understanding of the Mosaic Law and Israelite customs and the difference in how the monarchy in Israel functioned compared to those in the surrounding kingdoms. Ahab went back home after the owner

of the property refused to sell and simply moped. Jezebel looked at him in surprise, then had the man murdered so that Ahab could confiscate the property. This was radically new—and illegal—behavior in an Israelite monarch.

Later, after Elijah challenged and killed her priests of Baal at Mount Carmel, Jezebel issued a decree of death against the prophet: "May the gods deal with me, be it ever so severely, if by this time tomorrow I do not make your life like that of one of them" (1 Kings 19:2). Elijah went into hiding and her threat was never carried out.

After the deaths of Ahab and her son Ahaziah, her grandson Joram became king. One of Ahab's generals, Jehu, rebelled and killed Joram. When she heard about it, Jezebel knew her death was near. After calmly painting her eyes, she arranged her hair, and then waited by the window for Jehu to appear. Jehu ordered that she be tossed from the window. Her broken body was then consumed by dogs, leaving behind only her skull, hands, and feet. Jezebel's name has taken on negative connotations. Her primping just before her execution is the origin of the English phrase "a painted Jezebel," referring to a scheming, brazen woman with low morals.

AHAB

Ahab was king of the Northern Kingdom of Israel and husband of Jezebel, and sparred frequently with the prophet Elijah.

Ahab was the seventh king of the Northern Kingdom of Israel. Ahab's father Omri gets little mention in the Bible, but was so politically and militarily successful that the Assyrians from Omri's time on commonly referred to the Northern Kingdom of Israel as "Beth Omri"—House of Omri. Ahab, like his father, proved a strong ruler, expanding on his father's victories. His alliance with the Phoenicians of Tyre and Sidon, solidified by his marriage to their king's daughter, **Jezebel,** was politically advantageous but religiously disastrous for Israel. The worship of Baal and Asherah, a fertility goddess, became widespread. Persecution of those who worshiped Yahweh became common as well, particularly those who claimed to be prophets.

Elijah was Ahab's biggest nemesis throughout his reign, continually voicing criticism of his policies. Early in his reign, Elijah announced bad news to Ahab: no more rain. "As the Lord, the God of Israel, lives, whom I serve, there will be neither dew nor rain in the next few years except at my word" (1 Kings 17:1). Elijah immediately went into hiding, spending most of the next three years either in the wilderness or living with a widow. At the end of three years, after Yahweh had beaten Baal in a challenge, Elijah told Ahab that the drought was over and rain was coming. Meanwhile, Elijah went back into hiding, fearful that Ahab's wife, Jezebel, was going to kill him.

Ahab waged three successful wars against the nation of Aram. During the third war, the Arameans believed that their initial difficulties were due to the fact that they had attacked Israel in the hills and "Their gods are gods of the hills. That is why they were too strong for us. But if we fight them on the plains, surely we will be stronger than they" (1 Kings 20:23). They soon learned that Israel's God was not as limited by geography as they imagined. Having been completely trounced by the Israelites, the Aramean king Ben-Hadad approached Ahab in sackcloth and ashes. Although a prophet of Yahweh had told Ahab that Ben-Hadad needed to be put to death, Ahab instead made a treaty of peace with the king and sent him on his way.

One of the prophets who had been in hiding approached one of his companions and told the companion to strike him with a weapon (both prophets are unnamed in the Bible). His companion refused. The prophet told him, "Because you have not obeyed the Lord, as soon as you leave me a lion will kill you" (1 Kings 20:36). It happened as he foretold. The prophet then found another man and made the same peculiar request; the second man did as he was asked. Then the prophet stood by the side of the road, his head bandaged, waiting for Ahab to pass by. When the prophet saw Ahab, he said: "Your servant [I] went into the thick of the battle, and someone came to me with a captive and said, 'Guard this man. If he is missing, it will be your life for his life, or you must pay a talent of silver.' While your servant was busy here and there, the man disappeared." Ahab replied, "That is your sentence. You have pronounced it yourself" (1 Kings 20:39–40). The prophet quickly revealed himself and told the king that since he had released Ben-Hadad, a man of God's choosing must die in his place, "Therefore it is your life for his life, your people for his people" (1 Kings 20:42). The king returned to his palace in Samaria, unhappy and angry.

After three more years of peace and an alliance with the Southern Kingdom of Judah, Ahab attacked Aram again, despite prophetic warning against the venture. Ahab was killed in the battle, after having reigned as king for 22 years.

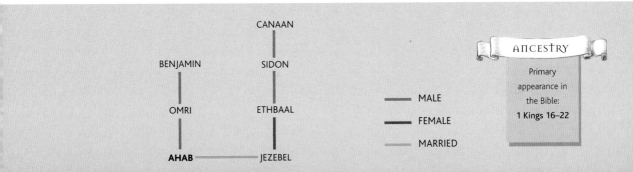

CANAAN

BENJAMIN   SIDON

OMRI   ETHBAAL

AHAB ———— JEZEBEL

—— MALE

—— FEMALE

—— MARRIED

ANCESTRY

Primary appearance in the Bible: 1 Kings 16–22

**Ahab in Battle
Against the Arameans**

*Ahab, king of the Northern
Kingdom of Israel, died in battle
against Aram. (German etching,
c. 1500–1699)*

MICHAIAH

Michaiah was one of many prophets in Israel during the time of Ahab. Ahab had made a military alliance with Jehoshaphat, the king of Judah, against Aram. Ahab invited Michaiah and several other prophets to come and pronounce God's message about the upcoming battle. While all the others promised success and victory, Michaiah told a story about Yahweh musing on how to entice Ahab to his death. Several angels said one thing, several another, until one stood up and volunteered to be a lying spirit in the mouths of Ahab's prophets to foretell victory. Yahweh praised him and told him that yes, that would work. Then Michaiah told Ahab that Yahweh had decreed his death during the upcoming war. An angry Ahab sent Michaiah to prison on a bread and water diet, but the prophecy came true and Ahab was killed (1 Kings 22:8–29).

ELIJAH

Elijah was a prophet of Yahweh who criticized Ahab and Jezebel for abandoning the Jewish God Yahweh for the worship of Baal.

Elijah Carried to Heaven in a Fiery Chariot
"As they were walking along and talking together, suddenly a chariot of fire and horses of fire appeared and separated the two of them, and Elijah went up to heaven in a whirlwind."
2 Kings 2:11
(Flemish School, sixteenth century)

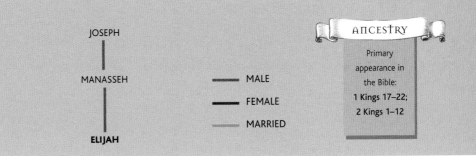

JOSEPH

MANASSEH

ELIJAH

—————— MALE

—————— FEMALE

—————— MARRIED

ANCESTRY

Primary
appearance in
the Bible:
1 Kings 17–22;
2 Kings 1–12

Elijah first appears in the Bible when he warns **Ahab,** king of the Northern Kingdom of Israel, that because of his wickedness there would be no rain for several years, unless Elijah said otherwise (Genesis 17:1). Ahab blamed Elijah for the suffering the drought brought to his land and wanted to find the prophet and kill him.

However, Elijah went into the wilderness east of the Jordan River to hide. There, he found a stream to supply him with water, and ravens brought him food every day, but as the drought intensified, his stream finally dried up. God then told Elijah to go to Zarephath in Sidon. There, he found a widow on the verge of starvation. He asked her for food and she refused, explaining that she had barely enough flour and oil to make one last loaf of bread for herself and her son. Elijah insisted, explaining that neither the oil nor the flour would ever run out again. From then on, the oil jar was always full, and the flour jar was never empty. Later, the widow's son suddenly became ill and died. When she complained to Elijah, he raised her son back to life.

In the third year of the drought, God finally sent Elijah back to Ahab. Elijah told Ahab to gather the 450 prophets of Baal and to meet him at Mount Carmel to determine whether Baal or Yahweh was the real God. Elijah and the prophets of Baal each built an altar, cut up a couple of bulls, gathered wood, and then prayed to their respective deities for fire to fall from heaven on their offerings.

Elijah allowed the prophets of Baal to go first. After preparing the sacrifice, they spent the day dancing around it, shouting to Baal, and cutting themselves with knives, hoping to get his attention. Elijah watched silently for a while, then started taunting them. "Shout louder! Surely he is a god! Perhaps he is deep in thought, or busy, or traveling. Maybe he is sleeping and must be awakened?" (1 Kings 18:27).

After the worshipers of Baal had finally given up from exhaustion, Elijah built an altar for Yahweh, then had volunteers fill four large jars full of water. He had them drench the altar and the wood, and then had them repeat the process twice more. Finally, Elijah quietly prayed to Yahweh. Fire promptly fell from the sky, consuming the wood, the sacrificed bulls on the wood, and even the stones and some of the surrounding dirt.

The people responded by repeating endlessly: "The Lord— he is God!" (1 Kings 18:39).

Elijah then ordered the crowd to kill the prophets of Baal, which they were happy to do. Elijah turned to a shocked Ahab and told the king that it was finally going to rain soon. Before Ahab could get home to tell his wife **Jezebel** everything that had happened, the drought ended.

When Jezebel heard what had happened to the prophets of Baal, she sent a message to Elijah: "May the gods deal with me, be it ever so severely, if by this time tomorrow I do not make your life like that of one of them" (1 Kings 19:2). In terror, he ran for his life into the desert, about a day's journey from Beersheba. While there, God fed him, encouraged him, and sent him to appoint a successor for himself and for Ahab.

Not long after Ahab's death, Elijah left for heaven in a horse-drawn chariot made of fire. According to a later biblical prophet, Elijah was destined to return to announce the coming of the Messiah (Malachi 4:5). To this day at Passover, Jewish people set out a cup of wine called "Elijah's cup" and send the youngest child to the door to see if Elijah has come to announce the arrival of the Messiah. **Jesus** later argued that **John the Baptist** was this prophesied Elijah when John announced that Jesus was the Messiah.

ELISHA

Elisha was Elijah's servant who took Elijah's place as prophet. Elisha performed a variety of miracles, including bringing a dead child back to life.

Elisha is first mentioned in the Bible when God tells **Elijah** to pick Elisha as his servant and successor. Elisha held the position as prophet in Israel for about 60 years, performing miracles on a regular basis. He made a spring of water drinkable by tossing some salt into it; he cursed a group of youths who made fun of his baldness so that they were immediately mauled by bears; he multiplied the amount of oil a poor widow had, so that she was able to fill up multiple jars, enough to sell and pay off her debts; he multiplied twenty loaves of new barley so that a hundred men could be fed; and he made a borrowed lost axe head float in the water so it could be recovered. Elisha also cured the leprosy of a Syrian general named Naaman by having him dip himself in the Jordan River seven times. As a consequence of the miraculous healing, Naaman turned away from idolatry and became a strict worshiper of Yahweh. When Elisha's servant **Gehazi** stole from the general, Elisha cursed his servant with the leprosy removed from the Syrian.

When the king of Aram laid siege to Samaria, the capital city of the Northern Kingdom of Israel, the people of the city started to starve. One day, the king of Israel was walking along the city wall and a woman called out to him, begging for help. "This woman said to me, 'Give up your son so we may eat him today, and tomorrow we'll eat my son.' So we cooked my son and ate him. The next day I said to her, 'Give up your son so we may eat him,' but she had hidden him" (2 Kings 6:28–29).

The king went into mourning and vowed that he would kill Elisha that very day, but when he came to carry out his vow, Elisha told him that within 24 hours, food would once again be abundant and cheap in Samaria. One of the king's officers who was with him scoffed, commenting that even if God started raining food from the sky, it would not fix the mess. Elisha told the officer that he would see God's provision for himself, but that he would die before he could eat any of it.

Meanwhile, as sunset neared, four lepers decided that they would be better off surrendering to the Arameans. They knew that the Arameans would likely just kill them, but since they were going to die of starvation anyhow, what could it hurt? When they reached the Aramean camp, they discovered that God had made the Aramean army believe that a massive Hittite army had arrived to save Samaria. The enemy army had vanished, fleeing in panic, and abandoning all their food, clothes, gold, and silver. After feasting and doing a little plundering, the lepers decided they should bring the good news back to Samaria. The famine was over, and the officer who had scoffed at Elisha's prophecy was trampled to death by the mob of people rushing out of Samaria to get to the abandoned food.

Elisha continued proclaiming the word of God. When a family kindly allowed him to stay in their home, Elisha prayed that the wife would get her greatest desire: a child. Years later, when her young son took ill and died, he raised him back to life. Elisha finally died of old age, but the miracles did not stop with his death. A year after he was buried, when a dead body tumbled against Elisha's bones during a burial, the dead man sprang back to life (2 Kings 13:20–21).

Little Children Mocking Elisha

"As he was walking along the road, some youths came out of the town and jeered at him. 'Go on up, you baldhead!' they said. 'Go on up, you baldhead!' He turned around, looked at them, and called down a curse on them in the name of the Lord. Then two bears came out of the woods and mauled forty-two of the youths." 2 Kings 2:23–24 (Book illustration, c. 1860)

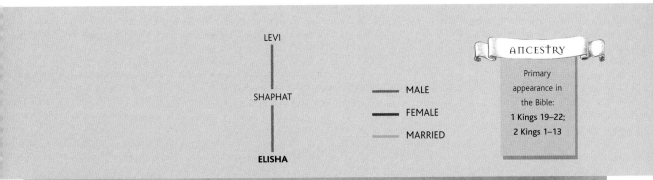

LEVI

SHAPHAT

ELISHA

MALE

FEMALE

MARRIED

ANCESTRY

Primary
appearance in
the Bible:
1 Kings 19–22;
2 Kings 1–13

GEHAZI

Gehazi was Elisha's servant who stole from the Syrian general Naaman after he came to Elisha to be cured of leprosy. Elisha then cursed Gehazi with leprosy for the rest of his life.

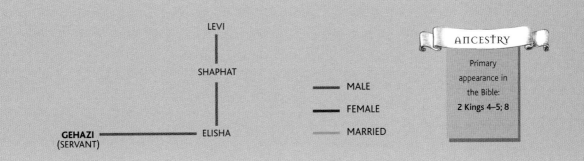

ANCESTRY

Primary appearance in the Bible: 2 Kings 4–5; 8

LEVI

SHAPHAT

ELISHA

GEHAZI (SERVANT)

MALE

FEMALE

MARRIED

Gehazi was **Elisha's** servant, fulfilling the same role for Elisha that Elisha had fulfilled for **Elijah.** One day Elisha decided that he should do something nice for the Shunammite woman who had provided him and Gehazi with a place to stay for several years whenever he traveled to the region where she lived. Gehazi related Elisha's words: "You have gone to all this trouble for us. Now what can be done for you? Can we speak on your behalf to the king or the commander of the army?" Her reply was simply, "I have a home among my own people" (2 Kings 4:13).

Gehazi pointed out that she had no children and that her husband was old, so Elisha told her to expect to give birth to a son within a year. She did not believe him, but it happened just as Elisha had predicted. Years later, her son became ill and died. She rode off to find Elisha. He saw her coming from a distance and sent Gehazi out to meet her and find out what was wrong. She told Gehazi nothing,

Elisha and Gehazi

Gehazi was Elisha's servant, but did not always obey orders. Elisha eventually cursed Gehazi and his descendants with leprosy. (Book illustration, c. 1860)

but when she finally arrived, she threw herself on the floor and grabbed Elisha's feet. Gehazi tried to push her away, but Elisha stopped him. After relating her sad story, Elisha gave Gehazi his staff and sent him to the boy with instructions to put the staff on him. Gehazi did as instructed but nothing happened. Elisha finally had to go in person to raise the boy from the dead.

Naaman, the commander of the Aramean army, had leprosy. A young Israelite slave girl told his wife that she knew of a prophet in Israel who would be able to cure him. Naaman went to his king and asked permission to go find this prophet. The king of Aram consented and gave him a letter to Joram, the king of Israel. The letter read: "With this letter I am sending my servant Naaman to you so that you may cure him of his leprosy" (2 Kings 5:6).

As soon as the king of Israel read it, he panicked. "Am I God?" he asked. "Can I kill and bring back to life? Why does this fellow send someone to me to be cured of his leprosy? See how he is trying to pick a quarrel with me!" (2 Kings 5:7). When Elisha heard the news, he told the king not to worry, because he could cure Naaman.

When Naaman arrived at Elisha's door, Elisha did not

even come out to see him. Instead, Elisha sent a messenger out with instructions to dip himself in the Jordan River seven times, after which he would be healed. Naaman left in a huff, but his servants convinced him to try it. After the seventh dip, he came up healed and hurried back to Elisha, thanking him and intending to pay him. Elisha refused all offers of payment and sent Naaman on his way.

Gehazi thought this was a mistake. He quickly chased after Naaman, made up a story, and got Naaman to give him two talents (about 190 pounds or 86 kg) of silver and two sets of clothes. He then hid them in his tent. Elisha confronted Gehazi about what he had done, denounced him, and cursed both him and his descendants with Naaman's leprosy.

Years later, while Gehazi was telling King Joram about Elisha's great deeds, the Shunammite woman came before the king to make a request. When Joram learned that this was the very woman whose son Elisha had raised from the dead, he immediately appointed people to handle her case. Thus, the suggestion that Elisha had made through Gehazi years earlier, that perhaps he could speak on her behalf to the king, came to pass.

PROPHETS BEFORE THE EXILE

The ancient Jewish prophets acted as the conscience of the people in the kingdoms where they lived, warning both people and rulers to turn to God and to treat one another with love. Their messages of warning and hope went largely unheeded. Both the Northern Kingdom of Israel and the Southern Kingdom of Judah were subjugated by their powerful neighbors; their upper classes were taken into captivity and endured a period of exile. The prophets preceding the exile did most of their prophesying between about 800 and 600 B.C.E. The prophets expressed most of their thoughts and ideas poetically using a technique referred to as "biblical parallelism." Instead rhyming the sounds at the end of each line of their poetry—which is a poetic convention more familiar to modern readers—they repeated or "rhymed" concepts using synonyms, colorful imagery, and astute metaphors. Due to this, their poetry can at times sound repetitious.

The Prophet Hosea

"I will ransom them from the power of the grave; I will redeem them from death. Where, O death, are your plagues? Where, O grave, is your destruction? I will have no compassion." Hosea 13:14 *(German etching, c. 1500–1699)*

HOSEA

The prophet Hosea's wife Gomer was unfaithful to him, and his experience became a symbol of how the people of Israel failed to worship Yahweh properly.

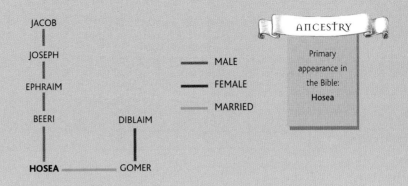

JACOB
JOSEPH
EPHRAIM
BEERI — DIBLAIM
HOSEA — GOMER

——— MALE
——— FEMALE
——— MARRIED

ANCESTRY

Primary appearance in the Bible:
Hosea

Hosea prophesied to the Northern Kingdom of Israel, and was the only prophet there who wrote down what he said. He composed his prophecies between 740 and 725 B.C.E., using his own bad marriage as a metaphor for God's relationship with the Northern Kingdom. It was common among the prophets of both the Northern and Southern Kingdoms to use adultery as a metaphor of Israel's tendency to worship other gods in addition to Yahweh.

God told Hosea to marry a prostitute named Gomer. Over the years, she gave birth to two sons and a daughter. Although it is not explicitly stated whether or not these three children born to Gomer were actually Hosea's biological children, most scholars suspect, given Gomer's prostitution and the whole purpose of Hosea's marriage, that they were the result of her chosen profession.

Hosea named his firstborn son Jezreel, because, God said, "I will soon punish the house of Jehu for the massacre at Jezreel, and I will put an end to the kingdom of Israel" (Hosea 1:4). Who was Jehu and what massacre upset God? Jehu had been a general in the army of the Northern Kingdom of Israel, serving first King **Ahab** and then his son, King Joram. One day, the prophet **Elisha** anointed Jehu as king and commanded him to wipe out Ahab's dynasty. To this end, Jehu rebelled against Joram and killed both him and his mother, **Jezebel.** Then Jehu murdered all the remaining members of the royal family in Jezreel: "So Jehu killed everyone in Jezreel who remained of the house of Ahab, as well as all his chief men, his close friends and his priests, leaving him no survivor" (2 Kings 10:11). According to Hosea, God was disturbed by this slaughter.

Gomer then gave birth to a daughter whom Hosea named Lo-Ruhamah, a Hebrew phrase meaning "unloved," because, God said, "I will no longer show love to the house of Israel, that I should at all forgive them" (Hosea 1:6). The lastborn son was named Lo-Ammi, a Hebrew phrase meaning "Not my people," because, as God said, "You are not my people, and I am not your God" (Hosea 1:9).

However, God's displeasure with the people of Israel was not permanent, anymore than the anger Hosea had for his unfaithful wife was permanent. After she left him, she fell on hard times and wound up a slave. God told Hosea to buy her back, take her home, and love her to illustrate God's ultimate intentions for misbehaving Israel. An important concept illustrated by Hosea's story is that God's judgment against his people was sometimes designed to be corrective. Writing to the Christian community in Rome, **Paul** argued that God's relationship with Israel was permanent, because "God's gifts and his call are irrevocable" (Romans 11:29).

God's hope in sending Hosea to prophesy—as with all the prophets he sent to his people— was that, when they witnessed Hosea's life experience and heard his words, they would repent of their idolatry and turn back to Yahweh. God always preferred to forgive, rather than punish. Unfortunately, his people refused to listen to Hosea and so in 722 B.C.E. the Northern Kingdom of Israel was destroyed by the Assyrian Empire. This destruction gave rise to the legend of ten lost tribes. In reality, no tribes were ever lost. Jerusalem simply reestablished political control over the northern tribes and even collected taxes from them (2 Chronicles 34:9).

JONAH

Jonah was a prophet who survived being swallowed by a whale.

Jonah was the son of Amittai. According to 2 Kings 14:25, he prophesied during the reign of Jeroboam II. His story, therefore, dates to somewhere between 775 and 750 B.C.E. Jonah was raised in Galilee, in the city of Gath Hepher, which is located just a few miles to the north of Nazareth. A Jewish tradition states that Jonah was the son of the widow of Zarephath, the same child that the prophet **Elijah** raised from the dead. There is no hard evidence to prove this, however.

Since the days of King Omri in 885 B.C.E., the Northern Kingdom had suffered sporadic attacks by Assyria and Syria. During the reign of Jeroboam II, Israel was living in relative peace and prosperity. Assyria, during Jonah's day, was on the rise as a world power. Nineveh, its capital, had a population of about 600,000. When Jonah went to Nineveh, the king of Assyria was most likely either Shalmanezer IV (783–773 B.C.E.) or Ashurdan III (773–755 B.C.E.). The Assyrians were viewed by the Israelites of Jonah's day as cruel oppressors who were bent on world conquest—a threat to Israel's existence.

One day God asked Jonah to warn the people of Nineveh that God planned to destroy the city for their wickedness. Jonah refused. He feared that if he delivered a prophecy from God, the Assyrians would repent and God would then forgive them— and Jonah did not want the enemies of Israel to be forgiven. He wanted them to be destroyed. Jonah ran away, convinced that God would kill him for his disobedience; deprived of his warning, Nineveh would suffer its just fate and be destroyed.

Jonah soon learned that there were worse things than dying, and that God's will could not be so easily thwarted. Boarding a ship at Jaffa (modern Tel Aviv), he sailed west. A storm blew up. Jonah told the sailors that the storm was doubtless on his account. To make it stop, all they needed to do was toss him overboard. At first they refused, but the storm grew worse, and so they finally tossed him into the water. Immediately the storm ceased, and a great fish swallowed him up. For the next three days, Jonah sat angrily inside the fish. Unable to take it any longer, he at last cried out to God for rescue.

The fish made its way back to Jaffa and spat him up on the shore. Once again, God asked Jonah to make the trip to Nineveh. Deciding that he did not want to be eaten again—or worse—he obeyed God, went to Nineveh, and told the Assyrians that they were doomed. Just as he feared, they repented and God forgave them. God then criticized Jonah for his lack of love and compassion.

In the New Testament, **Jesus** used Jonah's three days and nights in the belly of the great fish as a metaphor for the three days and nights that he would spend in the grave between his Crucifixion and Resurrection (Matthew 12:40).

The Hebrew phrase in the story translated as "great fish" in modern translations was not always so rendered. In the 1611 King James Version, Matthew 12:40 says that Jonah "was three days and three nights in the whale's belly." The Greek translation used by the Gospel writer describes the creature that swallowed Jonah with a word that means "whale," and the committee appointed to translate that part of the New Testament followed that sense of the term. Although whales are mammals and not fish, the ancient people of Israel did not make that distinction. They used "fish" for both creatures.

Jonah and the Whale

"And the Lord commanded the fish, and it vomited Jonah onto dry land." Jonah 2:10 (Unknown artist, 1606)

ZEBULUN

AMITTAI

JONAH

— MALE

— FEMALE

— MARRIED

ANCESTRY

Primary
appearance in
the Bible:
Jonah

ISAIAH

The prophet Isaiah warned Israel that its people needed to stop worshiping idols and oppressing the poor, or else God would send them into captivity.

The Prophet Isaiah Seated Under an Arch

"Then the Lord said, 'Just as my servant Isaiah has gone stripped and barefoot for three years, as a sign and portent against Egypt and Cush, so the king of Assyria will lead away stripped and barefoot the Egyptian captives and Cushite exiles, young and old, with buttocks bared—to Egypt's shame.'" Isaiah 20:3–4 (English manuscript, late eleventh century)

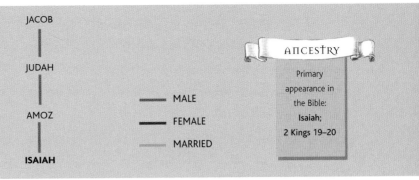

JACOB
|
JUDAH
|
AMOZ
|
ISAIAH

—— MALE
—— FEMALE
—— MARRIED

ANCESTRY

Primary
appearance in
the Bible:
Isaiah;
2 Kings 19–20

saiah was a prophet for more than 60 years—from about 740 B.C.E. until around 680 B.C.E. He prophesied during the reigns of at least five kings in the Southern Kingdom of Judah, including the reign of Hezekiah, during whose time a revival of exclusive Yahweh worship took place among the upper classes. His prophecies covered a wide range of topics, including several judgments against the nations that surrounded the Northern Kingdom of Israel and the Southern Kingdom of Judah. He also issued numerous warnings to both Judah and Israel to repent and turn back to worshiping Yahweh exclusively. As with all prophets, his messages bore a social aspect: He warned the rich and powerful to protect and care for the poor and disadvantaged.

Isaiah's prophetic messages were occasionally illustrated by events or actions in his life, whether it was giving his children unusual names to illustrate a coming judgment, or going about naked for three years in order to let the people of Egypt see how they would some day be taken away into exile.

Both **Jesus** and the New Testament authors mined Isaiah's words for prophecies regarding the Messiah. His message of a suffering servant (Isaiah 52:13–53:12) was interpreted in the New Testament as a prophecy of Jesus' death for the sins of humanity. When Ahaz, the king of Judah, feared invasion by the Syrians, God offered him the opportunity to ask for a sign. Ahaz refused, so Isaiah gave him one anyway, explaining that a young woman "will give birth to a son" (Isaiah 7:14) and that by the time the child was weaned, the enemy Ahaz feared would be destroyed. Shortly after, Isaiah's wife gave birth to a son. Before he was weaned, the Syrian menace was gone. The New Testament author of Matthew took this story and used it as a prophecy that Jesus would be born of a virgin (Matthew 1:23).

Isaiah's words have also been used by some modern commentators attempting to find an explanation for the origin of Satan. Isaiah's colorful condemnation of the king of Babylon has been improbably interpreted as a reference to Satan's fall from grace, thanks to an odd choice by the translators of the 1611 King James Version. In Isaiah 14:12, the Hebrew word for "morning star" or "shining star" has been replaced with the Latin word for "morning star" or "light-bearer": "Lucifer." Although this is the only place in the Bible that the word appears, and even though in context it plainly references the king of Babylon, in modern English this Latin term has become another name for Satan. Thus, Isaiah's condemnation of a Babylonian king was taken out of its context and misinterpreted as a story about Satan's origins.

Isaiah's prophecies were not all warnings about impending judgment. He also predicted that the punishments of God would be followed by restoration. Such predictions were not limited just to the people of Israel. Isaiah promised that Egypt and Assyria would some day be joined with Israel as God's special people (Isaiah 19:23–25).

As was often the case with prophets, Isaiah's words were not always accepted by his contemporaries. Later Jewish tradition reports that Isaiah met an unfortunate end during the reign of King Manasseh: He was executed by being placed in a log that was then sawn in half.

Most modern scholars since the mid-nineteenth century have assumed that the Old Testament book bearing Isaiah's name is a composite work, with the first section, through chapter 39, having been written by the prophet Isaiah, but the remaining chapters by an unknown author or authors at a post-exilic date.

JEREMIAH

*Jeremiah was a prophet when the Babylonians were coming to destroy Israel.
The government disliked his gloomy message and kept locking him in jail.*

God called Jeremiah to be a prophet when he was still young, during the thirteenth year of the reign of King Josiah of the Southern Kingdom of Judah, which would be around 628 B.C.E. Jeremiah has been called "the weeping prophet" and certainly there are many tears shed in his prophecies, but Jeremiah does not do most of the crying in his book. Rather, he records the tears of God, who weeps over the fate of his people.

Jeremiah's message is an unhappy one: Babylon was going to take the people of Judah into exile. He encouraged them to accept their fate. Not surprisingly, his words were interpreted by his government as defeatist and traitorous, and so he was often incarcerated. Jeremiah's words came true. Judah's resistance to the Babylonian domination, and a later rebellion against that rule, led to Jerusalem's destruction and the burning of the Temple.

A Vision of the Prophet Jeremiah: Greek Fire Being Poured Over Jerusalem

"Even if you were to defeat the entire Babylonian army that is attacking you and only wounded men were left in their tents, they would come out and burn this city down."
Jeremiah 37:10 *(Souvigny Bible, twelfth century)*

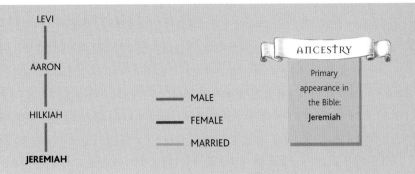

LEVI

AARON

HILKIAH

JEREMIAH

ANCESTRY

Primary
appearance in
the Bible:
Jeremiah

━━━ MALE

━━━ FEMALE

━━━ MARRIED

According to the words in the book that bears his name, God told Jeremiah at the beginning of his term as prophet that he would be unsuccessful; that is, no one would accept his message, his warnings would go unheeded, and the nation of Judah, the Southern Kingdom, would be destroyed and carried off into exile. Jeremiah explained that this punishment was like that of a parent disciplining a child: " 'For I know the plans I have for you,' declares the Lord, 'plans to prosper you and not to harm you, plans to give you hope and a future' " (Jeremiah 29:11).

God was never going to abandon his people: " 'If I have not established my covenant with day and night and the fixed laws of heaven and earth, then I will reject the descendants of **Jacob** and **David** my servant and will not choose one of his sons to rule over the descendants of **Abraham, Isaac** and Jacob. For I will restore their fortunes and have compassion on them" (Jeremiah 33:25–26). Jeremiah predicted that the period of captivity was only temporary, and that after 70 years the nation would be restored to its homeland.

Jeremiah's confidant, friend, and secretary was a man named Baruch, who recorded all that Jeremiah prophesied and who may be responsible for the order and arrangement of Jeremiah's prophecies in the Bible.

The last we hear of Jeremiah is shortly after the Babylonians have conquered Judah and taken most of the upper classes into captivity. Some of the remaining bureaucrats approached him and asked him what God wanted them to do now. They insisted that they would do whatever God told them. After praying, Jeremiah informed them that God wanted them to settle down in the land and just relax. They responded by calling Jeremiah a liar, saying that God could not possibly have told him that, and then they kidnapped him and carried him to the Egyptian city of Alexandria, where Jeremiah later died.

Many of Jeremiah's prophecies are taken up by writers in the New Testament. In fact, the concept of a New Testament comes from the words of Jeremiah. In Jeremiah 31:31–34, he described a "new covenant" or, to use the older English phrasing, a "new testament," that God would make with his people. The author of the New Testament Hebrews makes use of this passage and applies it to the work of **Jesus** in dying for the sins of humanity (Hebrews 8:6–10:4).

OTHER PROPHETS

Joel (444–400 B.C.E.) He described a locust invasion and called upon the people to repent before the coming judgment of God.

Amos (760–746 B.C.E.) A shepherd who warned of Israel's impending doom because of the people's idolatry and mistreatment of the poor.

Obadiah (c. 587 B.C.E.) Prophesied against the nation of Edom for their mistreatment of the people of Judah during the Babylonian deportations.

Micah (740–700 B.C.E.) Predicted the fall of the Northern Kingdom of Israel and the destruction of its capital, Samaria, which occurred when the Assyrians conquered it in 722 B.C.E.

Nahum (c. 610 B.C.E.) Predicted the fall of Assyria.

Habakkuk (605–589 B.C.E.) He complained about the evil of Judah's idolatry, wondering when God would do something about it. God explained that he would destroy Judah by using the Babylonians. Habakkuk was puzzled how God could use a people more wicked than Judah's as their judge.

Zephaniah (630–625 B.C.E.) He predicted the collapse of the Assyrian Empire and warned against idolatry.

Haggai (520–516 B.C.E.) During the rebuilding of the Temple after the exile, he prophesied encouragement to the leaders and people of Israel.

Zechariah (520–516 B.C.E.) A contemporary of Haggai, he also prophesied encouragement to the people during the rebuilding of the Temple.

Malachi (740–670 B.C.E.) Probably not an actual prophet, the book so identified with this name is actually an anonymous composition added to the Bible in order to have twelve minor prophets. A phrase in Malachi 3:1 is translated into English as "my messenger"—the same words that in 1:1 are transliterated as the name Malachi.

Period of the Exile

As Egypt's power faded and the Assyrian and Babylonian Empires rose, the twin kingdoms of Israel and Judah fell victim to their larger neighbors. The Assyrians invaded and destroyed the Northern Kingdom of Israel around 722 B.C.E. According to Assyrian records, they carried about 23,000 people into captivity—mostly the upper classes. After the Babylonians conquered the Assyrians, the Babylonians attacked the Southern Kingdom of Judah, transferring some of the Jews to Babylon in 605 B.C.E. and 597 B.C.E. When the Babylonians finally destroyed Jerusalem and burned the Temple of Solomon to the ground around 586 B.C.E., even more Jews found themselves transported to Babylon. These new deportees, numbering no more than 30,000, were mostly members of the royal family, government officials, the rich upper class, priests, and other religious leaders.

Nebuchadnezzar Speaking to His Court

Nebuchadnezzar was famous for his monumental buildings in the capital city of Babylon, as well as his destruction of Jerusalem and its Temple. (Undated illustration)

NEBUCHADNEZZAR

Nebuchadnezzar was the king of Babylon who destroyed Jerusalem and the Jewish Temple around 586 B.C.E. He also deported the Jewish people and took them as captives.

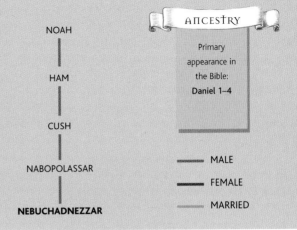

NOAH

HAM

CUSH

NABOPOLASSAR

NEBUCHADNEZZAR

ᴀɴᴄᴇsᴛʀʏ

Primary appearance in the Bible: Daniel 1–4

— MALE

— FEMALE

— MARRIED

Nebuchadnezzar ruled Babylonia from 605 to 562 B.C.E. His father Nabopolassar had established the Neo-Babylonian Empire after defeating the combined forces of Assyria and Egypt at Carchemish in 605 B.C.E. Nebuchadnezzar conquered Judah, then burned Jerusalem and destroyed its Temple around 586 B.C.E.

He was famous for the monumental buildings within his capital city, especially the Hanging Gardens of Babylon, one of the seven wonders of the world according to the first-century Greek poet Antipater of Sidon. Nebuchadnezzar built the gardens in order to cheer up his homesick wife, Amyitis. The daughter of the king of the Medes, she had married Nebuchadnezzar in order to create an alliance between their nations. The land she came from was green and mountainous, unlike the flat, sun-baked terrain of Babylonia. Nebuchadnezzar decided to recreate her homeland by building an artificial mountain with gardens.

Of the Jewish people that Nebuchadnezzar deported from their homeland, the Bible reports

that **Daniel** became the most famous. Nebuchadnezzar had a dream one night but could not make sense of it. He called in his astrologers and asked them to interpret it for him. They agreed and asked him to tell them the dream.

Nebuchadnezzar refused. He told them that if they were really the servants of the gods, they could find out what his dream was from them. If and when they were able to relate his dream, he would have confidence in their interpretation of it. The astrologers protested that this was an outrageous request. Nebuchadnezzar reacted to their outrage by ordering their execution and that of all the other wise men.

When Daniel learned of this, and thus of his own pending execution, he managed to get an audience with the king. Thanks to God telling Daniel the king's dream, he was able to tell Nebuchadnezzar what his dream was and what it meant. A grateful Nebuchadnezzar commuted the death sentences against all the wise men in Babylon and appointed Daniel as their new supervisor.

Later, Daniel's companions, Shadrach, Meshach, and Abednego, got into trouble with Nebuchadnezzar when they refused to bow down to a giant golden statue the king had built. As was his way, Nebuchadnezzar had them thrown into a furnace. Miraculously they survived, and so the king promoted them and issued a decree praising the God they worshiped.

According to the author of Daniel, Nebuchadnezzar's initial contempt for the God of the Jews finally changed to adoration following his recovery from a brief mental illness that had caused him to scamper about his gardens and eat grass like a cow.

After Nebuchadnezzar's death in 562 B.C.E., he was succeeded by his son Amel-Marduk and then his son-in-law Neriglissar. Finally, Nabonidus took the throne in 555 B.C.E., but he was more interested in archaeology than governing an empire, and left his son Belshazzar in charge. Unfortunately, Belshazzar was not really interested in ruling either, and so Cyrus, the king of Persia, managed to conquer Babylonia less than 25 years after Nebuchadnezzar's death.

EZRA

Ezra was a priest who led the movement to restore Yahweh worship following the Babylonian exile. In legend he is described as having reestablished the Old Testament after it was lost.

God Appearing to Ezra

"Day after day, from the first day to the last, Ezra read from the Book of the Law of God." Nehemiah 8:18 *(French illuminated Bible, 1526)*

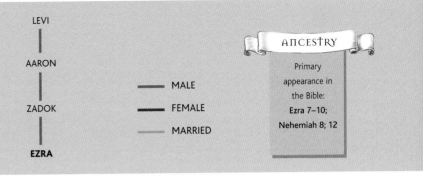

LEVI
|
AARON
|
ZADOK
|
EZRA

—— MALE

—— FEMALE

—— MARRIED

AΠCESTRY

Primary
appearance in
the Bible:
Ezra 7–10;
Nehemiah 8; 12

Ezra, a priest and descendant of Aaron, returned to Jerusalem together with about 5,000 other exiles during the seventh year of the reign of Artaxerxes I (also known as Artakhshathra I or Artaxerxes I Longimanus), king of the Persian Empire from 465 B.C.E. to 424 B.C.E. He arrived in Jerusalem with orders from the Persian king to check that Yahweh was being properly worshiped in the recently rebuilt Temple. The king gave him gold and silver to purchase sacrificial animals and anything else that might be necessary. The Persian treasury was to supply whatever additional funds he might need. Ezra quickly set about organizing the religious and civil affairs of the Jewish people. About fourteen years later, the Persian king gave one of his attendants, Nehemiah, permission to return to Jerusalem to help in its restoration and act as governor of Judea. After he had arrived in around 445 B.C.E., Nehemiah built a new city wall.

Ezra led in the public reading of the Torah—the Law of Moses—to the assembled crowd during the dedication ceremony for the new Jerusalem city wall. Following the dedication ceremony, the people celebrated the Jewish festival called Sukkot, a week-long holiday during which the Israelites moved into temporary shelters made of branches. Sukkot recalled their 40 years of wandering in the desert as they made their way to the Promised Land. At that time, they also committed themselves to the strict observance of the Law of Moses.

Ezra believed that Israel had gone into Babylonian captivity as a result of failing to follow all the detailed instructions in that Law. Therefore, Ezra was determined to keep that from ever happening again. During this period in Jewish history, the synagogue system was organized and legend suggests that Ezra played a significant role in its establishment. The purpose of the local synagogues was to ensure regular instruction in the law of God, in the hope that with a proper, weekly religious education, Israel would never again turn away from God. This system of local synagogues was later adapted by the early Christians to form their church communities.

Ezra was harshly legalistic in his implementation of the Law. For instance, he writes, "The leaders came to me and said, 'The people of Israel, including the priests and the Levites, have not kept themselves separate from the neighboring peoples with their detestable practices, like those of the Canaanites, Hittites, Perizzites, Jebusites, Ammonites, Moabites, Egyptians, and Amorites. They have taken some of their daughters as wives for themselves and their sons, and have mingled the holy race with the peoples around them. And the leaders and officials have led the way in this unfaithfulness.' When I heard this, I tore my tunic and cloak, pulled hair from my head and beard, and sat down appalled" (Ezra 9:1–3). Ezra ordered those who had married nonIsraelites to divorce their foreign wives. He also ordered those women and any children they had borne be expelled from the community.

According to Jewish legend, Ezra organized and edited all the books of the Old Testament, even though the final selection and arrangement occurred many years later. The story is told that the entire Old Testament had been lost during the exile in Babylon and that Ezra was able to find people who had memorized it, so that it could be restored to writing. It does seem likely that the switch from the old paleo-Hebrew alphabet to the newer Aramaic square script— what is today the familiar Hebrew alphabet—occurred during this era. Whether Ezra himself had a hand in it is impossible to say.

ESTHER

When Xerxes I, the king of Persia, got angry with his queen, Vashti, he decided to have a contest to pick her replacement. Esther, a young Jewish woman, won the contest.

Named Hadassah at birth, Esther was a Jewish woman whose name was changed when she joined the harem of Persian King Xerxes I (reigned 485–465 B.C.E.). Hadassah means "myrtle" in Hebrew. Her new Persian name, Esther, may have been derived from various words for "myrtle" or "star." She was a member of the tribe of **Benjamin.**

There are two versions of the story of Esther, one written in Hebrew and another in Greek. In the Hebrew version, neither God's name Yahweh nor the word "God" ever appears in the text. However, in the early Greek translation produced around 200 B.C.E., several new chapters along with frequent usage of the word "God" have been added. These additions appear in both the Roman Catholic and Eastern Orthodox Bibles. Protestants and Jews regard these additions as apocryphal, and it does seem likely that the Hebrew version preserves the original form of the story.

When the queen of Persia, Vashti, lost favor with Xerxes, his advisors suggested staging a contest to find a replacement (in older translations Xerxes is called Ahasuerus). They gathered all the most beautiful young women in the Persian Empire and, after twelve months of beauty treatments, each of the young women was sent to the king. The girl he liked the most was to become the new queen.

Esther wound up being the king's favorite out of all the women of his empire, so he crowned her the new queen. Her cousin Mordecai, who had raised her after the death of her parents, was a minor bureaucrat in the palace. He had warned her to keep her Jewish heritage a secret.

Not long after Esther's coronation, **Haman,** one of the king's chief officials, became enraged at Mordecai for a perceived slight—Mordecai had not bowed before him—and so decided to kill both him and all the Jews in the empire because their customs seemed strange to Persians. He convinced Xerxes to allow a decree to be issued that all the Jews be exterminated, then he set about building a gallows just for hanging Mordecai. It is unlikely that Haman explained precisely what he wanted to do to the Jews, and it is unlikely that Xerxes asked him. The king gave Haman his signet ring, so he could issue decrees in the monarch's name.

Mordecai told Esther about the plot and encouraged her to make an appeal to Xerxes. Although she was reluctant—anyone who approached the king of Persia without being invited beforehand risked a death sentence—she went in anyway. Xerxes was very happy to see her and asked her what he could do for her. She requested that a small private banquet be arranged for her and the king, with just one guest: Haman.

Haman was excited when he heard the news, but on the second day of the party, Esther revealed her heritage and told the king what Haman had been plotting. Xerxes quickly ordered the execution of Haman.

Although no decree made by a Persian king could be rescinded, including the one to exterminate the Jews, Xerxes found a way to fix the problem, thanks to an idea he got from Mordecai. He ordered that the Jews be heavily armed, so that they could fight back against anyone who tried to harm them. So, the Jewish people were spared—and actually inflicted vengeance on many of their enemies. From that time on, they began celebrating a new annual holiday: Purim.

Coronation of Esther as Jewish Queen of Persia by King Xerxes

After a year of beauty treatments, Xerxes chose Esther as his favorite and crowned her as his new queen. (Vincenzo Morani, 1809–70)

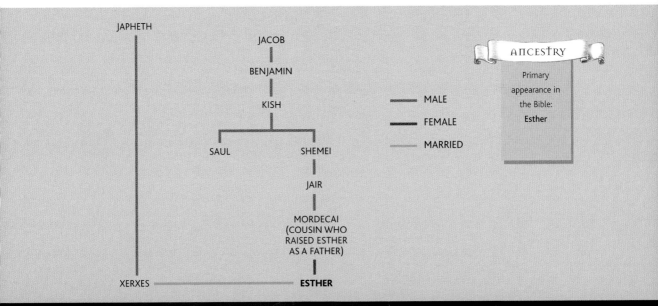

JAPHETH

JACOB

BENJAMIN

KISH

SAUL   SHEMEI

JAIR

MORDECAI
(COUSIN WHO
RAISED ESTHER
AS A FATHER)

XERXES ——————— **ESTHER**

MALE

FEMALE

MARRIED

ANCESTRY

Primary
appearance in
the Bible:
Esther

HAMAN

Haman was an important Persian official during the reign of Xerxes I. He attempted to exterminate all of the Jews. Although descended from Noah, Haman was not a Jew since his lineage was through Noah's son Japheth rather than Shem and the Jewish patriarchs Abraham, Isaac, and Jacob.

Haman is the archetype of evil in Judaism. During the reign of the Persian King Xerxes I (485–465 B.C.E., also known as Ahasuerus), Haman was honored above all the other nobles. While everyone else bowed before Haman, Mordecai the Jew refused. Deeply offended, Haman decided to kill not just Mordecai but all the Jews, and he convinced the Persian government to issue a decree ordering their extermination.

Haman then built a very tall gallows just so he could hang Mordecai on it. Unknown to Haman, however, the king's queen, **Esther,** happened to be Jewish—and Mordecai was her cousin and had raised her as his daughter. Mordecai passed word to Esther of Haman's plan, so she arranged for a special banquet with just her, the king, and Haman. Haman was overjoyed, believing that he was receiving special favor from the king.

The night before the banquet, Xerxes had trouble sleeping and asked that the daily archives be read to him. While they were being read, he was reminded of how Mordecai had uncovered an assassination plot against him. Xerxes asked if Mordecai had ever been rewarded for his service. Discovering that he had not, Xerxes asked Haman, who just then happened to be coming in the door, what should be done for the man that the king wished to honor.

Believing that the king wanted to honor him, Haman told the king what he would like: A high official should parade the honored man on the king's horse, proclaiming all the while that "this is what the king does for someone he wishes to honor!" (Esther 6:9). So, Xerxes sent Haman to do precisely that for Mordecai. Humiliated after parading Mordecai all around the city, Haman went home. His

wife told him that this was an ill omen, indicating that he would be destroyed by the Jews. Right then, Haman was summoned to the banquet with Queen Esther and King Xerxes.

There, Esther revealed that Haman was plotting to kill both her and all her people. Furious, the king stormed out of the room. Upon his return, he found Haman on the couch with Esther, pleading for his life. Xerxes interpreted this close proximity to Esther as Haman's attempt to rape her, and so he ordered Haman's immediate execution on the gallows he had built for Mordecai. Haman's estate was then given to Esther. Later, Esther asked that Haman's ten sons also be hanged on the same gallows.

Later Jewish legends include many tales about Haman. For instance, one explains that he had been so destitute once that he had sold himself to Mordecai as a slave. In synagogues, the book of Esther is read aloud during Purim, the annual Jewish holiday that celebrates the Jews' survival and victory over Haman. Whenever the name Haman is uttered, the congregation boos, hisses, and waves noise makers to drown out the sound of his name. A type of pastry known as "Haman's Ears" are traditionally eaten on this holiday as well.

MORDECAI

Esther's uncle Mordecai took Haman's place in the bureaucracy of Persia. He saw to the survival of the Jewish people by concocting a plan to undermine Haman's original decree to exterminate all the Jews. Mordecai extracted the king's permission for the Jewish people to mass together and arm themselves against any who might try to kill them. Few, therefore, decided to obey the original decree against the Jews, and those who did were summarily slaughtered.

NOAH
|
JAPHETH
|
HAMAN

━━━ MALE

━━━ FEMALE

━━━ MARRIED

ANCESTRY

Primary
appearance in
the Bible:
Esther

King Xerxes Giving a Banquet for Esther

Esther arranged a private banquet for herself, the king, and Haman. There she revealed her Jewish heritage and Haman's plot to destroy the Jews. (Flemish School, seventeenth century)

Prophets during the Exile

While the Israelites endured the Babylonian exile for nearly 70 years from 605 B.C.E. until 537 B.C.E., God spoke to his captive people through prophets. Their message was both one of criticism for past sins, as well as hope for the future: Their present punishment would only be temporary. God instructed his people, through his prophets, to accept their new land of exile, to build homes, bear children, and to create a new life for themselves. When the time came and Cyrus the Great, king of the Persian Empire, finally granted the Israelites permission to return to their homeland in 537 B.C.E., only a small percentage of the Jews actually chose to go back home, so comfortable had many of them become in their place of exile.

Ezekiel's Vision

"Wherever the spirit would go, they would go, and the wheels would rise along with them, because the spirit of the living creatures was in the wheels." Ezekiel 1:20 *(Raphael, 1483–1520)*

EZEKIEL

Ezekiel wrote prophecies about the people of Israel and Judah, comparing their unfaithfulness to God as being similar to a wife who becomes a prostitute.

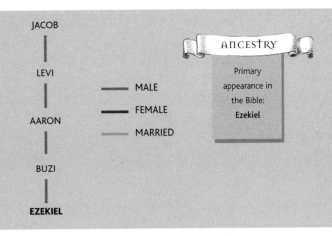

JACOB

LEVI

AARON

BUZI

EZEKIEL

━━━ MALE

━━━ FEMALE

━━━ MARRIED

ANCESTRY

Primary appearance in the Bible: Ezekiel

zekiel was the son of Buzi, a priest. He was one of the exiles from the Southern Kingdom of Judah who settled at Tel-Abib, on the banks of the Chebar Canal in Mesopotamia, probably around 597 B.C.E. His prophetic call came during the fifth year of King Jehoiachin of Judah's captivity in Babylonia, around 594 B.C.E. Although he held a prominent place among the exiles, Ezekiel complained that people listened to him only for entertainment, as if they were just listening to "love songs" (Ezekiel 33:32). His ministry extended over 23 years. He was probably a contemporary of the prophets **Daniel, Jeremiah,** and Obadiah. The time and manner of his death are unknown. His tomb is said to be near Baghdad, at a place called Keffil.

Ezekiel's prophecies were designed to lead the people away from their tendency to worship idols. God often called upon him to act out his prophecies. For instance, he had to get a brick, set it down in a public place, and pretend to attack it as if he were an army laying siege to it. The point of this childish exercise was to illustrate how Jerusalem would suffer attack by

the Babylonian army. He was told not to cry over his wife's death to illustrate how the people would have no opportunity for mourning rituals when Jerusalem and the Temple were destroyed. He compared Israel and Judah to prostitutes in the most explicit and graphic language in the Bible for their tendency to chase after other gods.

Ezekiel reminds the Israelites of a Mosaic statute that limits the extent of punishment: "Fathers shall not be put to death for their children, nor children put to death for their fathers; each is to die for his own sin" (Deuteronomy 24:16). Ezekiel also points out that just as forgiveness can come at any moment, with past guilt wiped clean, judgment for a misdeed may also fall suddenly, with past righteousness equally forgotten.

Ezekiel is best known for the opening chapter of the book that bears his name, where he had a vision of wheels within wheels (Ezekiel 1:16). Although some have speculated about extraterrestrial visitation, Ezekiel is merely describing his encounter with God on his throne in heaven, a vision similar to earlier representations of God enthroned. For instance, in

Exodus 24, **Moses,** his brother Aaron, and 70 elders saw something resembling what Ezekiel records. The described wheels are similar to those seen on representations of other ancient Near Eastern royal thrones. The odd creatures that accompany the wheels are identified later in the story as cherubs, a class of angels seen throughout the Near East. In the Bible, cherubs are frightening monsters, not the cuddly beings of modern popular mythology.

The last few chapters of Ezekiel's prophecies describe a cataclysmic battle between good and evil, followed by a restored Israel, lifted to prominence, with a rebuilt Jerusalem and Temple. His description of the New Jerusalem included very detailed measurements based on his tour of the city when he was guided by an angel. The words he used for that final battle between good and evil, for the restored city and Temple, complete with a river flowing from God's throne and trees on its banks providing shade and the fruit for healing the nations, was adopted by the author of Revelation, the last book in the New Testament, to describe the Kingdom of Heaven.

DANIEL

Daniel was one of the Israelite captives taken to Babylon. Educated by the Babylonians, he became a high official in their government.

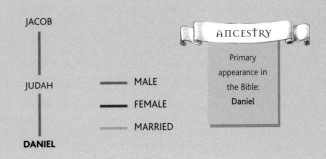

JACOB

JUDAH

DANIEL

——— MALE

——— FEMALE

——— MARRIED

ANCESTRY

Primary appearance in the Bible: **Daniel**

Daniel was descended from one of the noble families of the Southern Kingdom of Judah and was probably born in Jerusalem around 623 B.C.E., during the reign of Josiah. In the first deportation of the Jews by **Nebuchadnezzar**, the king of Babylonia, immediately after the victory of the king's father, Nabopolassar, over the Egyptians at the second battle of Carchemish, Daniel and three of his friends were carried off to Babylonia around 605 B.C.E.

Daniel received training in the schools of the wise men of Babylonia to prepare him for service to the Babylonian Empire. He was given the Babylonian name Belteshazzar, which means "prince of Bel" or "Bel protect the king." Strict in his observance of the Law of Moses, Daniel soon gained the confidence of those who supervised him and he joined the ranks of the wise men of Babylon.

One night, Nebuchadnezzar had a disturbing dream and called several of his wise men

in to interpret it. Rather than telling them the dream, he demanded that they tell it to him instead, so that he would then be assured of their claimed abilities. After all, if these wise men really had a connection to the gods, it should be easy to get the gods to reveal the dream itself, not just its interpretation. When the wise men failed to do as Nebuchadnezzar asked, he ordered the execution of all the wise men in his kingdom. Daniel prayed to Yahweh and received both the dream and the interpretation. After Daniel told all of it to Nebuchadnezzar, the king rescinded the order of execution and promoted Daniel to the rank of governor over the province of Babylonia.

Many years afterward, on the night before Nebuchadnezzar's grandson Belshazzar was overthrown and killed by the Persians, Daniel was called in at the insistence of the queen mother to interpret mysterious handwriting that had appeared on the wall. Belshazzar rewarded Daniel with a purple robe and elevated him to the rank of "third ruler," not that it mattered since Belshazzar was dead by morning and the Persians had taken over.

The Persians, under the leadership of Cyrus the Great, conquered Babylon. However,

they kept most of the old Babylonian bureaucracy in place. Therefore, Daniel kept his position of authority in the government. Daniel's fidelity to God exposed him to persecution once again. When Cyrus issued a decree that for a month no one could pray to anyone but Cyrus, Daniel disobeyed and continued praying to Yahweh instead. Turned in by other officials who were jealous of Daniel's high position, he was cast into a den of lions overnight. However, the lions did not harm him. The next morning Cyrus released Daniel and then cast his informers into the lions' den instead. They were immediately attacked and eaten by the hungry beasts.

Daniel's prophecies predicted times of trouble for the Jewish people, as well as good times: their restoration to their homeland and a glorious future when the kingdoms of the world would be replaced by the Kingdom of God. His vision of a series of beasts, some with multiple heads and horns, representing a series of world empires, was adapted by the author of the New Testament Revelation. The time and circumstances of his death are not recorded. Several additional stories of Daniel were added to the ancient Greek translation of the book of Daniel and they are included in the Apocrypha.

Daniel in the Lions' Den

"So the king gave the order, and they brought Daniel and threw him into the lions' den." Daniel 6:16 (Jacopo Guarana, 1720–1808)

Apocrypha

After the Jewish people returned from exile, Israel (the whole region) was never again an independent nation. It remained subject to great powers, first the Persians, then the Greeks, and finally the Romans. During this period, Hebrew scholars continued to record the Israelites' experiences, and their texts formed the official collection of Hebrew scripture. Between the third and first centuries B.C.E., Hebrew scholars living in Alexandria, Egypt, translated this scripture into Greek for the benefit of Jews who had spread throughout the region. Their translation, called the Septuagint (meaning "seventy" in Latin because of a tradition that there were 72 scholars), contained additions to the texts of Esther and Daniel and other books, and these became known as "apocryphal texts." Later Judaic and Protestant leaders rejected these works, but Roman Catholic and Eastern Orthodox churches accepted them as part of the Old Testament. Other apocryphal writings are from the New Testament era.

Judas Maccabeus

"As soon as Maccabeus got his army organized, the Gentiles could not withstand him, for the wrath of the Lord had turned to mercy."
2 Maccabees 8:5 *(J. F. Schreiber, late nineteenth century)*

JUDAS MACCABEUS

Judas Maccabeus, also called "the Hammer," led the successful rebellion against the Seleucid Emperor Antiochus Epiphanes.

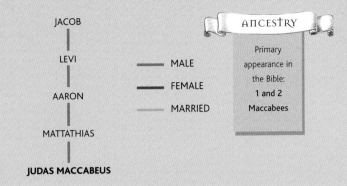

JACOB
|
LEVI
|
AARON
|
MATTATHIAS
|
JUDAS MACCABEUS

—— MALE

—— FEMALE

—— MARRIED

ANCESTRY

Primary appearance in the Bible:

1 and 2 Maccabees

When Antiochus IV became emperor of the Seleucid Empire in 175 B.C.E., he passed an edict that all Jews must worship the Greek gods. Failure to obey meant death. A priest from Modiin named Mattathias publicly refused. He began an armed insurrection, killing many of the Greeks and destroying their temples. He and his family escaped into the wilderness where others rallied to his cause. Judas Maccabeus, his third son, led the rebellion after his father died. Maccabeus means "hammer" and he merited this sobriquet because of his ferocity in battle.

Ultimately succeeding in his father's goals after many battles, Judas Maccabeus entered Jerusalem, where he discovered that Emperor Antiochus had profaned the Jewish Temple by sacrificing a pig on the altar. According to Jewish tradition, on the 25th day of Kislev (December 14) in 164 b.c.e., the Jews began the process of cleansing and rededicating the Temple. Only one day's supply of oil was available to burn in the sacred menorah (candelabra), but it miraculously lasted for the full eight days needed.

This event is commemorated by the festival of Hanukkah (also called the Festival of Lights). **Jesus** spent at least one Hanukkah in Jerusalem (John 10:22), where the holiday is referred to as the Feast of Dedication.

Judas waged guerrilla operations against the Seleucids until the spring of 161 b.c.e., when he sent a delegation to Rome to request recognition of the independent state of Judea and military aid. Rome granted the request in exchange for their allegiance. However, this only inspired the Seleucids to send an army of 20,000 men against the Jews. Judas Maccabeus fought them at the Battle of Elasa. Surrounded by enemy troops, he died in battle. His two brothers took command, and after a few more years of war the Jews finally achieved independence from the Seleucids. However, the Romans that Judas had asked to come help, never left. They eventually subjugated the new Jewish state and turned it into a Roman province.

The Punishment of Antiochus

"And so it came about that he fell out of his chariot as it was rushing along, and the fall was so hard as to torture every limb of his body." 2 Maccabees 9:7 *(Gustave Doré, 1832–83)*

ANTIOCHUS IV EPIPHANES

Antiochus' father was defeated by the Romans about 190 B.C.E. As a teenager, Antiochus was taken to Rome as a hostage. Ransomed, he became king in 175 B.C.E. "Epiphanes" meant "exalted one." Behind his back, people called him "Epimanes"—"the insane one." Besides the disastrous attempt to impose Greek religion on the Jews, his reign was noted for the near-conquest of Egypt, halted only by the threat of Roman intervention. His fame was the consequence of failure, compounded by insanity. Many stories are told of his odd behavior: He was by nature an eccentric, unreliable despot, given to being both cruel and tyrannical. There are legends that he died insane in Persia around 163 B.C.E.

JUDITH

Judith pretended to seduce the enemy general Holofernes, plied him with wine, and when he was comatose, decapitated him with his own sword to save her people from destruction.

Judith Kills Holofernes

"She went up to the bedpost near Holofernes' head, and took down his sword that hung there. She came close to his bed, took hold of the hair of his head, and said, 'Give me strength today, O Lord God of Israel!' Then she struck his neck twice with all her might, and cut off his head." Judith 13:6–8 (Valentin de Boulogne, 1591–1632)

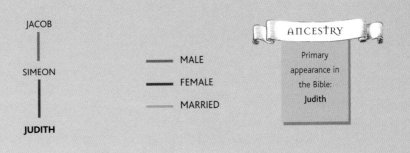

JACOB
|
SIMEON
|
JUDITH

—— MALE

—— FEMALE

—— MARRIED

ANCESTRY

Primary appearance in the Bible: Judith

Nebuchadnezzar, king of Assyria, in the eighteenth year of his reign, sent Holofernes, his commander-in-chief, to conquer Judah. Holofernes lay siege to the Judean city of Bethulia and cut off its water supply. After 34 days, its citizens begged their rulers to surrender. They responded that if nothing improved in five days, they would. Upon hearing how demoralized the people and leaders of Bethulia had become, Judith, a righteous and strikingly beautiful widow, asked the city leaders to visit her. She berated them for their lack of faith in God and warned that if Bethulia fell, all of Judah would fall with it. Then Judith vowed that within the few days that were left, she had a plan to rescue the city.

Dressing up in her best finery, Judith loaded down her servants with food and drink and headed for the Assyrian camp. She told the first soldier she met that she was fleeing Bethulia because she knew that everyone in it was doomed. She also explained that she had an idea and wanted to tell Holofernes how he could capture the city with practically no effort or loss of life.

The soldiers brought Judith to Holofernes. Immediately attracted to her, he invited her to dine with him. For three days she declined his invitation, but on the fourth day she accepted, dressed herself attractively, and went to eat with him in his tent. As Holofernes attempted to seduce her, he drank far more wine than "he had ever drunk in any one day since he was born" (Judith 12:20).

Alone with her at last and anticipating his conquest, he suddenly passed out on his bed. Judith prayed, asked God for strength, then took his sword and with two swift strokes, cut off his head. Her servant stuffed Holofernes' head in a food bag and then they hurried from the Assyrian camp and made their way back to Bethulia.

Upon their arrival, Judith announced their victory and showed off the head of the dead commander. Judith ordered the city rulers to hang his head from the city wall, and when morning dawned, to go out and attack the Assyrians. The next morning, when the Assyrians realized that their commander was dead, their morale plummeted and the Israelites quickly routed them.

Although many men wanted to marry her, Judith remained faithful to the memory of her dead husband and died a widow. During the remainder of her very long life, Israel was never again attacked.

Judith Shows the Head of Holofernes

"Then she pulled the head out of the bag and showed it to them, and said, 'See here, the head of Holofernes, the commander of the Assyrian army, and here is the canopy beneath which he lay in his drunken stupor. The Lord has struck him down by the hand of a woman. As the Lord lives, who has protected me in the way I went, I swear that it was my face that seduced him to his destruction, and that he committed no act of sin with me, to defile and shame me.'" Judith 13:15–16 *(Gustave Doré, 1832–83)*

SUSANNA

Because Susanna refused the advances of two lecherous old men, they falsely accused her of adultery. The prophet Daniel saved her, just as she was about to be executed for this crime, by proving her innocence.

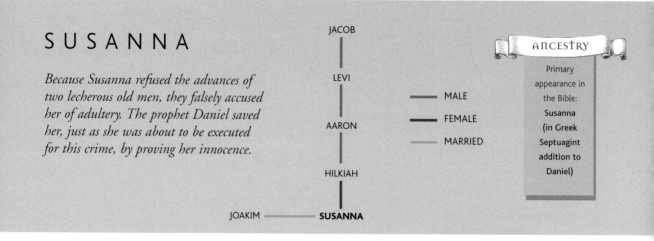

JACOB

LEVI

AARON

HILKIAH

JOAKIM ———— **SUSANNA**

——— MALE

——— FEMALE

——— MARRIED

ANCESTRY

Primary appearance in the Bible: Susanna (in Greek Septuagint addition to Daniel)

Susanna was a beautiful and devout woman married to a rich and important man named Joakim. Their garden was a regular meeting place for the important Jews of Babylon. Two of the Jewish elders who frequently visited became infatuated with Susanna and conspired to find a way to seduce her.

One hot day, Susanna went out to the garden and decided to take a bath. Sending her two maids to get supplies for bathing, she had them shut the garden door. While they were gone, the two elders sneaked into the garden and demanded to have sex with her. They told her that if she refused, they would publicly accuse her of having an affair with a young man. She told them that she would rather obey God and suffer at their hands than to disobey God and be spared.

The two elders began shouting, and people came running to find out what the commotion was about. The elders claimed to have just witnessed Susanna engaging in intercourse and when they had gone to apprehend the young man who had been with her, he had overpowered them and escaped—and that Susanna had refused to reveal his name. Found guilty based on the eyewitness accounts of these two well-respected elders, Susanna was led out to her execution.

Daniel intervened. He ordered the two men to be separated and then questioned them individually. Daniel asked the first one, "Under what tree did you see them being intimate with each other?" The accuser replied, "Under a mastic tree." When the second elder was asked the same question, he answered, "Under an evergreen oak." Thus discovered to be false witnesses, they were promptly executed and Susanna was fully exonerated (Susanna 1:54–59).

Susannah's Innocence Recognized

"Then the whole assembly raised a great shout and blessed God, who saves those who hope in him. And they took action against the two elders, because out of their own mouths Daniel had convicted them of bearing false witness; they did to them as they had wickedly planned to do to their neighbor. Acting in accordance with the law of Moses, they put them to death. Thus innocent blood was spared that day." Susanna 1:60–62 *(Valentin de Boulogne, 1591–1632)*

TOBIT

Tobit was a righteous Jew living in the city of Nineveh in Assyria. He provided proper burials for Jews killed by the Assyrian king, Sennacherib. Tobit suffered several horrible setbacks, but in the end he was blessed for his faithfulness.

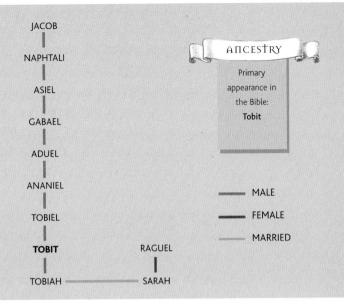

JACOB
|
NAPHTALI
|
ASIEL
|
GABAEL
|
ADUEL
|
ANANIEL
|
TOBIEL
|
TOBIT ——— RAGUEL
| |
TOBIAH ——— SARAH

ANCESTRY

Primary appearance in the Bible: **Tobit**

——— MALE
——— FEMALE
——— MARRIED

The Angel Raphael Leaving Tobit and His Family
"'I am Raphael, one of the seven angels who stand ready and enter before the glory of the Lord.' The two of them were shaken; they fell face down, for they were afraid. But he said to them, 'Do not be afraid; peace be with you. Bless God for evermore.'" Tobit 12:15–17 (Rembrandt, 1606–69)

Furious at Tobit's burial services to the Jews that Sennacherib had killed, the king seized Tobit's property and sent him into exile in Media. On his return to Nineveh after Sennacherib's death, Tobit buried a man who had been murdered on the street. That night, while he slept, bird droppings fell into his eyes, blinding him. Discouraged, he prayed to die.

Meanwhile, in Media, a young woman named Sarah was also praying to die. Each of her seven marriages had ended when the demon Ashmodai killed her husbands on their wedding nights. God heard both their prayers, and sent the angel Raphael to heal Tobit and to free Sarah from the demon.

Disguising himself as a relative of Tobit named Azariah, Raphael joined Tobiah, Tobit's son, on his journey to collect some money that his father had left on deposit back in Media. Along the way, Raphael had instructed Tobiah to take the heart, liver, and gall bladder of a fish that leaped up and tried to swallow him as he bent to wash in a river. When they got to Media, Raphael explained it was Tobiah's right to marry Sarah, because he was her closest relative. Raphael also told him to burn the heart and liver of the fish in order to drive away the demon on their wedding night. It worked. The demon fled to Egypt, where Raphael tied him up.

Meanwhile, Tobiah's father-in-law Raguel had dug a grave, because he expected Tobiah to go the way of all his daughter's previous husbands. Come morning, surprised to find his son-in-law still alive and well, he ordered a double-length wedding feast while sending his servants to have the grave secretly filled. Tobiah could not leave the feast, so he sent Raphael to recover his father's money. After the feast, Tobiah and Sarah returned to Nineveh. There, Raphael told Tobiah to drain the bile from the gall bladder and use it to cure his father's blindness, then revealed his true identity and returned to heaven. Tobit lived happily to the age of 112.

THE NEW TESTAMENT

Christians, whether Roman Catholic, Eastern Orthodox, or Protestant, agree on the contents of the New Testament (although Martin Luther, the man who started the Protestant Reformation, did have doubts about whether Hebrews, James, Jude, or Revelation should remain part of the Bible). The New Testament was composed over a period of no more than 100 years by several people.

It was written in common Greek, rather than in literary Greek, so that average people could read it. At the time the New Testament was composed, Greek was the main language used in the eastern half of the Roman Empire. Jesus and his disciples used Aramaic (a Semitic tongue related to ancient Hebrew) as their regular spoken language in Israel. In their day, Hebrew had been relegated to liturgical use in synagogues.

During the New Testament era, the Jews were divided into three major sects: Pharisees, Sadducees, and Essenes. The Pharisees had originated during the time of Antiochus IV Epiphanes. They believed in the resurrection of the dead and accepted the existence of angels and demons. Strict and legalistic in their interpretation of the law, they controlled the synagogues.

The Sadducees accepted only the five books of Moses as scripture. They did not believe in either the resurrection of the dead or the existence of angels and demons. They controlled the Temple in Jerusalem.

The Essenes had beliefs similar to the Pharisees but believed that Judaism had been hopelessly corrupted. They separated themselves from Jewish society and lived in remote regions, waiting for the Messiah to come, clean house, and conquer the world.

The first four books of the New Testament are called "Gospels"; they present the Christian understanding of Jesus as the long-anticipated Jewish Messiah by describing his teachings, miracles, and resurrection.

Acts, the next book of the New Testament, showcases some of the early work of the Christian community in bringing their message of Jesus to the Jewish and Roman worlds. Revelation is classified as apocalypse.

The remaining books of the New Testament are letters, written to specific individuals or Christian communities; seven are general letters, since no recipient is specified. The letters are traditionally referred to as epistles, an older word for "letters." The authors of the New Testament were all Jewish, except for Luke, who was the author of Acts and the Gospel that bears his name.

Christianity began as a sect of Judaism and was treated as such by the Roman authorities. In its first decades, the new faith was composed almost exclusively of Jews. Only gradually, thanks to missionary activity, did increasing numbers of Gentiles, who were not Jews, come to embrace the faith; they ultimately became dominant among those who came to be known as Christians.

After the refusal of Christians to participate in the rebellion against Rome that led to the Roman destruction of Jerusalem and its Temple in 70 C.E., Christians were no longer regarded as a sect of Judaism by other Jews, but rather as belonging to a different and rival faith.

CONTENT AND CATEGORIZATION OF THE NEW TESTAMENT BOOKS

Gospels: Matthew; Mark; Luke; John

History: Acts

Pauline letters: Romans; 1 Corinthians; 2 Corinthians; Galatians; Ephesians; Philippians; Colossians; 1 Thessalonians; 2 Thessalonians; 1 Timothy; 2 Timothy; Titus; Philemon

General letters: Hebrews; James; 1 Peter; 2 Peter; 1 John; 2 John; 3 John; Jude

Apocalypse: Revelation

NEW TESTAMENT GENEALOGIES

The New Testament is the name given to the final section of the Bible, as organized by Christians. It consists of 27 books: four Gospels of Jesus; one work, Acts, that lays out the history of the first Christians through the time of Paul; an apocalyptic book, Revelation; and a collection of Letters attributed to Paul, John, Peter, James, Jude, and one anonymous author. Composed between about 45 C.E. and 100 C.E., these books were gradually collected into a single collection over a period of several centuries. This genealogy gives a simplified overview of the relationships of the characters in the New Testament. Additional information is provided within each character's article.

The Genealogy of the Virgin Mary
A family tree tracing Mary's ancestry back to the patriarchs of the Old Testament. Biblical genealogies have often been represented in art and were particularly popular in medieval times. (Gerard David, c. 1460–1523)

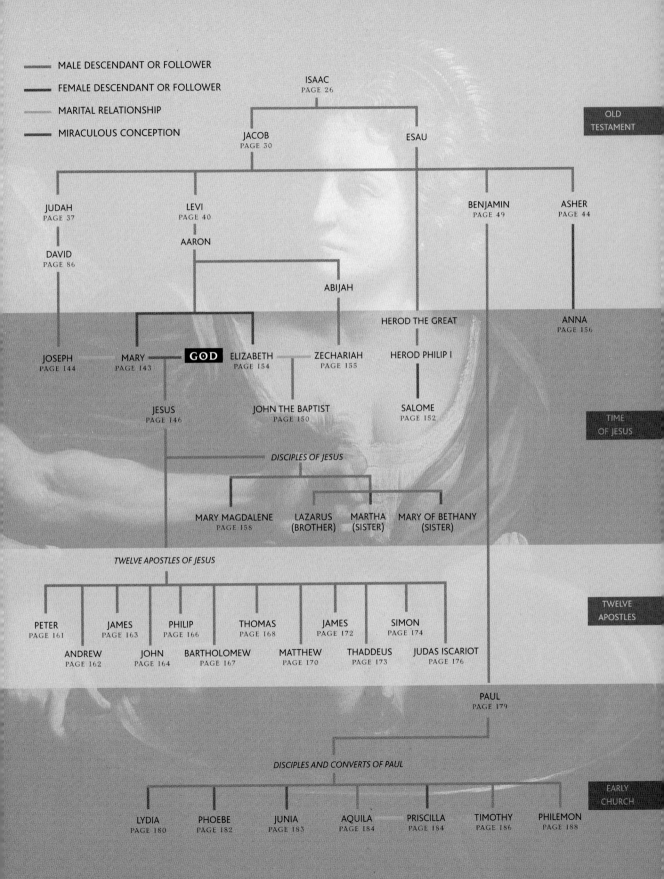

MALE DESCENDANT OR FOLLOWER

FEMALE DESCENDANT OR FOLLOWER

MARITAL RELATIONSHIP

MIRACULOUS CONCEPTION

ISAAC
PAGE 26

OLD
TESTAMENT

JACOB
PAGE 30

ESAU

JUDAH
PAGE 37

LEVI
PAGE 40

BENJAMIN
PAGE 49

ASHER
PAGE 44

DAVID
PAGE 86

AARON

ABIJAH

HEROD THE GREAT

ANNA
PAGE 156

JOSEPH
PAGE 144

MARY
PAGE 143

GOD

ELIZABETH
PAGE 154

ZECHARIAH
PAGE 155

HEROD PHILIP I

JESUS
PAGE 146

JOHN THE BAPTIST
PAGE 150

SALOME
PAGE 152

TIME
OF JESUS

DISCIPLES OF JESUS

MARY MAGDALENE
PAGE 158

LAZARUS
(BROTHER)

MARTHA
(SISTER)

MARY OF BETHANY
(SISTER)

TWELVE APOSTLES OF JESUS

PETER
PAGE 161

JAMES
PAGE 163

PHILIP
PAGE 166

THOMAS
PAGE 168

JAMES
PAGE 172

SIMON
PAGE 174

TWELVE
APOSTLES

ANDREW
PAGE 162

JOHN
PAGE 164

BARTHOLOMEW
PAGE 167

MATTHEW
PAGE 170

THADDEUS
PAGE 173

JUDAS ISCARIOT
PAGE 176

PAUL
PAGE 179

DISCIPLES AND CONVERTS OF PAUL

EARLY
CHURCH

LYDIA
PAGE 180

PHOEBE
PAGE 182

JUNIA
PAGE 183

AQUILA
PAGE 184

PRISCILLA
PAGE 184

TIMOTHY
PAGE 186

PHILEMON
PAGE 188

Time of Jesus

Augustus, the adopted son of Julius Caesar and the first Roman emperor, sat on his throne when Jesus was born in Bethlehem. The Jewish nation was a subject province in the new empire. Judea, the region around Jerusalem, was ruled by a Roman governor, while the region of Galilee was overseen by a puppet king. Many Jewish people chafed under the Roman yoke and longed for relief. Hope that a Messiah would arrive to liberate them and drive out the Romans was widespread. Many charismatic leaders arose claiming to be such a man, but they inevitably disappointed people's expectations, and the Romans remained in control. Some Jewish people joined violent insurrectionist movements such as the Zealots, but the bulk of the population simply endured the domination, convinced that, sooner or later, Yahweh would do something to change the status quo.

Madonna and Child

"She gave birth to her firstborn, a son. She wrapped him in cloths and placed him in a manger, because there was no room for them in the inn." Luke 2:7 *(Cima da Conegliano, c. 1459–1518)*

MARY

Mary was the wife of Joseph and the mother of Jesus, who was conceived miraculously through the intervention of God.

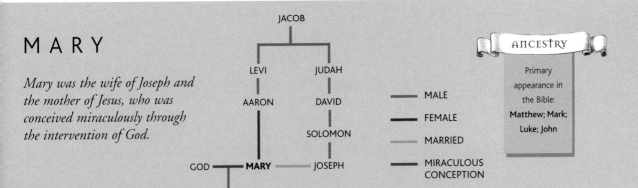

JACOB

LEVI   JUDAH

AARON   DAVID

SOLOMON

GOD — **MARY** — JOSEPH

JESUS

—— MALE

—— FEMALE

—— MARRIED

—— MIRACULOUS CONCEPTION

ANCESTRY

Primary appearance in the Bible:

Matthew; Mark; Luke; John

Mary is the subject of much veneration among Christians. She realized God's goodness to her: "From now on all generations will call me blessed" (Luke 1:48). However, Mary appears only briefly in the four Gospels and receives just a single mention in the first chapter of Acts.

Mary is often referred to as the "Virgin Mary" or "Mother of God," though neither designation is ever used in the Bible. She was apparently from the tribe of **Levi** and a descendant of Aaron. The angel Gabriel announced to Mary that she would become pregnant and give birth to a son whom she was to call **Jesus** (the Greek form of the Hebrew name Joshua, meaning "he saves") because he would "save his people from their sins" (Matthew 1:21). She objected that she was an unmarried virgin at the time. Gabriel explained that Jesus' birth would happen miraculously, through the intervention of God. Although the Catholic and Eastern Orthodox churches teach that Mary remained a virgin her entire life, modern Protestants generally reject this, based on the Gospel writers' references to Jesus' brothers and sisters.

A decree from the Roman Emperor Augustus forced Mary and her new husband **Joseph** to travel to Bethlehem, where she gave birth to Jesus. Jesus' first miracle happened nearly 30 years later when he and his mother were guests at a wedding in Cana. Their hosts ran out of wine and Mary asked Jesus to take care of the problem. He converted several large jars of water into good-quality wine.

At the beginning of his ministry, Mary and Jesus' brothers expressed concern for his sanity (Mark 3:21, 31). At his death, Jesus gave the apostle **John** the responsibility of caring for Mary, because her husband Joseph had apparently died by that time. She was with the other disciples on the day of Pentecost, and after that Mary disappears from the biblical story.

Mary's parents are unnamed in the four canonical Gospels, but according to the apocryphal Gospel of James, she was the daughter of Joachim, of the tribe of Judah, and Anna, of the tribe of Levi, who were both old and previously unable to have children. They took her to live in the Temple in Jerusalem when she was three years old, just as Hannah had taken her son **Samuel,** who became one of Israel's judges.

According to Roman Catholic and Eastern Orthodox tradition, somewhere between three and fifteen years after Jesus rose from the dead, Mary died, surrounded by all the apostles. When they opened her tomb, they found it empty, so they concluded that she had been taken into heaven.

Mary has several feast days, including September 8 (nativity) and August 15 (assumption into Heaven). She is a patroness for motherhood and against floods.

HEROD THE GREAT

The Roman Emperor Augustus appointed Herod the Great as king of Judea, despite Herod's support for Mark Antony after the death of Julius Caesar. Although he was not an Israelite, Herod embraced Judaism. He built a port on the coast of Israel called Caesarea; remodeled the Temple in Jerusalem; and constructed a summer palace on Mount Masada. He was noted for his paranoia and cruelty. Augustus reportedly commented that it was safer to be one of Herod's pigs than one of his sons. When the Magi went to Herod's palace in Judea on the birth of Jesus, expecting to visit the king's newborn son, Herod was afraid that a baby had been born who would eventually usurp him as the legitimate king. To escape from Herod's plan to kill Jesus, Mary and Joseph fled to Egypt and remained there until Herod's death.

JOSEPH

Joseph was the supposed father of Jesus. He initially did not believe
Mary's wild story of how she got pregnant and he planned to leave her.

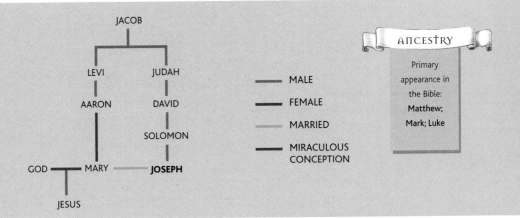

JACOB

LEVI   JUDAH

AARON   DAVID

SOLOMON

GOD ━━ MARY ━━ **JOSEPH**

JESUS

━━━ MALE

━━━ FEMALE

━━━ MARRIED

━━━ MIRACULOUS
CONCEPTION

ANCESTRY

Primary
appearance in
the Bible:
Matthew;
Mark; Luke

oseph appears only in the
birth narratives of **Jesus.**
He was a carpenter and
thus not a poor man. The New
Testament describes him as
righteous, and from what little
we see of him in the Bible, he
comes across as very kind. When
he learned that his wife-to-be,
Mary, was pregnant—and not
by him—he was unwilling to
humiliate her. Instead, he
considered leaving her. Only
when an angel intervened,
explaining to him that God had
made her pregnant miraculously—
that she had not been unfaithful
to him—was he willing to stay.

Near Mary's time of giving
birth, Joseph was forced to take
her with him to Bethlehem
because Augustus Caesar, the first
Roman Emperor, had ordered a
census. All adults had to return
to their ancestral hometowns in
order to register, and because
Joseph was a descendant of
David, the ancient king of Israel

St. Joseph's Dream

*"An angel of the Lord appeared to
him in a dream and said, 'Joseph
son of David, do not be afraid to
take Mary home as your wife.'"*
Matthew 1:20 *(Georges de la Tour,
1593–1652)*

from Bethlehem, that is where he
had to go. Finding no room in
the inns, thanks to the unusually
large influx of travelers, the
couple had to make do with a
stable where Mary gave birth.
A feeding trough became a bed
for the infant. Shepherds arrived,
explaining angels sent them to
see the newborn Messiah.

Some months later, Magi came
bearing expensive gifts. When
they left, an angel warned Joseph
to flee to Egypt to escape King
Herod who planned to murder
the baby to protect his throne.
Joseph kept his family there until
Herod's death, at which point he
moved them back to Nazareth,
returning to his business as a
carpenter. The time and manner
of his death are unknown.

In Roman Catholic tradition,
Joseph is the patron saint of
workers. He has two feast days:
March 19 (as the husband of
Mary) and May 1 (as the patron
of workers). In some religious
images, Joseph is depicted bearing
a staff topped with flowers. This
is derived from an early legend
about how Joseph became
engaged to Mary: The walking
sticks of widowers throughout
Israel were gathered; Joseph's,
out of all of them, burst into
flowers, so Mary chose him.

MAGI FROM THE EAST

Although they gave three gifts, the Bible does not
say how many Magi came to visit the young Jesus.
In popular tradition, their names are Caspar,
Melchior, and Balthasar. The 1611 King James
Version calls them "wise men," though elsewhere
it translates the same term as "sorcerers." Modern
translations simply call them the "Magi," from
which we get the word "magic."

So who were they? The Magi were Zoroastrian
priests and astrologers who interpreted astrological
signs. Unlike ordinary star gazers who saw nothing
significant in the sky at that time, they saw the
famous "Star of Bethlehem" and believed it
predicted that a king was about to be born in
Judea. Naturally, the Magi went to King Herod's
palace in Judea, expecting to find the king's son.
Herod was as surprised by their news as they were
to discover that there was no baby there.

Herod knew he held the throne of Israel
illegitimately, only because the Roman Emperor
Augustus had put him on it. The legitimate king
would be a descendant of David: the baby whom
the Magi had come to visit. That is why Herod
sent them to Bethlehem, David's hometown, with
instructions to let Herod know where the baby was.
Herod planned to kill the baby in order to destroy a
potential rival.

However, after visiting Jesus, the Magi did not
report back to Herod. In a dream, the Magi were
warned that Herod planned to kill the newborn
Messiah, so they returned to their homeland by a
different route (Matthew 2:12). Herod then ordered
the murder of all male children in Bethlehem under
the age of two.

JESUS

Jesus was the son of God and of Mary. Christians believe that he died to save men and women from their sins and to reconcile them with God.

Jesus was born in the Judean village of Bethlehem some time before 4 B.C.E., since Herod the Great was still king at the time of his birth and he died in 4 B.C.E. Jesus was raised by a carpenter named **Joseph;** his mother was named **Mary.** For the first years of his short life, little is recorded beyond his presentation at the Temple shortly after his birth and one visit to Jerusalem at the age of twelve when he got left behind and was found three days later in deep conversation with the rabbis.

When Jesus was about 30, his cousin, **John the Baptist,** announced that Jesus was the long-awaited Jewish Messiah. "Messiah" in Hebrew means "Anointed One." In the ancient world, priests and kings commonly had oil poured on their heads as part of a ceremony that installed them into their official positions. In Israel, it was believed that these anointed people had been appointed to their positions by God. The word "Christ" is simply derived from a Greek word that means the same as the Hebrew word. In the first century C.E., the Messiah or Christ was popularly conceived as a leader who would mount a successful rebellion against Rome and establish Israel as the preeminent

political power in place of the hated Romans. Several of John the Baptist's disciples became followers of Jesus.

During the three years of his public ministry, Jesus picked twelve men to become his apostles (ambassadors), though hundreds followed him. Wealthy women supplied funds to pay for Jesus' peripatetic ministry. Jesus proclaimed the good news that the Kingdom of God was at hand and that those who were sick would be healed. His message was of love and the forgiveness of sins. He also vilified the religious establishment, repeatedly denouncing religious leaders as hypocrites who legalistically twisted the Bible in order to justify their own bad behavior.

Although many religious leaders believed that abstaining from pleasure—what is called asceticism—was a path to God, Jesus' life and practice seemed at odds with that belief. Jesus was often found at parties and was repeatedly criticized by the religious authorities as a result. He commented, "For John the Baptist came neither eating bread nor drinking wine, and you say, 'He has a demon.' The Son of Man came eating and drinking, and you say, 'Here is a glutton and a drunkard, a friend of tax collectors and "sinners"'"

(Luke 7:33–34). His disciples were also questioned about why they did not fast like the disciples of the other religious leaders (Matthew 9:14).

Jesus became well-known for his miraculous healings, which included raising dead people back to life, most notably Lazarus, the brother of Martha and Mary of Bethany. The religious establishment sent representatives to examine and question Jesus. They came to the conclusion that he was simply one more of a long line of false messiahs because he failed to match their list of expectations of the Messiah to come. Although not disputing that he was healing people, they decided that he accomplished his miracles by means of demons.

The religious leaders had made accommodations with the ruling Romans, thereby insuring

Jesus Expelling Traders from the Temple

"Jesus entered the temple area and drove out all who were buying and selling there. He overturned the tables of the money changers and the benches of those selling doves. 'It is written,' he said to them, ' "My house will be called a house of prayer," but you are making it a "den of robbers." ' " Matthew 21:12–13 *(El Greco, 1541–1614)*

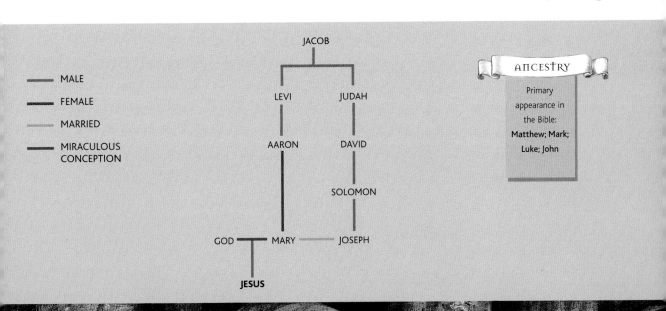

MALE

FEMALE

MARRIED

MIRACULOUS
CONCEPTION

JACOB

LEVI   JUDAH

AARON   DAVID

SOLOMON

GOD —— MARY —— JOSEPH

JESUS

ANCESTRY

Primary
appearance in
the Bible:
**Matthew; Mark;
Luke; John**

The Flagellation of Christ

"But God demonstrates his own love for us in this: While we were still sinners, Christ died for us. Since we have now been justified by his blood, how much more shall we be saved from God's wrath through him! For if, when we were God's enemies, we were reconciled to him through the death of his Son, how much more, having been reconciled, shall we be saved through his life! Not only is this so, but we also rejoice in God through our Lord Jesus Christ, through whom we have now received reconciliation." Romans 5:8–11 *(Caravaggio, 1571–1610)*

that the Jews could practice their religion without being forced to follow Roman conventions of emperor worship. Despite Jesus' repeated denials of political aspirations, they feared that Jesus' growing popularity might lead to a widespread popular uprising against Rome. Knowing Roman power, they feared that when such a rebellion was inevitably crushed, the Jewish people would also lose many of the concessions the Romans had made to the Jewish faith.

Therefore, in order to protect the nation, they conspired with the Roman government to have Jesus arrested and put to death as a rebel.

Pontius Pilate, the Roman governor in Jerusalem, questioned Jesus about his movement. Jesus told Pilate that "My kingdom is not of this world. If it were, my servants would fight to prevent my arrest" (John 18:36). Finding that the charges of rebellion were unfounded, Pilate initially sought to release Jesus, but given the pressure of both a mob and the religious leaders, who suggested that they might bring charges about his loyalty to the Roman emperor, Pilate finally ordered that Jesus be crucified. Crucifixion was a common form of execution used by the Romans. Although condemned criminals had been known to linger for days on a cross, Jesus succumbed within a matter of hours.

The religious leaders expected that Jesus' movement, like those of other pretenders to messiahship before him, would simply fade away with his death. Within days, however, his disciples were proclaiming that Jesus had not stayed dead, but rather had risen from the grave. Their message was not one of political or military revolution. Instead, they proclaimed that Jesus was the ultimate sacrifice; he died to save humanity from sin. That he rose from the dead, they argued, demonstrated that God had accepted his sacrifice. This was radically different from the common interpretation of who and what the Messiah was supposed to be and to do.

Jesus referred to himself both as "Son of Man" and "Son of God." This is consistent with the Christian concept that Jesus was both human and divine. Jesus was accused of blasphemy for calling himself the Son of God and thereby "making himself equal with God" (John 5:18).

The Trinity

An altarpiece painting depicting an enthroned God the Father holding his crucified Son, with the Holy Spirit above the head of Christ in the shape of a dove. (Unknown artist, fifteenth century)

JESUS AS MAN AND GOD

Christians came to believe that God had become the human being who was born a baby in Bethlehem. The author of the Gospel of John uses language similar to that of the creation narrative of Genesis to introduce Jesus and then explicitly identifies him as God. However, mainstream Christianity has also consistently affirmed that Jesus was just as much human as he was divine. **Paul** describes Jesus' physical body and suffering, and he also describes him as the creator of the universe (Colossians 1:15–17 and 1:21–26). Likewise, both **Peter** (Acts 2:21) and Paul (Romans 10:13) quote a passage from the prophet Joel that states "And everyone who calls on the name of the Lord will be saved" (Joel 2:32) and then apply it to Jesus. They thus equate Jesus with Yahweh, the God of the Old Testament. However, the authors of the New Testament affirm that Jesus was born (Luke 2:1–16), grew up (Luke 2:52), wept (John 11:35), got hungry (Mark 11:12), slept (Matthew 8:24), suffered and died (Hebrews 2:9, 18), and thus was fully and completely human (Philippians 2:5–8).

Jesus is repeatedly called "Lord" by the New Testament writers. In Judaism of the first century, this word was a synonym for "God." The doctrine of the Trinity arose in early Christianity as a way of reconciling the apparent contradiction between an insistence that there is only one God, and an insistence that the Father, Jesus, and Holy Spirit are each God as well.

JOHN THE BAPTIST

John the Baptist, a prophet and Jesus' cousin, publicly announced that Jesus was the Messiah.

**St. John
the Baptist**

"And so John came, baptizing in the desert region and preaching a baptism of repentance for the forgiveness of sins."
Mark 1:4
(Leonardo da Vinci, 1452–1519)

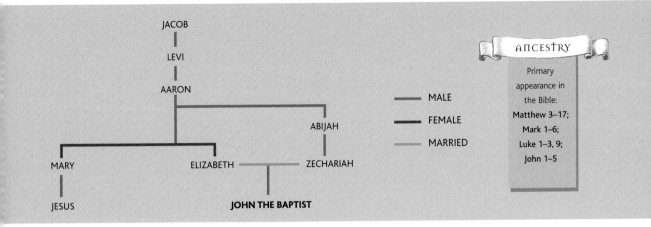

An angel announced the impending birth of John the Baptist to his elderly parents, **Elizabeth** and **Zechariah.** Because of their age and the appearance of an angel, they considered his birth miraculous.

John grew up to become a prophet who lived along the Jordan River. He gathered a number of followers and not a few enemies due to his repeated denunciations of the religious establishment in Jerusalem. He was noted for proclaiming that the Messiah was coming and that the Israelites needed to repent of their sinful ways. When those listening to him repented, he would take them into the Jordan River and baptize them. Baptism was a standard Jewish ritual, practiced for a number of reasons, most commonly for repentance, conversion to Judaism, or for initiation into ministry (for instance, when someone became a rabbi). Although many suspected that John himself might be the Messiah, he consistently denied it. Ultimately he announced that his cousin, **Jesus** of Nazareth, was the promised Messiah.

John lived in the wilderness and did not go into town, so he ate what he could find, often only grasshoppers and wild honey. He wore animal skins. John's denunciation of mainstream religion in Israel and the fact that he lived away from civilization, have led some scholars to speculate that he was influenced by the Essenes, if not actually a member of their sect. The Essenes believed that Judaism had become corrupted, so they lived in remote areas away from the rest of Jewish society while waiting for the Messiah to come and clean up all the corruption.

John the Baptist's preaching against the puppet king, Herod Antipas, led to his arrest. Jesus praised John and told his followers that John was the **Elijah** who would precede the Messiah. Herod was reluctant to do anything more than keep John in prison, however, and would occasionally bring him out to listen to him talk. However, one day he was having a banquet, got drunk, and offered his stepdaughter, **Salome,** anything she wanted. Herod's wife hated John with a passion for how he had denounced her relationship with Herod Antipas. She used this opportunity to see to it that John was executed. Following instructions from her mother, Salome asked for John's head on a platter and, having promised her anything she asked for, Herod felt constrained to fulfill her gruesome request.

The New Testament reports that John continued to baptize people during the time that Jesus was preaching and healing, and that John's disciples, for the most part, had not joined Jesus' ministry. After Christianity had been established following Jesus' resurrection, the author of Acts reports that John's disciples were only slowly assimilated into the Jesus movement. In Ephesus, a city in what is now Turkey, a man named Apollos appeared proclaiming the message of John the Baptist; two Christians, **Aquila** and his wife **Priscilla,** instructed Apollos in the Way of Jesus. Later, when **Paul** arrived in Ephesus, he found more disciples of John. After telling them about Jesus, they were baptized in Jesus' name and received the Holy Spirit.

For Roman Catholics, John's feast days are June 24 (nativity) and August 29 (beheading); among the Eastern Orthodox, his main feast day is January 7. He is the patron of baptism, monastic life, and epileptics.

SALOME

Salome was the stepdaughter of King Herod Antipas. At the urging of her mother, Salome asked for John the Baptist's head on a platter.

Her mother's political ambitions brought Salome to her evil deed. Herodias, her mother, was the daughter of Aristobulus IV, a son of Herod the Great and Berenice, a daughter of Herod's sister.

Herodias married Herod II Boethus, her uncle who was the son and heir to the throne of Herod the Great, around 1 C.E. After he was assassinated in 6 C.E., she married another uncle, Herod Philip I. Salome was born to them around 14 C.E. About 23 C.E., Herodias divorced Herod Philip I and married another uncle, Herod Antipas.

HEROD ANTIPAS

Herod Antipas was the son of Herod the Great, who had sought to kill the infant **Jesus.** Herod Antipas was tetrarch throughout the time of Jesus. Tetrarchy is a system of government where power is divided between four people. Judea became a tetrarchy following the death of Herod the Great in 4 B.C.E. because his kingdom was divided between his sons, each of whom got a piece of the kingdom. After he had executed John the Baptist, Herod Antipas heard about Jesus and wondered if possibly Jesus was John resurrected. When Jesus was later arrested, the Roman governor Pontius Pilate sent Jesus to see Herod Antipas, who happened to be in Jerusalem for Passover. He was excited to meet Jesus, because he hoped Jesus would perform some miracles. Disappointed by Jesus' refusal to do any tricks, he sent Jesus back to Pilate to be executed.

The primary motivation for her change in husbands was political. Herodias was of Hasmonean descent. The Hasmonean Kingdom (140–37 B.C.E.) had been a semiautonomous Jewish state in ancient Judea. Its ruling dynasty had been established under the leadership of Simon Maccabeus, whose brother **Judas Maccabeus** defeated the Seleucid army during the Maccabean Revolt in 165 B.C.E.

Thus, Herodias' Hasmonean descent was a very good asset for Herod Antipas' ambitions to the royal crown. Herodias' marriage with Herod Antipas improved her status because she became his queen. However, the people of Israel saw the marriage as a violation of Mosaic Law. **John the Baptist** became a vociferous critic of their relationship.

Although Salome appears in the New Testament, her name is never given there. She is simply referred to as the "daughter of Herodias." The first-century Jewish historian Josephus preserves her name, however, and writes that she was married twice, first to Herod Philip II, also known as Philip the Tetrarch, the half-brother of her stepfather Herod Antipas. Later, she married Aristobulus of Chalcis, the son of Herod of Chalcis and brother of Agrippa, who, in Acts, is recorded as

ordering the execution of the apostle **James** the Great. Salome would eventually have three sons with Aristobulus: Herod, Agrippa, and Aristobulus.

Before she was married, her stepfather Herod Antipas had finally arrested and imprisoned John the Baptist for his never-ending denunciations. However, John the Baptist was very popular with the people and Herod was not, so Herod kept him alive, fearful of a rebellion.

One day, during his birthday celebration, Herod Antipas had Salome dance as entertainment in front of him and his guests. Excited by her performance, and thoroughly drunk, he promised her anything she might ask up to half his kingdom. Salome's mother told her to request John the Baptist's head on a platter. Herod felt constrained to keep his promise, given all the witnesses to his offer, and so he ordered John's decapitation. Salome took the platter with John's head and gave it to her mother.

Salome Receiving the Head of St. John the Baptist

"On Herod's birthday the daughter of Herodias danced for them and pleased Herod so much that he promised with an oath to give her whatever she asked." Matthew 14:6–7 *(Guercino, 1591–1666)*

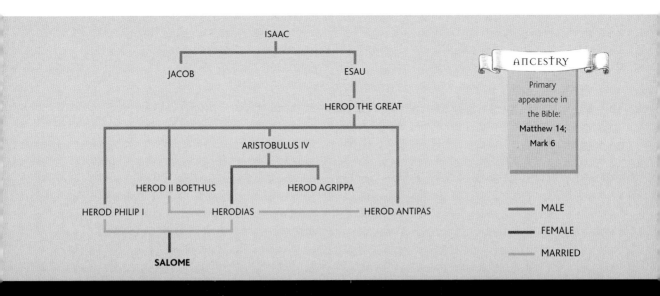

ISAAC

JACOB

ESAU

HEROD THE GREAT

ARISTOBULUS IV

HEROD II BOETHUS

HEROD AGRIPPA

HEROD PHILIP I

HERODIAS

HEROD ANTIPAS

SALOME

ELIZABETH

Elizabeth was the mother of John the Baptist and a cousin of Mary, Jesus' mother.

JACOB

LEVI

AARON

ABIJAH

MARY — ELIZABETH — ZECHARIAH

JESUS — JOHN THE BAPTIST

ANCESTRY

Primary appearance in the Bible:
Luke 1

—— MALE
—— FEMALE
—— MARRIED

E lizabeth was a descendant of Aaron, the high priest. She and her husband, **Zechariah,** are described as righteous. Like **Sarah,** the wife of **Abraham,** Elizabeth was childless and well past the time when she would have normally been able to bear children. Like Abraham, Elizabeth's husband Zechariah was visited by a representative of God, the angel Gabriel, who told him that Elizabeth would get pregnant and give birth to a son who was to be called John, later known as **John the Baptist.** Gabriel also told them that John would do great things and was to be raised as a Nazarite from birth. The Nazarite vow (Numbers 6) was normally a voluntary and short-term decision on the part of an individual to abstain from wine and other fermented drinks. In the Old Testament, both **Samson** and **Samuel** were made Nazarites from birth.

While Elizabeth was pregnant with John, her cousin **Mary** visited her. Mary was pregnant with **Jesus,** and when she arrived, Elizabeth's baby "leaped in her womb" (Luke 1:41).

Elizabeth was then filled with the Holy Spirit and told Mary, "Blessed are you among women and blessed is the child you will bear!" (Luke 1:42).

According to legend, when King Herod set out to kill the infant Jesus, he heard about the special circumstances of John's birth and tried to hunt him down as well. Elizabeth took an eighteen-month-old John to a mountain wilderness. She spoke to the mountain and a cave opened up in it to hide her from Herod. A stream flowed from the cave and a date palm sprang up at its entrance.

Meanwhile, Zechariah was killed in the Temple. His spilled blood turned into a stone as a testimony against Herod. Forty days later, Elizabeth died in the wilderness. An angel took care of John the Baptist as he grew up in the wilderness.

Elizabeth is revered as a saint in Catholic, Eastern Orthodox, and Anglican traditions. She is considered the patroness of expectant mothers. For Roman Catholics, her feast day is November 5. Among Eastern Orthodox, it is September 8.

The Visitation
"When Elizabeth heard Mary's greeting, the baby leaped in her womb, and Elizabeth was filled with the Holy Spirit." Luke 1:41 (Castilian, fifteenth century)

ZECHARIAH

Zechariah was the father of John the Baptist. He lost his voice for a time because of his lack of faith.

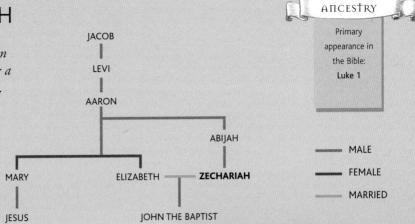

JACOB

LEVI

AARON

ABIJAH

MARY — ELIZABETH — **ZECHARIAH**

JESUS

JOHN THE BAPTIST

ANCESTRY

Primary appearance in the Bible:
Luke 1

MALE

FEMALE

MARRIED

Although Zechariah is a common name in the Old Testament—more than twenty Zechariahs are mentioned—there is only one person in the New Testament who went by that name. In the Gospel of Luke, Zechariah (also spelled Zacharias) was a priest descended from Abijah, a descendant of **Moses'** brother Aaron. He was the husband of Elizabeth, also a descendant of Aaron. Zechariah was a righteous man. Both he and his wife were old and well past the time of having children when their son **John the Baptist** was born.

The performance of various duties at the Jerusalem Temple alternated from family to family. Due to the large number of eligible descendants of Aaron, usually a priest would have the opportunity of officiating in the Temple only once during his lifetime. So it was during Zechariah's once-in-a-lifetime task of lighting incense in the Temple that the angel Gabriel appeared to him and announced that his elderly wife would soon give birth to a son, whom he was to name John. Zechariah did not believe what Gabriel had told him and asked for a sign, so the angel made Zechariah unable to speak until the boy was born.

On the day of their son's circumcision, when Elizabeth insisted that the baby should be called John, Zechariah's startled relatives asked him whether she was right to give him that name, since no one else in the family had it. Zechariah then wrote on a tablet that her name choice was correct. At that point, he was suddenly able to speak again and uttered a hymn of praise to God. In the hymn, Zechariah said that John would be a prophet who would "go on before the Lord to prepare the way for him" (Luke 1:76).

According to legend, Herod had Zechariah killed in the Temple, where his spilled blood turned into a stone as a testimony against Herod. Forty days later, Elizabeth died in the wilderness. An angel took care of John the Baptist as he grew up. Revered as a saint by Roman Catholics (but not a patron saint), his feast day is November 5, the same as that of Elizabeth, his wife.

Zechariah Writes John the Baptist's Name

"He asked for a writing tablet, and to everyone's astonishment he wrote, 'His name is John.' Immediately his mouth was opened and his tongue was loosed, and he began to speak, praising God." Luke 1:63–64 (Hispano–Flemish workshop, late fifteenth century)

ANNA

Anna was a female prophet who announced that Jesus was the Messiah.

Anna is described in the Gospel of Luke as a descendant of **Asher,** and the daughter of Phanuel. The name Phanuel means "face of God." Nothing else is known of her father. In the book of 1 Enoch (which is quoted from once in the New Testament, by the author of Jude, and is an apocryphal book included in the Ethiopian Orthodox Bible), Phanuel is listed as one of the four archangels of the Lord of Spirits. He is said to preside over "repentance, and the hope of those who will inherit eternal life" (1 Enoch 40).

Anna had remained a widow following her husband's death after only seven years of marriage. The name of her husband is unknown. The name Anna is the Greek form of the Hebrew name Hannah, the mother of the judge **Samuel.** It means "grace" or "favor" and is derived from the same Hebrew root that gives us the name John. Anna is said to have prayed and fasted at the Temple both night and day. Jewish women were allowed access only to the Court of Women, which was the first inner court reached upon entering the Temple.

Anna was 84 years of age when **Joseph** and **Mary** brought their son **Jesus** to the temple to be circumcised eight days after his birth, in obedience to the Mosaic Law. She was generally recognized as a prophet by her contemporaries. Upon seeing Jesus, she thanked God and from that point on spoke about Jesus to all "who were looking forward to the redemption of Jerusalem" (Luke 2:38).

Throughout Jesus' life, women played prominent roles. It is a woman who first knew that he was to be the Messiah when the angel Gabriel told his mother Mary what was about to happen. Women provided the finances that supported Jesus in his public ministry. Women first learned about and reported his resurrection. Here, with Anna, a woman became his first missionary to proclaim the Good News.

In Roman Catholicism, her feast day is September 1; among the Eastern Orthodox, it is February 3. She is the patroness of hermits. We know nothing about the circumstances of her death. Some have speculated that when Jesus stayed behind in the Temple for three days at the age of twelve to converse with the rabbis, he stayed with Anna.

St. Augustine (354–430 C.E.) of Hippo, a city in North Africa, was an early and influential Christian theologian. He wrote a letter to a woman named Juliana on "Holy Widowhood," praising women who remained widows and did not remarry, using Anna as an example who was blessed by God to bear witness to the coming of the Messiah. Some commentators have suggested that Anna served as a model for the apostle **Paul**'s rule regarding church support of widows. He wrote to **Timothy,** one of his traveling companions whom tradition says became Bishop of Ephesus in Turkey: "No widow may be put on the list of widows unless she is over sixty, has been faithful to her husband, and is well known for her good deeds, such as bringing up children, showing hospitality, washing the feet of the saints, helping those in trouble, and devoting herself to all kinds of good deeds" (1 Timothy 5:9–10). In the early Christian community "widow" also became an ordained ministry, like deacon or bishop.

The Presentation of Jesus at the Temple

"There was also a prophetess, Anna, the daughter of Phanuel, of the tribe of Asher. She was very old; she had lived with her husband seven years after her marriage." Luke 2:36
(Giovanni di Paolo, 1403–83)

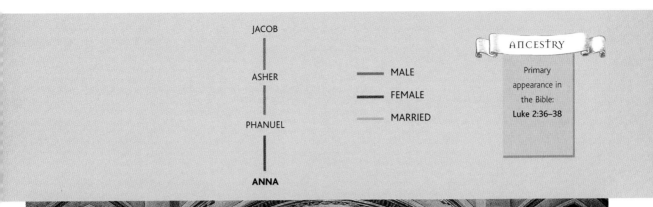

JACOB

ASHER

PHANUEL

ANNA

—— MALE

—— FEMALE

—— MARRIED

ANCESTRY

Primary
appearance in
the Bible:
Luke 2:36–38

MARY MAGDALENE

Mary Magdalene was one of Jesus' followers. She was the first witness to his resurrection from the dead.

Christ Appears to Mary Magdalene
"'Woman,' he said, 'why are you crying? Who is it you are looking for?'" John 20:15 *(Style of Orcagna, fourteenth century)*

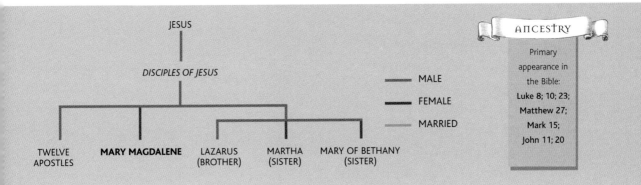

JESUS

DISCIPLES OF JESUS

TWELVE APOSTLES | **MARY MAGDALENE** | LAZARUS (BROTHER) | MARTHA (SISTER) | MARY OF BETHANY (SISTER)

—— MALE
—— FEMALE
—— MARRIED

ANCESTRY

Primary appearance in the Bible:
Luke 8; 10; 23;
Matthew 27;
Mark 15;
John 11; 20

Miriam—the English variant is Mary—was a common name during **Jesus'** time. Several Marys and unnamed women, saints and sinners, were followers of Jesus.

Mary of Magdala, or Mary Magdalene, is identified in the New Testament as an important leader in the Christian movement. She is one of the wealthy women who financially supported Jesus and his disciples in their public ministry (Luke 8:1–3). Jesus was buried in haste after crucifixion, and Mary Magdalene was one of the three women who went to the tomb afterward to take care of his dead body. The tomb was empty and she became the first person to meet and speak with the risen Christ (John 20:17).

Luke's Gospel records when Mary Magdalene became a disciple of Jesus. When Jesus was healing people of evil spirits and physical infirmities during his public ministry, he drove seven demons out of her (Luke 8:2). In those days, "demons" were thought to cause madness or illness, and "seven" throughout the Bible generally signifies "a great deal" when people are involved, or "perfection" in connection with God's work, as in the seven days of creation. Before meeting up with Jesus, from Luke's account, Mary could have been either a great sinner, or just very sick, or both.

Over the course of history, and even in New Testament times, people have connected incidences in other Marys' and other women's lives with Mary Magdalene. She has often been connected with the unnamed "public sinner" who washed Jesus' feet with her hair at the house of Simon the Pharisee (Luke 7:36–50). In John's Gospel, this woman is identified as Mary of Bethany, the sister of Lazarus and Martha (John 11:1–2). Mary of Magdala has also been mistakenly identified as the adulteress brought before Jesus in John 8 whom Jesus refused to condemn to death by stoning. These women's sexual sin later gave rise to the image of Mary Magdalene as a prostitute.

Many have speculated that Mary Magdalene was romantically interested in Jesus, which is not unreasonable. Early Christians would not have been scandalized by the thought of Jesus being married or having children. In fact, his humanity has always been firmly emphasized in Christian doctrine, just as much as his divinity. Later Gnostics, who were considered heretics by Christianity, would have been appalled at the idea of Jesus marrying. Gnostics believed that the physical body and sexual activity were inherently evil.

Roman Catholic, Eastern Orthodox, and Anglican churches consider Mary Magdalene a saint. Her feast day is July 22. She is the patroness of women, penitent sinners, and apothecaries.

A tradition concerning Mary Magdalene explains the origin of Easter eggs. Following the death and resurrection of Jesus, Mary was invited to a banquet given by the Roman Emperor Tiberius Caesar. When she met him, she held an egg in her hand and exclaimed "Jesus is risen!" Caesar laughed, and said that Jesus rising from the dead was as likely as the egg in her hand turning red. The egg immediately turned bright red. Alternatively, the custom is explained by the story that she had placed a basket of eggs at the foot of Jesus' cross. Blood dripping from his wounds turned the eggs red and she later took those eggs to Tiberius.

FEMALE DISCIPLES

In addition to Mary Magdalene, the author of the Gospel of Luke writes that among Jesus' female disciples were "Joanna the wife of Cuza, the manager of Herod's household; Susanna; and many others. These women were helping to support them [Jesus and his disciples] out of their own means" (Luke 8:3).

THE TWELVE APOSTLES

Jesus had many disciples. From that larger group, he chose twelve to become his apostles. They paralleled the twelve sons of Jacob who were patriarchs of the Twelve Tribes that formed the nation of Israel. "Apostle" is a word that in Greek means "sent one," a meaning close to the modern word "ambassador." The Twelve stayed with Jesus during his entire public ministry, received special instructions not given to the larger group of disciples, and were eyewitnesses to his resurrection. They all subsequently became leaders in the early Christian Church, except for Judas Iscariot, who had betrayed Jesus to his enemies and then committed suicide. Therefore, following Jesus' resurrection, the remaining eleven apostles chose Matthias from among the other disciples of Jesus to replace Judas (Acts 1:26).

The Tears of St. Peter

"Then Peter remembered the word Jesus had spoken: 'Before the rooster crows, you will disown me three times.' And he went outside and wept bitterly." Matthew 26:75 *(El Greco, 1541–1614)*

PETER

Jesus invited Simon, a fisherman from Galilee, to follow him, renaming him Rock. Peter is derived from the Latin petrus, "rock." He is also called Cephus, "rock" in Greek.

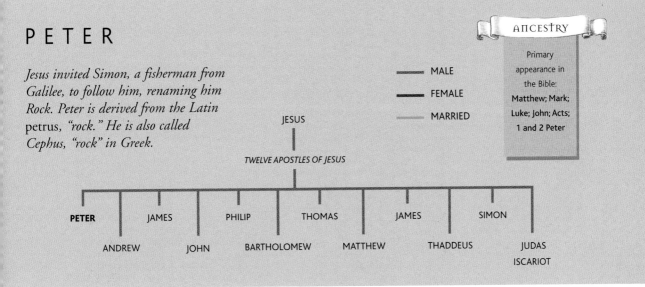

ANCESTRY

Primary appearance in the Bible: Matthew; Mark; Luke; John; Acts; 1 and 2 Peter

——— MALE

——— FEMALE

——— MARRIED

JESUS

TWELVE APOSTLES OF JESUS

PETER · ANDREW · JAMES · JOHN · PHILIP · BARTHOLOMEW · THOMAS · MATTHEW · JAMES · THADDEUS · SIMON · JUDAS ISCARIOT

Peter was one of the first people whom **Jesus** asked to become a disciple. His brother **Andrew** was responsible for introducing Peter to Jesus. Together with **James** the Great and **John,** Peter was one of Jesus' closest companions. A fisherman by trade, with an outgoing personality, he was noted to be impulsive and had a tendency to talk first and think second.

One day during a storm, as he and other disciples were rowing across the Sea of Galilee, they noticed Jesus walking by on the surface of the water. Terrified, Peter told Jesus that if it were really him and not just a ghost, then he should tell Peter to come out to join him on the water. Jesus told him to come on out. Peter stepped out of the boat and walked for some distance before he panicked. He cried out to Jesus as he started to sink. Jesus, of course, rescued him and carried him back to the boat (Matthew 14:25–32).

Peter, John, and James were the only three apostles whom Jesus took to Mount Tabor when he transfigured and revealed himself in his glory. Peter and John were the only two who followed Jesus to his interrogation after he was arrested. Peter had told Jesus at the Last Supper that although everyone else might desert him in his hour of need, he could count on Peter never to abandon him. Jesus responded to Peter that he would, in fact, wind up denying that he knew Jesus before the rooster crowed the next morning.

While Peter was probably plotting and trying to figure out a way to rescue Jesus from his arrest over the course of that last night, three people asked him if he were a disciple. He denied it three times. After the last denial, the rooster crowed and Jesus looked right at him. Peter broke down in tears and ran off.

After Jesus rose from the dead, he made a point of asking Peter three times, "Do you love me?" Three times, Peter affirmed that he did, the last time nearly in tears: "Lord, you know all things; you know that I love you" (John 21:15–17). Peter went on to become a leader in the early church and preached the first Christian sermon in Jerusalem on the day of Pentecost when the Holy Spirit arrived. Peter was arrested several times for preaching about Jesus. Once, an angel rescued him from prison, surprising both him and the church that was praying for him. He spent most of his life in Jerusalem after Jesus' resurrection, but at some point he moved to Rome. He was married, and his house in Capernaum was used as a church.

Roman Catholics believe that Peter was the first pope. According to tradition, Peter was crucified upside down in Rome during the reign of Emperor Nero. He is buried in Rome, in St. Peter's Basilica.

Peter's feast days are June 29 (Feast of Peter and Paul), February 22 (Feast of the Chair of Peter), and November 18 (Feast of the Dedication of the Basilicas of Peter and Paul). He is the patron of fishermen, bakers, butchers, shoemakers, watchmakers, and foot problems.

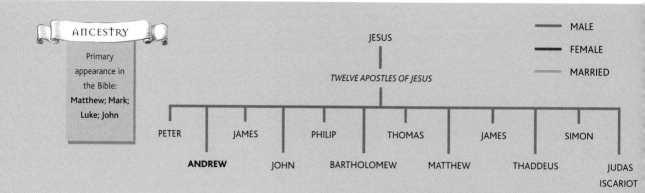

ANCESTRY

Primary appearance in the Bible: Matthew; Mark; Luke; John

JESUS

TWELVE APOSTLES OF JESUS

PETER
ANDREW
JAMES
JOHN
PHILIP
BARTHOLOMEW
THOMAS
MATTHEW
JAMES
THADDEUS
SIMON
JUDAS ISCARIOT

— MALE
— FEMALE
— MARRIED

ANDREW

Andrew was Peter's brother. He was also a fisherman and a disciple of John the Baptist before joining Jesus.

Andrew was the first disciple whom **Jesus** asked to join him, and he introduced his brother **Peter** to Jesus. Born in Bethsaida by the Sea of Galilee, Andrew had been a disciple of **John the Baptist** before joining up with Jesus. During the feeding of the five thousand, Andrew pointed out the boy with the five loaves and two fish to Jesus, and Jesus miraculously multiplied the food and fed the entire crowd.

The church historian Eusebius (c. 275–339 C.E.) reports that Andrew wound up preaching in Asia Minor and in Scythia, along the Black Sea as far as the River Volga. He later became a patron saint of Romania and Russia. Tradition indicates that Andrew was the first bishop of Byzantium (now Istanbul) and was crucified on an X-shaped cross.

After the Synod of Whitby in the seventh century, the Celtic Church believed that their patron saint, Columba, had been outranked by Peter. They therefore decided that the patron of the Celtic Church would thenceforth be Peter's older brother, Andrew.

About the middle of the tenth century, Andrew also became the patron saint of Scotland. One legend explains that, during a battle in the eighth century, the Scottish King Ungas saw a cloud shaped like an "X," convincing him that Andrew was watching over them, so he promised that if they won the battle he would make Andrew their patron saint. The 1320 Declaration of Arbroath, which declared Scottish independence from England, cited Scotland's conversion to Christianity by St. Andrew, "the first to be an Apostle," as evidence that Scotland was held in especially high regard by God.

Many parish churches in Scotland, of various Christian denominations, are named after St. Andrew. St. Andrew's Day is observed on November 30 by both Roman Catholic and Eastern Orthodox churches. It is also the national day of Scotland.

St. Andrew and St. Francis
Andrew was crucified on an X-shaped cross that became known as St. Andrew's cross. (El Greco, 1541–1614)

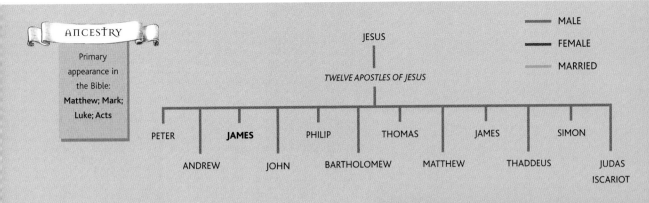

MALE
FEMALE
MARRIED

JESUS

TWELVE APOSTLES OF JESUS

PETER · **JAMES** · PHILIP · THOMAS · JAMES · SIMON

ANDREW · JOHN · BARTHOLOMEW · MATTHEW · THADDEUS · JUDAS ISCARIOT

JAMES THE GREAT

James was one of the sons of Zebedee and was usually listed with his brother John.

James is also called St. James the Great in order to distinguish him from the other two people of the New Testament who are named James: **Matthew**'s brother, St. James the Less, and **Jesus**' brother, St. James the Just, who is believed to be the author of the Letter of James. James is an English variant of the Hebrew name Jacob. Oddly, his brother **John** never mentions him in the Gospel attributed to John.

James was one of Jesus' earliest disciples, together with his brother John. Jesus nicknamed them both the "sons of thunder" (Mark 3:17), perhaps because of their tempers. One day Jesus was not welcomed at a Samaritan village and James and John asked Jesus, "Lord, do you want us to call fire down from heaven to destroy them?" (Luke 9:54). Jesus rebuked them for making such a suggestion.

James was a fisherman, and both he and his brother John left their father's business in order to follow Jesus (Matthew 4:21–22). James, John, and **Peter** were with Jesus at the transfiguration when Jesus met with **Elijah** and **Moses** and changed into a bright figure (Matthew 17:1–8). James, again with Peter and John, was with Jesus when Jesus raised Jairus' daughter from the dead (Mark 5:35–43). The three also stayed at Jesus' side as he prayed in the Garden of Gethsemane the night that **Judas Iscariot** betrayed Jesus (Mark 14:32–33).

Herod Agrippa I executed James by sword around 44 C.E., making him the first martyr among the apostles. There is a legend that James had first traveled to Spain and preached the gospel there before returning to Palestine. After his execution, tradition states that his body was miraculously transferred to Iria Flavia in northwest Spain, and then later to Compostela. During the Middle Ages, Compostela became one of the most famous places of pilgrimage in the world. James's feast day is July 25. He is the patron saint of blacksmiths, laborers, soldiers, and veterinarians.

St. James the Great as Pilgrim

"It was about this time that King Herod arrested some who belonged to the church, intending to persecute them. He had James, the brother of John, put to death with the sword." Acts 12:1–2 *(El Greco, 1541–1614)*

JOHN

John and his brother James the Great were the two sons of Zebedee.
Jesus refers to them as the "sons of thunder" (Mark 3:17).

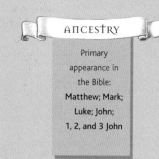

ANCESTRY

Primary
appearance in
the Bible:
Matthew; Mark;
Luke; John;
1, 2, and 3 John

The Call of St. John

John received inspiration to write Revelation while on the island of Patmos.
(Douce Apocalypse, English manuscript, thirteenth century)

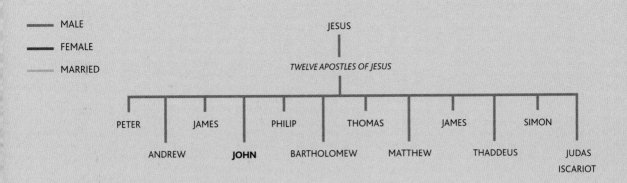

MALE
FEMALE
MARRIED

JESUS

TWELVE APOSTLES OF JESUS

PETER
JAMES
PHILIP
THOMAS
JAMES
SIMON

ANDREW
JOHN
BARTHOLOMEW
MATTHEW
THADDEUS
JUDAS ISCARIOT

ohn, the younger brother of **James** the Great, was one of **Jesus'** earliest disciples. He had been a disciple of **John the Baptist**. His father Zebedee was a fisherman and apparently a man of some wealth. John and James both worked for their father. When Jesus asked them to join him as his disciples, he explained that they would no longer be fishermen, but rather "fishers of men" (Matthew 4:19).

John considered himself to be Jesus' best friend. He regularly refers to himself as "the beloved disciple" in the Gospel that bears his name. According to John's Gospel, Jesus secretly confessed to John at the Last Supper that **Judas Iscariot** was the one who would betray Jesus (John 13:21–26).

John, James, and **Peter** were with Jesus at the transfiguration when Jesus revealed himself in his glory. Together with his brother and Peter, he was there when Jesus raised Jairus' daughter back to life and when Jesus raised Lazarus, the brother of Martha and Mary of Bethany, from the dead. With Peter, he followed Jesus and watched his trial and conviction, then stood at the foot of the cross when Jesus died. Just before Jesus died,

he gave John the responsibility of taking care of his mother, **Mary.**

John raced Peter to the tomb where Jesus had been laid after the first reports came from **Mary Magdalene** and the other women that it was empty. John beat Peter there but deferred to let Peter enter first (John 20:3–8). In a meeting after the resurrection, Jesus told Peter how Peter would die. Peter asked Jesus, "What about him?" and pointed at John. Jesus replied, "If I want him to remain alive until I return, what is that to you?" The rumor then spread that John would not die before Jesus returned (John 21:18–23).

Tradition states that John was once boiled in oil without serious harm. He was briefly exiled for his faith to the island of Patmos during the reign of the Roman Emperor Domitian. While exiled there, John claimed that he received the vision that he recorded in Revelation, also called the Apocalypse. John outlived all the other disciples, and alone among them, did not suffer martyrdom. According to tradition, he died of natural causes in Ephesus, in what is now Turkey, around 100 C.E.

John is traditionally regarded as the author of several of books

in the New Testament: the Gospel of John; the Letters designated 1, 2, and 3 John; and Revelation, the final book in the Bible, also called the Apocalypse. His feast day is December 27, among Roman Catholics; among the Eastern Orthodox, it is May 8. He is the patron of authors, theologians, publishers, booksellers, editors, and painters, as well as of friendships.

APOCALYPSE

Both Hebrew and Christian scriptural authors composed apocalyptic literature that offered hope to those who suffered during times of persecution. Revelation is the only example of this in the New Testament. Revelation dates to the period when Roman officials persecuted Christians, and in it "Babylon" was a code word used to avoid problems with Roman officials. Christians grasped that Rome was a new Babylon acting the same way the Babylon of old did when it attacked Israel, Jerusalem, and the Temple.

A parallel to ancient apocalyptic literature exists in the Negro spirituals that were written before the American Civil War. The Jordan River, for instance, became code in these songs for the Ohio River, which if crossed meant freedom for the slaves. Likewise, the "chariot" of "Swing Low, Sweet Chariot" referred to the underground railroad that rescued slaves. While the slavemasters imagined their slaves were singing hymns to God, they were actually plotting escape.

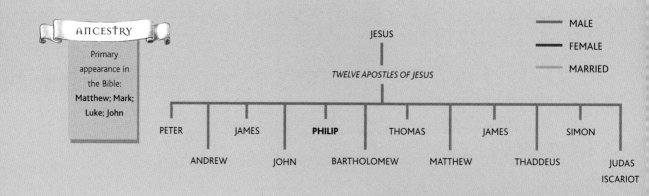

ANCESTRY

Primary
appearance in
the Bible:
Matthew; Mark;
Luke; John

JESUS

TWELVE APOSTLES OF JESUS

——— MALE
——— FEMALE
——— MARRIED

PETER   JAMES   **PHILIP**   THOMAS   JAMES   SIMON

ANDREW   JOHN   BARTHOLOMEW   MATTHEW   THADDEUS   JUDAS ISCARIOT

PHILIP

Philip, one of the earliest of the twelve apostles, was from Bethsaida in Galilee.

Like **Andrew** and **Peter,** Philip was a native of Bethsaida. He was one of the first of the twelve apostles whom **Jesus** called to follow him. In John's Gospel, he introduced a man named Nathanael to Jesus. Nathanael is sometimes identified with the apostle **Bartholomew.**

Philip seems to have held a prominent place among the apostles, but little is known of him. At the feeding of the five thousand, Jesus asked him where they could buy bread for the crowd. Philip told him that eight months' wages would not be enough to purchase the bread to feed them all. At the Last Supper, Philip asked Jesus to show them the Father. Jesus responded that those who had seen Jesus had also seen the Father (John 14:8–11). Nothing more is said about Philip.

The Christian writer Clement of Alexandria (c. 150–215 C.E.) reports that Philip was married and had children, including a married daughter. According to later Christian tradition, Philip both preached and worked miracles after Jesus' death and resurrection. He is reported to have traveled to Galilee, Greece, Azota, Syria, and Phrygia.

According to legend, in Phrygia, a region of modern Turkey, Philip and Bartholomew preached the Gospel message. Through prayer, they managed to kill a large serpent in a temple devoted to serpent worship. They also healed many people of snake bites. The city governor and a pagan priest, angered by their actions, ordered Philip and Bartholomew to be crucified. During their crucifixion, a large earthquake shook the city and Philip prayed for everyone's safety. When the earthquake ended, the people demanded that Philip and Bartholomew be freed. Although Bartholomew was released and survived, Philip asked not to be let free and died. According to tradition, he was buried in Hieropolis, Turkey.

Philip's feast day is May 3. He is the patron saint of hatters and pastry chefs.

St. Philip the Apostle
Philip and Bartholomew were crucified in Phrygia, but when an earthquake struck the city, Philip prayed for the people's safety. In gratitude, Bartholomew was released from his cross, but Philip did not survive. (Albrecht Durer, 1471–1528)

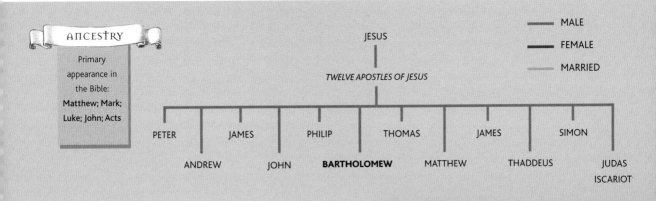

ANCESTRY

Primary
appearance in
the Bible:
Matthew; Mark;
Luke; John; Acts

JESUS

TWELVE APOSTLES OF JESUS

— MALE
— FEMALE
— MARRIED

PETER | JAMES | PHILIP | THOMAS | JAMES | SIMON

ANDREW | JOHN | **BARTHOLOMEW** | MATTHEW | THADDEUS | JUDAS ISCARIOT

BARTHOLOMEW

Bartholomew, another of the twelve apostles, was often associated with Philip. He was martyred in Armenia.

Bartholomew was also known as Nathanael. In the Gospels of Matthew, Mark, and Luke, **Philip** and Bartholomew are always mentioned together, while Nathanael is never mentioned. In the Gospel of John, Philip and Nathanael are mentioned together, but there is no mention of Bartholomew. Since the name Bartholomew is Aramaic for "son of Talmai," it may be that it was simply Nathanael's patronymic. Little is said about Bartholomew in the New Testament; he merely occurs in lists of the apostles and as one of the witnesses of **Jesus'** ascension into heaven following the resurrection.

In John 1:45–51, when Philip tells Bartholomew (Nathanael) that he has found the Messiah, Bartholomew is very sceptical. He comments to Philip, "Nazareth! Can anything good come from there?" Nevertheless, he follows Philip. When Jesus meets Bartholomew, he says that Bartholomew is "a true Israelite, in whom there

is nothing false." Jesus makes the puzzling comment to Bartholomew that "I saw you while you were still under the fig tree before Philip called you." Some have suggested that this phrasing is from a Jewish figure of speech referring to studying the Torah.

Following Jesus' ascension, according to Syrian tradition, Bartholomew embarked on a missionary tour of India, taking a copy of the Gospel of Matthew with him. He is also said to have brought Christianity to Armenia, where he was martyred. In works of art, Bartholomew is often represented with a large knife or with his own skin hanging over his arm. This is because of the tradition that while he was a missionary in Armenia, he was flayed alive, then crucified upside down. This grizzly fate led to his being adopted as the patron saint of tanners. Roman Catholics celebrate the festival of St. Bartholomew on August 24; the Eastern Orthodox celebrate it on June 11.

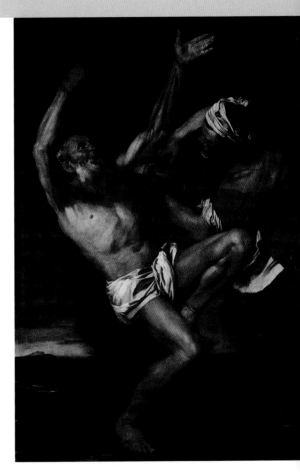

The Martyrdom of St. Bartholomew

Bartholomew survived one crucifixion, alongside Philip in Phrygia, but was eventually martyred in Armenia by being flayed alive and then crucified. (Jusepe de Ribera, 1591–1652)

THOMAS

Thomas was also known as Judas Thomas Didymus
(the twin) but is better known as Doubting Thomas.

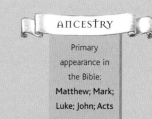

ANCESTRY

Primary
appearance in
the Bible:
Matthew; Mark;
Luke; John; Acts

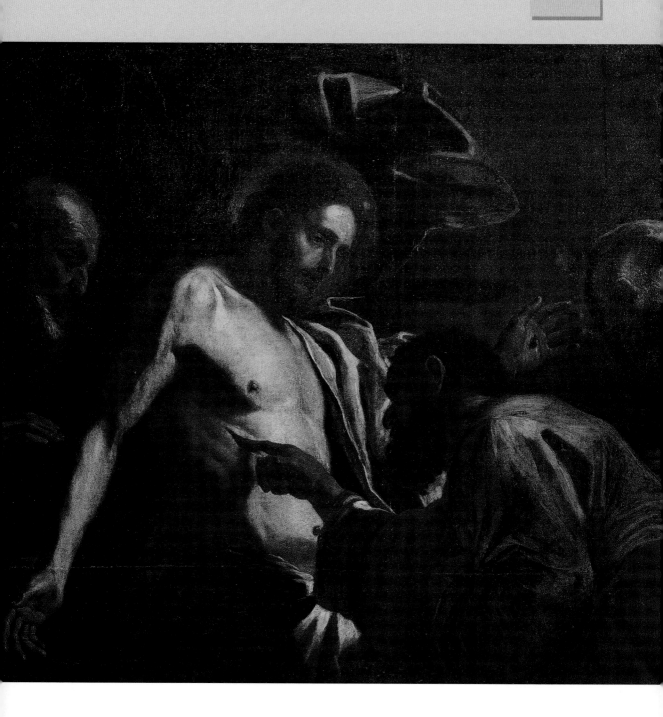

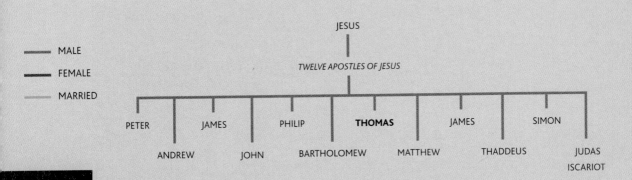

MALE
FEMALE
MARRIED

JESUS

TWELVE APOSTLES OF JESUS

PETER
ANDREW
JAMES
JOHN
PHILIP
BARTHOLOMEW
THOMAS
MATTHEW
JAMES
THADDEUS
SIMON
JUDAS
ISCARIOT

Thomas comes across as a pessimist in the Gospel of John. When **Jesus** decided to go to Bethany after learning that Lazarus, the brother of Martha and Mary of Bethany, had died, Thomas reacted by telling the other disciples, "Let us also go, that we may die with him" (John 11:16). Of course, once Jesus got to Bethany, he raised Lazarus from the dead.

During the Last Supper, Jesus was attempting to explain to his disciples what was about to happen to him, and that he was going to prepare a place for them and return for them. He then commented that they knew where he was going and how to get there. Thomas responded, "Lord, we don't know where you are going, so how can we know the way?" Jesus told him, "I am the way and the truth and the life. No one comes to the Father except through me. If you really

The Doubting of St. Thomas
"Then he said to Thomas, 'Put your finger here; see my hands. Reach out your hand and put it into my side. Stop doubting and believe.' Thomas said to him, 'My Lord and my God!'" John 20:27–28 (Mattia Preti, 1571–1610)

knew me, you would know my Father as well. From now on, you do know him and have seen him" (John 14:5–7).

After his resurrection, Jesus appeared to all the disciples except Thomas. When the others told Thomas that Jesus was alive, he refused to believe it and responded, "Unless I see the nail marks in his hands and put my finger where the nails were, and put my hand into his side, I will not believe it" (John 20:25). It is on account of this statement that he is now known as "Doubting Thomas."

A week later, Jesus appeared to Thomas and told him to put his finger in his hands and side. Thomas did not stick his fingers into Jesus' wounds (despite being depicted doing so in numerous paintings). Instead, he fell to his knees and exclaimed that Jesus was his Lord and God (John 20:28).

According to the tradition recorded in the Acts of Thomas, written about 200 C.E., Thomas traveled to India as a missionary. Today, the Christians of India revere him as their founder. Tradition also asserts that he was present at the assumption of Jesus' mother, **Mary.** The other apostles were miraculously

transported to Jerusalem to witness her death, but Thomas was left in India. However, after her burial he was transported to her tomb, where he witnessed her bodily ascension into heaven. As she rose, she dropped her girdle (an article of outer clothing that encircled the waist). In a reversal of the story of Thomas's doubts regarding Jesus' resurrection, the other apostles were skeptical of Thomas's story until they saw the empty tomb and the girdle. Thomas's receipt of the girdle is commonly depicted in medieval and early Renaissance art.

Several apocryphal works claim to have been written by Thomas. The best known of these is the Gospel of Thomas, written in Coptic and unearthed in Egypt at a place called Nag Hammadi in 1945. Although some scholars suggest that it predates the Gospels in the New Testament, most identify it as a later Gnostic work. Thomas is believed to have been martyred in India around 53 C.E. His feast day is July 3 for Roman Catholics, October 6 for the Eastern Orthodox. He is considered the patron saint of India, architects, people in doubt, and theologians.

MATTHEW

The apostle Matthew was a tax collector. Sometimes called Levi, he was a son of Alphaeus and the brother of St. James the Less.

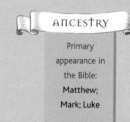

ANCESTRY

Primary
appearance in
the Bible:
Matthew;
Mark; Luke

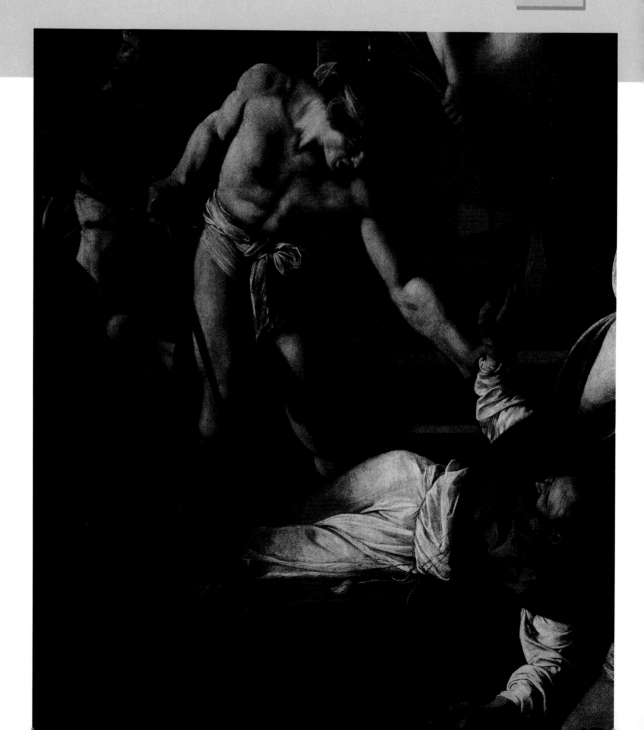

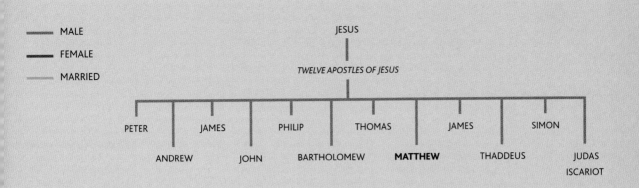

JESUS

TWELVE APOSTLES OF JESUS

| MALE | FEMALE | MARRIED |

PETER

ANDREW

JAMES

JOHN

PHILIP

BARTHOLOMEW

THOMAS

MATTHEW

JAMES

THADDEUS

SIMON

JUDAS ISCARIOT

Matthew's name means "gift of Yahweh." In the Gospel of Luke he is called Levi, while in Mark's Gospel both designations appear. Besides being one of **Jesus'** twelve apostles, Matthew is traditionally regarded as the author of the Gospel of Matthew. Given that he is listed as a son of Alphaeus, it is assumed that he is therefore also the brother of **James** the Less. His mother's name was Mary, a very common name among women in first-century Judea. She is listed as one of the women who witnessed Jesus' crucifixion and who also went to Jesus' tomb to finish embalming him, only to discover that he had risen.

Before being called as a disciple, Matthew was a tax collector in Capernaum. This would have made him something of an outcast in Jewish society. The Roman government gave individual tax collectors contracts for various regions in the empire. They were required

to turn over a specified amount of money annually, but how they acquired those funds from their assigned area was up to them, and anything extra was theirs to keep. Consequently, tax collectors would take as much money as they could get from their territory, and they were not adverse to threatening people in order to get it. They were hated as traitors by most Jews, and the Zealots commonly targeted them for assassination.

One day, when Jesus came into town from the Sea of Galilee, he passed Matthew's tax booth and asked him to become one of his disciples. Matthew agreed and left his business. Later that same day he threw a party to which he invited Jesus and his disciples. He also invited many other tax collectors and prostitutes, prompting religious leaders to criticize Jesus severely. They asked his disciples, "Why do you eat and drink with tax collectors and 'sinners'?" Jesus' reply was simple, "It is not the healthy who need a doctor, but the sick. I have not come to call the righteous, but sinners to repentance" (Luke 5:30–32).

Matthew illustrates Jesus' power over evil: After he forgave sinners, they turned their backs

on their old ways of life. Thanks to his relationship with Jesus, Matthew became an entirely different person. Where before he had collaborated with the Roman government for the sake of wealth, he now renounced it and joined hands with **Simon the Zealot,** an apostle who would have been Matthew's deadly enemy before their conversions.

Little more is reported about Matthew in the New Testament. The last time he is mentioned is in a list of those who were in the upper room when the Holy Spirit came upon the disciples on the Day of Pentecost. He is also one of the few apostles mentioned by name in the Gospel of Thomas, perhaps indicating that he held some level of prominence in the early Christian community. According to tradition, Matthew preached extensively following Christ's resurrection and was later martyred. Some legends describe how he was killed in Ethiopia, while others say he died for the faith in Hierapolis, Turkey.

His feast day is September 21 for Roman Catholics, November 16 for the Eastern Orthodox. Matthew is the patron saint of bankers, accountants, stock brokers, and tax collectors.

The Martyrdom of St. Matthew
It is claimed that the remains of the martyred St. Matthew are located in a crypt in the cathedral in Salerno, Italy. (Caravaggio, 1571–1610)

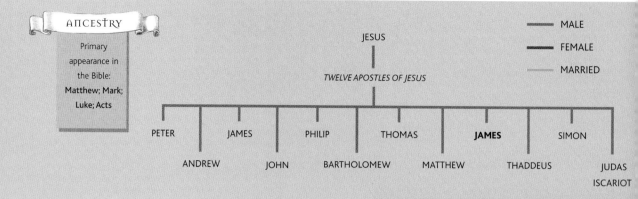

ANCESTRY

Primary appearance in the Bible: Matthew; Mark; Luke; Acts

JESUS

TWELVE APOSTLES OF JESUS

PETER   ANDREW   JAMES   JOHN   PHILIP   BARTHOLOMEW   THOMAS   MATTHEW   **JAMES**   THADDEUS   SIMON   JUDAS ISCARIOT

— MALE
— FEMALE
— MARRIED

JAMES THE LESS

James, the son of Alphaeus and brother of Matthew, was no relation to the other apostle James, the brother of John.

This James is called James the Less to distinguish him from the other men with the same name in **Jesus'** world—the apostle **John**'s brother, St. **James** the Great, and Jesus' brother, St. James the Just. James the Less was a brother of the apostle **Matthew** (Alphaeus being their father) and the son of a woman named Mary, not to be confused with **Mary,** the mother of Jesus.

James appears in the lists of the twelve apostles. His mother is listed as one of the women who watched Jesus' crucifixion. She also went to Jesus' tomb to finish embalming his body, only to discover that the tomb was empty. Over the years, some have attempted to identify James the Less with James the Just, the brother of Jesus and leader of the early Jerusalem church, as well as the author of the book of James. Most modern scholars doubt this identification, however.

The church historian Eusebius (c. 275–339 C.E.), quoting from Hegesippus (c. 110–c. 180 C.E.),

another early chronicler of the church whose works are all lost except as quoted by Eusebius, reports that James "was always a virgin, and was a Nazarite, or one consecrated to God. In consequence of which he never shaved, never cut his hair, never drank any wine or other strong liquor; moreover, he never used any bath, or oil to anoint his limbs, and never ate of any living creature except when of precept, as the paschal lamb: he never wore sandals, never used any other clothes than one single linen garment. He prostrated so much in prayer that the skin of his knees and forehead was hardened like to camels' hoofs."

According to tradition, James traveled to Egypt to preach about Christianity and was crucified in Ostrakine. A carpenter's saw is a symbol often associated with him because tradition also says that he was sawn into pieces after his crucifixion. For Roman Catholics, his feast day is May 3. He is the patron saint of pharmacists and the dying.

St. James the Less at the Last Supper

James, son of Alphaeus, is also known as James the Less to distinguish him from others with that name in the New Testament. (Andrea del Castagno, c. 1421–57)

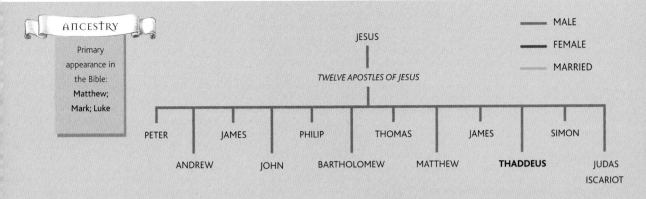

ANCESTRY

Primary
appearance in
the Bible:
Matthew;
Mark; Luke

JESUS

TWELVE APOSTLES OF JESUS

MALE
FEMALE
MARRIED

PETER · ANDREW · JAMES · JOHN · PHILIP · BARTHOLOMEW · THOMAS · MATTHEW · JAMES · **THADDEUS** · SIMON · JUDAS ISCARIOT

THADDEUS

Thaddeus, by virtue of his persistence in the face of difficult challenges, is the patron saint of desperate cases and lost causes.

Thaddeus was also known as Judas Thaddeus. The New Testament authors take pains to distinguish this Judas from **Judas Iscariot,** who betrayed **Jesus.** Thaddeus is also referred to as St. Jude and is often identified as the author of the Letter of Jude and the Judas who is listed as a brother of Jesus, thus making Thaddeus a brother of James the Just, the leader of the early church in Jerusalem. The church chronicler Eusebius (c. 275–339 C.E.) quotes that Thaddeus was the bridegroom at the wedding at Cana where Jesus performed his first miracle, turning water into wine.

Thaddeus, as St. Jude, is sometimes credited with taking Christianity to Armenia. In the Roman Catholic church, Jude is the patron saint of desperate cases and lost causes. His attribute is a club and he is often shown in icons with a flame around his head. This flame is designed to indicate that he was present at the Day of Pentecost, when he received the Holy Spirit

with the other apostles. He is sometimes represented holding an axe, because of the tradition that he was martyred with an axe. Occasionally, he is shown holding a scroll or book that is supposed to represent the New Testament Letter attributed to him. Other times he is shown holding a carpenter's rule, because if he actually was Jesus' brother, then like Jesus, he was probably a carpenter, too.

As St. Jude, Thaddeus is sometimes invoked in desperate situations because his letter in the New Testament stresses the importance of perseverance in the face of trials. Roman Catholics avoided prayers on his behalf because he was often confused with Judas Iscariot, and so he was sometimes called the "forgotten saint." Devotion to him only began among Catholics during the 1800s, spreading from Europe to the United States in the 1920s. His feast day is celebrated by Roman Catholics on October 28; for the Eastern Orthodox, it is June 19.

Thaddeus

Thaddeus is also known as St. Jude. According to legend, some time after his death, Thaddeus's body was brought to Rome and buried on the site of what is today St. Peter's Basilica. (Fresco in Church of San Martino al Tagliamento, Pordenone, Italy, late Renaissance)

SIMON THE ZEALOT

Simon the Zealot was one of Jesus' twelve apostles. Zealots were first-century terrorists, noted for assassinating Romans and Roman sympathizers.

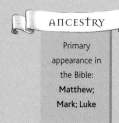

ANCESTRY

Primary
appearance in
the Bible:
Matthew;
Mark; Luke

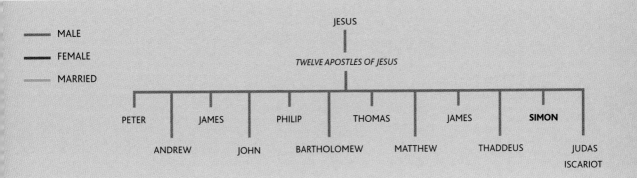

The name Simon, a Greek form of the Hebrew name Simeon, means "listening." Simon the Zealot is only mentioned four times in the New Testament. In two of those four occurrences, the 1611 King James Version, following the church father Jerome who translated the Bible from Greek and Hebrew into Latin in the early fifth century, calls him "the Canaanite" because of Jerome's failure to understand the word that appears in the Greek text of Matthew 10:4 and Mark 3:18. The word there, *kananaois*, is an Aramaic word transliterated into Greek. Like the Greek term Zealot, which is used to describe Simon in Luke 6:15 and Acts 1:13, it meant someone who was jealous on behalf of God. However, Jerome thought the word meant someone from either the village of Cana or from Canaan. Newer translations call Simon a Zealot in all four places that his name appears.

The Zealots belonged to a first-century C.E. political

St. Simon

Simon the Zealot, according to tradition, was martyred by being sawed in half and so is usually depicted with a saw. (Domenico Fetti, c. 1589–1623)

movement that sought to incite the Jewish people to rebel against the Roman Empire and expel it by force from Israel. They believed that the Jewish homeland should be ruled only by a Jewish king descended from **David.** The Zealots were founded by Judas of Galilee (also called Judas of Gamala) and Zadok the Pharisee around 6 C.E. The Sicarii, or "dagger men," were Zealots who made a practice of assassinating anyone they believed was collaborating with the Romans. When they got the opportunity, they assassinated Romans as well. The Zealots finally instigated a revolt against Rome in 66 C.E. The Romans crushed them, burned Jerusalem, and destroyed the Temple in 70 C.E. The last remaining Zealots died by suicide on Masada in 73 C.E.

Although there is a legend that suggests Simon died in the Jewish revolt against Rome in 66 C.E., this is improbable. Christians are known to have refused to participate in that rebellion, and in fact, it was Christian refusal to participate that led to the final rupture between mainstream Judaism and those Jews who followed **Jesus** as the Messiah.

Simon was a member of this terrorist group before he became

a disciple of Jesus. Even more than other Jews, Simon was therefore looking for a political leader who would overthrow the Romans. He doubtless saw in Jesus a man who was likely to fulfill his political aspirations. Like the other disciples, it would not be until after Jesus' crucifixion and resurrection that Simon would modify his understanding of who and what the Messiah was. From being a terrorist, he was transformed into a preacher of the Gospel that Jesus had died to rescue people from their sins, not lead an army against foreign oppression.

A widespread tradition reports that, after teaching about Christianity in Egypt, Simon joined **Thaddeus** in Persia and Armenia, where both were martyred. Other traditions speculate that Simon traveled as far as Africa, or that he visited Britain in Glastonbury and was martyred in Lincolnshire. Other legends say that Simon was martyred by being sawed in two in Persia. As a result, in art he is usually depicted with a saw.

Among Roman Catholics, Simon shares the same feast day, October 28, with Thaddeus. Among the Eastern Orthodox, his feast day is May 10. He is the patron saint of lumbermen and tanners.

JUDAS ISCARIOT

Judas Iscariot was the disciple who betrayed Jesus in exchange for a nominal payment.

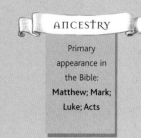

ANCESTRY

Primary appearance in the Bible: Matthew; Mark; Luke; Acts

The name Judas is simply another form of the Hebrew name Yehudah, which sometimes appears in English translations as Judah or Jude. It was a very common proper name in the first century C.E. The name Iscariot may refer to the Judean town of Kerioth, or to the Sicarii, a group of Jewish nationalist insurrectionists. Others have suggested a connection with the tribe of **Issachar,** or simply that it was his family name.

That Judas ultimately betrayed **Jesus** to the authorities seems to have come as a surprise to the other disciples. He had been given the responsibility of carrying the group's money and only after his death did they discover that he had embezzled from it (John 12:4–6). At the Last Supper, when Jesus announced that one of his disciples would betray him, everyone was shocked at the idea: Not one of them suspected it would be Judas.

Judas agreed to turn Jesus over to the religious leaders in Jerusalem—who subsequently handed him over to the Romans—in exchange for 30 pieces of silver, the normal price of a slave. The author of Matthew explains that Judas, filled with remorse, returned the money to those who had given it

to him and committed suicide by hanging himself. The religious leaders then used the money to purchase a plot of ground as a cemetery for the poor (Matthew 27:5–9). The author of Acts quotes **Peter** as explaining, "With the reward he got for his wickedness, Judas bought a field; there he fell headlong, his body burst open and all his intestines spilled out. Everyone in Jerusalem heard about this, so they called that field in their language *Akeldama,* that is, Field of Blood" (Acts 1:18–19).

Most modern Christians perceive Judas as a traitor, and his name has entered the English language as a synonym for betrayer. Some later Gnostics, as for instance in the Gospel of Judas, argued that Judas was merely doing what Jesus had asked him to do. However, this Gnostic interpretation is at odds with how Judas is portrayed in the New Testament.

Why did Judas betray Jesus? In the Gospels, Jesus talks about creating a new kingdom and saving his people. The Messianic expectations of the Jews—an expectation shared by Jesus' disciples—was that the Messiah would overthrow the Romans and restore the Jewish homeland to the glory it had during the time of **David** and **Solomon.**

Judas had witnessed Jesus escape capture and stonings on several occasions. He had seen Jesus heal the sick and raise the dead. Therefore, some speculate that Judas was simply hoping that by selling him out to the authorities, he could force Jesus finally to begin his war with the Romans.

Only after Pentecost would Jesus' statement that his "kingdom is not of this world" (John 18:36) finally make sense to his disciples. Jesus did not come to overthrow the Romans through violence but to save people from their sins. The transformation of the human heart inevitably had political ramifications, but in ways that neither the disciples nor the Romans could have anticipated. Within 300 years of Jesus' resurrection, the Roman Empire, which had long persecuted Christians, was transformed and subsumed by it: a revolution more complete and total than any Zealot could have imagined.

The Kiss of Judas

"Now the betrayer had arranged a signal with them: 'The one I kiss is the man; arrest him.' Going at once to Jesus, Judas said, 'Greetings, Rabbi!' and kissed him." Matthew 26:48–49 *(Giotto di Bondone, c. 1267–1337)*

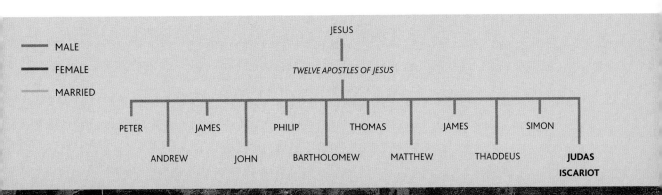

MALE

FEMALE

MARRIED

JESUS

TWELVE APOSTLES OF JESUS

PETER

ANDREW

JAMES

JOHN

PHILIP

BARTHOLOMEW

THOMAS

MATTHEW

JAMES

THADDEUS

SIMON

JUDAS ISCARIOT

THE EARLY CHURCH

In the early years, the Jewish followers of Jesus preached only to other Jews. Eventually, persecution against those who believed that Jesus was the Messiah drove them into the surrounding Roman provinces. As these Jewish followers of Jesus fled, they shared their new faith, first only with other scattered Jews who lived throughout the Roman Empire, and then later with some of their Gentile neighbors who were not Jews. As more people came to believe in the risen Jesus, the growing congregations of Christians began purposely sending missionaries to spread the faith through preaching. Paul became one of these missionaries, and he especially sought to convert Gentiles and founded several congregations that were predominantly Gentile. Within a generation, those who were not Jewish would come to dominate what had begun as a purely Jewish movement.

The Conversion of St. Paul

"As he neared Damascus on his journey, suddenly a light from heaven flashed around him. He fell to the ground and heard a voice say to him, 'Saul, Saul, why do you persecute me?'" Acts 9:3–4 *(German, fifteenth century)*

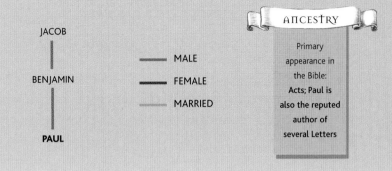

PAUL

After Jesus temporarily blinded him, Paul converted to the Christian faith that he had previously hated.

JACOB

|

BENJAMIN

|

PAUL

— MALE

— FEMALE

— MARRIED

ANCESTRY

Primary appearance in the Bible: Acts; Paul is also the reputed author of several Letters

Paul of Tarsus is responsible for beginning the process of bringing Christianity to Gentiles. His Hebrew name was Saul, but he is better known by the Greek form of his name, Paul. Paul was a Hellenized Jew and a Roman citizen from the city of Tarsus, in present-day Turkey. He was a member of the Jewish sect called the Pharisees and had been trained by the Rabbi Gamaliel in Jerusalem. He persecuted the early Christians, and was present at the execution of the first Christian martyr, Stephen, a deacon in the early church in Jerusalem. He viewed Christians as Jewish heretics.

On his way to Damascus to arrest Christians and bring them back to Jerusalem for trial, Paul had a vision. **Jesus** appeared to him in a blinding light and demanded to know why Paul was persecuting him. Jesus told Paul to go on to Damascus and wait for instructions. Paul discovered at this point that he was blind. Three days later, Ananias, a Christian in Damascus, reluctantly followed God's command to heal Paul of his blindness.

Paul's experience converted him to faith in Jesus as the Messiah and Son of God. After Ananias baptized him, Paul remained in Damascus, telling people about Jesus and creating such a disturbance within the Jewish community that they plotted to kill him. Paul was forced to flee by night, slipping over the city wall in a basket.

He then spent time with the early Christian community in Jerusalem, which reluctantly accepted him at the urging of Barnabas, one of their leaders. Paul did not stay in Jerusalem for long, however, and soon made his way back to his home town Tarsus. Later, Barnabas went to Tarsus looking for Paul and took him to Antioch where they taught for about a year. Later, the church commissioned them as missionaries. First with Barnabas, and then later with another traveling companion, Silas, Paul established churches in several cities in what is today Turkey, as well as in Greece. He was also arrested on a few occasions on account of his preaching.

On a later visit to Jerusalem, Paul got into trouble with the religious authorities and was arrested. Fearing for his life, and not trusting that he would get a fair trial in Judea, he made an appeal to Caesar, which was his right as a Roman citizen. The Roman governor of Judea subsequently sent him to Rome under guard. Tradition says that he was released and continued preaching and teaching for a number of years until he was finally arrested by Nero and beheaded around 65 C.E.

Paul is venerated as a saint by various groups, including Roman Catholics, Eastern Orthodox, Anglicans, and some Lutherans. Paul's Letters make up 16 of the 27 books of the New Testament. Among Roman Catholics, his conversion is celebrated on January 25. June 29 is the celebration of **Peter** and Paul as founders of the Church, and November 18 is the feast of dedication for the Basilicas of Peter and Paul. Paul is the patron saint of journalists and musicians, as well as the patron to protect against snakes.

CHRISTIANS AND MOSAIC LAW

In his Letters to Gentile Christian communities, Paul argued that it was unnecessary to practice some laws of Judaism—notably circumcision—in order to become a Christian. He argued that Jesus' death on the cross took away all sin. In fact, he argued that sacrifices and obeying the Mosaic Law had never had the ability to remove sin. Paul's message was primarily one of salvation by grace through faith. Good works, in his mind, seem to have been a consequence of God's activity and gift of grace in an individual's life (see 1 Corinthians 15:10 and Ephesians 2:8–10).

LYDIA

Lydia was a merchant woman and one of the earliest recorded converts to Christianity in Europe. She became a deacon and her home was used as a church.

PAUL

|

LYDIA
(CONVERT)

━━━━ MALE

━━━━ FEMALE

━━━━ MARRIED

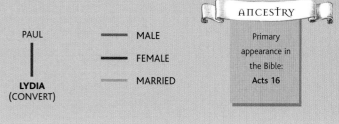

ANCESTRY

Primary
appearance in
the Bible:
Acts 16

After the split between **Paul** and his missionary companion Barnabas, Paul took Silas to Macedonia. There, the two missionaries came to the city of Philippi, a Roman colony. Paul's normal practice in a new city was to begin preaching in the local synagogue, but there was no synagogue in Philippi. For a synagogue to exist there had to be at least ten men; if there were not enough Jewish men to form the necessary quorum, then the Jews of the city would come together in an informal gathering called a "place of prayer."

Paul sat down and began to speak to some women who had gathered at such a place. One of them was Lydia, a dealer in purple cloth from the city of Thyatira, in Turkey. Purple cloth was the most expensive available in the first century C.E. She, like many people in the Roman Empire, had begun worshiping the Jewish God. She accepted the message that Paul was preaching, and, together with the other members of her household, she was baptized. She invited Paul and those traveling with him to stay in her house. The Christian community of Philippi continued to use her house for their worship services for several years.

Paul and Silas got into trouble with the local officials in Philippi when they cast a spirit out of a slave girl who made a lot of money for her owners by using the spirit for fortune-telling. They were beaten and imprisoned, but were quickly released once the officials realized that they were Roman citizens. After their release, they visited Lydia before leaving town. Paul would later write a Letter to the church in Philippi. That letter is now part of the New Testament. Lydia's feast day is on August 3 for Roman Catholics, and May 20 for Eastern Orthodox. She is the patron saint of cloth dyers.

BARNABAS AND SILAS

First Barnabas and then later Silas traveled with Paul during his missionary journeys throughout the Roman Empire. Barnabas was the man who first brought Paul to the attention of the church in Antioch and helped him gain acceptance in the Christian community, convincing them that the former persecutor was now one of them. Together, he and Paul went out to proclaim the message of **Jesus.** Subsequently, Paul and Barnabas had a falling out over whether John Mark (believed to be the author of the Gospel of Mark) would be acceptable as a companion on a later missionary trip. At that point, Paul and Barnabas went their separate ways and Silas became Paul's new companion on his later missionary journeys. Silas was with Paul when he preached to Lydia in Philippi, and was also imprisoned when Paul cast a spirit out of a slave girl there.

Paul Casts Out a Spirit from a Slave Girl

"He turned around and said to the spirit, 'In the name of Jesus Christ I command you to come out of her!' At that moment the spirit left her."
Acts 16:18 *(Johann Christoph Weigel, 1654–1726)*

Paul Preaches to a Group of Women by the River

"One of those listening was a woman named Lydia, a dealer in purple cloth from the city of Thyatira, who was a worshiper of God. The Lord opened her heart to respond to Paul's message." Acts 16:14 *(Johann Christoph Weigel, 1654–1726)*

PHOEBE

Phoebe was one of the very few female deacons mentioned by name in the early Christian community.

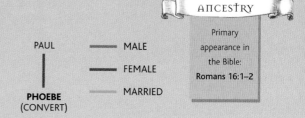

PAUL ——— MALE
PHOEBE ——— FEMALE
(CONVERT) ——— MARRIED

ANCESTRY

Primary appearance in the Bible: Romans 16:1–2

St. Phoebe, Deacon of Cenchrea

Phoebe was a patron of Paul in his missionary work and may have delivered Paul's Letter to the Romans. (Undated icon)

Phoebe was a deacon in the Christian community in Cenchrea, about four miles southeast of Corinth in Greece. In **Paul**'s Letter to the Christian community in Rome, he writes, "I commend to you our sister Phoebe, a deacon of the church in Cenchrea. I ask you to receive her in the Lord in a way worthy of the saints and to give her any help she may need from you, for she has been a great help to many people, including me" (Romans 16:1–2). The phrase translated "has been a great help" indicates she was a patron. This would have meant that she supported Paul in his ministry financially or politically. It has been suggested that she was responsible for delivering Paul's Letter to the Roman church.

Women played a prominent role in the early church, which is not surprising, given the fact that women were the first to see the resurrected **Jesus** and were responsible for supplying the money that made it possible for Jesus and his apostles to travel about Israel proclaiming the coming Kingdom of Heaven.

The English word "deacon" is a transliteration of a Greek word that means "servant." The reason that a word like "servant" was used to indicate someone with authority in the Christian community goes back to what Jesus taught about leadership: "You know that the rulers of the Gentiles lord it over them, and their high officials exercise authority over them. Not so with you. Instead, whoever wants to become great among you must be your servant, and whoever wants to be first must be your slave— just as the Son of Man did not come to be served, but to serve, and to give his life as a ransom for many" (Matthew 20:25–28). Phoebe's feast day is September 3 for Eastern Orthodox Christians.

JUNIA

Junia was a female apostle who was arrested with Paul and shared his prison time for proclaiming the Gospel message.

PAUL

| JUNIA
(ONE OF JESUS' DISCIPLES)

—— MALE

—— FEMALE

—— MARRIED

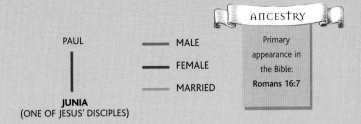

ANCESTRY

Primary appearance in the Bible:
Romans 16:7

Junia's brief mention in **Paul**'s Letter to the Romans reminds us that we are reading someone else's mail, peering over his shoulder, knowing less than those to whom he addressed the missive. Where was Paul incarcerated with Junia? For what reasons, and for how long? What did they do, and what did they talk about while they were locked up together?

At the end of the letter, Paul greets a number of people by name: seventeen men and nine women. In Romans 16:7 he writes, "Salute Andronicus and Junia, my kinsmen, and my fellow-prisoners, who are of note among the apostles, who also were in Christ before me" (1611 King James Version). The identification of Junia as an apostle is controversial. Some suggest that by "of note among the apostles" simply means that she was well thought of by them, not that she herself was one. There is even a question about whether she is actually a she.

Although the King James Version identifies her as female, most modern translations have changed her gender to that of a man named "Junias." However, while many modern commentators believe that it is improbable that a woman would be called an apostle, the church fathers—influential theologians and writers during the first five centuries of Christian history—who commented on this passage generally recognized her as female.

There are also objective reasons for thinking she really was a woman apostle. First, the female Latin name Junia occurs more than 250 times in Greek and Latin inscriptions from Rome alone, but the masculine name Junias never appears anywhere at all. Second, when Greek manuscripts were first given accent marks, the scribes put the feminine form on her name, not the masculine form, indicating a traditional understanding of her gender.

Apostles are usually thought to be those who were part of the original group of disciples. It is a word that in Greek means "one who is sent." It is loosely equivalent to the English word "ambassador." Junia's gender, and her role in the early church, are likely to remain contentious for the foreseeable future.

Perhaps Junia was one of the "many others" mentioned in Luke 8:1–3: "The Twelve were with him, and also some women who had been cured of evil spirits and diseases: **Mary** (called Magdalene) from whom seven demons had come out; Joanna the wife of Cuza, the manager of Herod's household; Susanna; and many others. These women were helping to support them out of their own means." Junia is venerated as a saint by the Eastern Orthodox. Her feast day is May 17.

Sts. Andronicus, Paul, and Junia

Paul was imprisoned with Andronicus and Junia, but it is not revealed where this took place or for what charge. There is controversy over the gender of Junia and whether she was an apostle of Jesus. (Undated icon)

AQUILA AND PRISCILLA

Aquila and his wife, Priscilla, were tentmakers, like Paul. They were both converts to Christianity and became leaders in the early church.

Aquila and his wife Priscilla were tentmakers in Rome who were forced to leave the city when Emperor Claudius expelled all Jews from Rome in 49 C.E. They settled in Corinth and set up their business there.

The Roman historian Suetonius, writing in the first and second centuries C.E., tells us that Claudius expelled the Jews from Rome because they were rioting on account of someone named "Chrestus"—perhaps referring to disputes between Christian and nonChristian Jews.

As was customary in first-century Judaism, the job of rabbi was an unpaid position. Those who served in that capacity, like **Paul,** were expected to have a profession. In Paul's case, it was tentmaker. When Paul arrived in Corinth, he found work with the local tentmakers Aquila and Priscilla. It is unclear whether they were Christians before they met Paul, or if he converted them through his teaching.

Toward the end of his first Letter to the Christian community in the Greek city of Corinth, Paul passed along the greetings of Priscilla and Aquila to their friends in Corinth. This indicates that they had joined Paul on his missionary journey as he traveled in Asia Minor, and in fact, according to Acts,

they wound up settling for a time in Ephesus.

In his Letter to the Roman Christian community, written a few years after his Letter to the Corinthian church, Paul sent greetings to Priscilla and Aquila and noted that they had risked their lives on his behalf.

Obviously they had by then returned to their home in Rome, because after the Emperor Claudius died in 54 C.E., the prohibition on Jews living in Rome had been lifted. The house of Aquila and Priscilla in Rome was used as a church.

After Paul had moved on, Acts records that an evangelist by the name of Apollos arrived in Ephesus. He was well-spoken and was well-received in the local synagogue. Although what he said about **Jesus** was accurate, he seemed to know only about the baptism of **John** and nothing after that, so Priscilla and Aquila invited him to their home and "explained to him the way of God more adequately" (Acts 18:26).

Priscilla, assisted by her husband, became one of the earliest known teachers of Christian theology after Paul. In one of his Letters to **Timothy,** then serving as a pastor in Ephesus, Paul makes the statement that "I do not permit a woman to teach or to have

authority over a man; she must be silent" (1 Timothy 2:12). However, given the examples of women serving as leaders in both the Old and New Testaments, Priscilla acting as a teacher to Apollos, and women serving as prophets elsewhere in the Bible, not to mention Paul's own statements elsewhere that men and women were equal, it has been suggested that Paul's words to Timothy related to a specific, local problem in Timothy's congregation. Many theologians now believe that Paul's words should not be interpreted as a universal statement about the status and role of women in either the church or society.

Legend relates that Aquila and Priscilla were martyred in Rome, perhaps during the time of Nero. Their feast day is July 8 for Roman Catholics, and February 13 for Eastern Orthodox.

St. Paul at Corinth with the Tentmakers Aquila and Priscilla

"There he met a Jew named Aquila, a native of Pontus, who had recently come from Italy with his wife Priscilla, because Claudius had ordered all the Jews to leave Rome. Paul went to see them, and because he was a tentmaker as they were, he stayed and worked with them." Acts 18:2–3 (Jan Sadeler, 1550–1600)

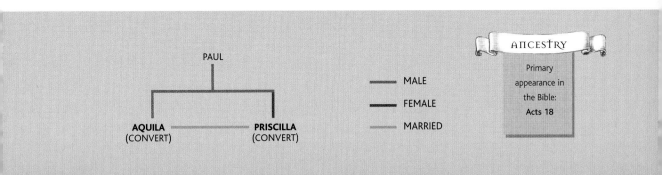

PAUL

AQUILA
(CONVERT)

PRISCILLA
(CONVERT)

MALE

FEMALE

MARRIED

ANCESTRY

Primary
appearance in
the Bible:
Acts 18

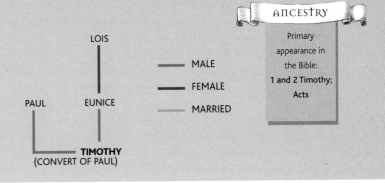

TIMOTHY

Timothy was one of Paul's converts. He became the pastor of the church in Ephesus. Two of Paul's Letters to him are now part of the New Testament.

LOIS

PAUL — EUNICE

— MALE
— FEMALE
— MARRIED

TIMOTHY
(CONVERT OF PAUL)

ANCESTRY

Primary appearance in the Bible:
1 and 2 Timothy; Acts

After his conversion to Christianity, Timothy accompanied **Paul** on many of his missionary journeys. He had learned his early Jewish faith from his mother and grandmother. Because his father was Greek, however, Timothy had not been circumcised as an infant. Paul arranged for the ritual because he thought it would ease relationships with Jewish people they met in their missionary travels.

Timothy was first mentioned during Paul's second visit to Lystra, a city in Turkey. It is likely that he became a Christian as a result of hearing Paul preach there. He was later ordained as a pastor and accompanied Paul in his missionary journey through Phrygia, Galatia, and Mysia.

According to later tradition, Paul ordained Timothy as Bishop of Ephesus in 65 C.E., where Timothy served for fifteen years.

Timothy

"Timothy, my son, I give you this instruction in keeping with the prophecies once made about you, so that by following them you may fight the good fight, holding on to faith and a good conscience."
1 Timothy 1:18–19 *(Michael Burghers, 1647–1727)*

In 80 C.E., Timothy tried to halt a pagan procession of idols there. This enraged the pagan worshipers. The angry crowd beat him and dragged him through the streets. In the end, they stoned him to death.

Paul's two Letters to Timothy are part of the New Testament. In them, we learn that Timothy worked in Ephesus, apparently serving as the pastor there. In the first letter, Paul gives Timothy instructions on how to serve well as a pastor, and what he thought the qualifications for church leadership were. In the second letter, it appears that Paul was in prison in Rome, expecting to be executed soon.

One controversial aspect of Paul's first Letter to Timothy is what Paul has to say about women acting as teachers in the Church (1 Timothy 2:11–15). For most of the Church's history, scholars have assumed from what Paul wrote to Timothy that women were not permitted to teach or preach. However, in recent decades, most scholars (though not all) have taken a different position on what Paul wrote: They have adopted the idea that Paul was addressing a specific problem in Timothy's church in Ephesus, rather than making a universal pronouncement on the role of women in the church or society.

Given the very low status of women in Greek society in the first century C.E., and the fact that women there were rarely permitted an education, many scholars now believe that Paul was simply warning Timothy not to allow unqualified and unlearned people to have positions of authority, rather than women in particular. That this interpretation is the more likely one is demonstrated by the positive things Paul had to say about women elsewhere, even in his very next Letter to Timothy, in which he commends the roles that Timothy's mother and grandmother played in his religious education: "I have been reminded of your sincere faith, which first lived in your grandmother Lois and in your mother Eunice and, I am persuaded, now lives in you also" (2 Timothy 1:5).

Timothy's feast day is celebrated on January 26. He is the patron saint of stomach and intestinal disorders, because of Paul's words to him in his first letter: "Stop drinking only water, and use a little wine because of your stomach and your frequent illnesses" (1 Timothy 5:23).

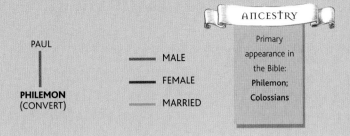

PHILEMON

Philemon was one of the members of the Christian community at Colossae. He was a slave owner.

PAUL

|

PHILEMON
(CONVERT)

——— MALE

——— FEMALE

——— MARRIED

ANCESTRY

Primary appearance in the Bible: **Philemon; Colossians**

Philemon was apparently a man of wealth; he was certainly a slave owner. It is assumed that he lived in Colossae because he was mentioned in a letter attributed to **Paul** that was sent to the Christian community in Colossae.

Paul suggested in his letter that Philemon's escaped slave Onesimus, whom Paul was sending back to him, should be freed. Paul does not make that request explicit, however, nor does he comment on the institution of slavery in general.

The Letter to Philemon thus raises a question: Why does the New Testament not explicitly address the issue of slavery and condemn it? Christianity spoke of equality before God and argued that Christians, as children of God, were the brothers of Christ, who was God himself.

Christianity was thus inherently radical and dangerous to the status quo—part of the

Paul Dictates a Letter to Philemon

"I appeal to you for my son Onesimus, who became my son while I was in chains. Formerly he was useless to you, but now he has become useful both to you and to me. I am sending him—who is my very heart—back to you."
Philemon 1:10–12 *(Johann Christoph Weigel, 1654–1726)*

reason why it was persecuted by the Roman government. However, the church never took a stand on the issue of slavery, even after Christianity became the official state religion. In fact, it would not be until the 1600s that Christians began working to end slavery.

One point that Paul makes in another of his letters may help to clarify why Paul and the early church did not do more to change social problems. He writes, "Be careful to do what is right in the eyes of everybody. If it is possible, as far as it depends on you, live at peace with everyone" (Romans 12:17–18).

Paul seems to have believed that Christians should never act in a way that might prevent others from being attracted to the Gospel message. Explicitly attacking social ills, though commendable, was secondary to telling people about **Jesus.** Paul did not want to say or do anything that would stop people from hearing his message. He believed the world was more likely to change if enough people had changes of heart, rather than by focusing on their faults. He knew that laws did not solve problems or prevent people from behaving badly.

Paul spent a lot of time in his letters contrasting grace with the Law, pointing out that no one was ever saved by just following

the rules. Making rules against murder or theft prevented neither. Only a changed heart kept such sinfulness at bay, so he decided to focus on changing hearts, rather than laws. In his Letter to Philemon, Paul emphasized that both Philemon and his runaway slave had changed hearts—and thus only hinted that perhaps there should be some changes in their behavior to go along with that.

According to tradition, Philemon became the Bishop of Colossae. Later, with Appia, Archippus, and Onesimus (his former slave), Philemon was martyred at Colossae during the first general persecution brought on by the Roman Emperor Nero. Philemon's feast day is celebrated on November 22.

ONESIMUS

Onesimus was an escaped slave who had belonged to Philemon. At some point he met Paul, and Paul converted him to Christianity. Onesimus decided to return to his master. Little is known of him, though the letter Paul wrote to Philemon implies that Onesimus, besides having run away, had also stolen from Philemon and had not been a very good slave. Paul wrote that since his conversion, Onesimus had improved his attitude, and that he was now a good worker. Paul offered to pay Philemon for anything his slave had taken and to bear responsibility for any wrong Onesimus had done him. According to tradition, Philemon freed Onesimus.

INDEX

**Page numbers in bold refer
to main illustrated references**

*Page numbers in italic refer
to other illustrations*

CREDITS

Author's acknowledgments
Thanks to my wife, Ruth, for all her support over so many years. This book's for you! Thanks to Dandi Moyers, for reading multiple drafts of this book and offering valuable corrections and comments. All authors should have such a helper. Thanks to my editors Kate Kirby and Michelle Pickering at Quarto Publishing for all their tireless efforts at making this book possible.

Bible quotations
Unless indicated otherwise, quotations of Old and New Testament scripture are taken from the Holy Bible, New International Version. Quotations in the Apocrypha chapter are taken from the Holy Bible, New Revised Standard Version.

Selected bibliography
Anchor Bible Commentary Series. 80 volumes. New York City: Doubleday. 1964–present.
Butler, Alvin. *Lives of the Saints.* Rockford, Illinois: Tan Books & Publishers. 1995.
Catholic Encyclopedia. New York City: The Encyclopedia Press. 1913.
Elliger, Karl, and Willhelm Rudolph, eds. *Biblia Hebraica Stutgartensia.* Peabody, Massachusetts: Hendrickson Publishers. 2006.
Freedman, David Noel, ed. *Anchor Bible Dictionary.* New York City: Anchor Bible. 1992.
— — —, Allen C. Myers, and Astrid B. Beck, eds. *Eerdmans Dictionary of the Bible.* Grand Rapids, Michigan: Eerdmans. 2000.
Holy Bible. New International Version. Grand Rapids, Michigan: Zondervan. 1983.
Holy Bible. New Revised Standard Version with the Apocrypha and the Deuterocanonical Books. Peabody, Massachusetts: Hendrickson Publishers. 2005.
Nestle, Eberhard, Erwin Nestle, and Kurt Aland. *Novum Testamentum Graece.* New York City: American Bible Society. 1993.
Word Biblical Commentary Series. 58 volumes. Nashville, Tennessee: Thomas Nelson. 1983–present.